IN
SEARCH
OF
EXCESS

IN SEARCH OF EXCESS

The Overcompensation of American Executives

GRAEF S. CRYSTAL

W · W · Norton & Company · New York · London

The text of this book is composed in Galliard with the display set in Centaur and Galliard. Manufacturing by The Haddon Craftsmen, Inc. Book design by Marjorie J. Flock.

First published as a Norton paperback 1992.

Library of Congress Cataloging-in-Publication Data

Crystal, Graef S.
   In search of excess: the overcompensation of American
executives / by Graef S. Crystal.
    p.   cm.
   Includes bibliographical references and index.
   1. Executives—Salaries, etc.—United States. I. Title.
HD4965.5.U6C77   1992
331.2'816584'00973—dc20   91-25569

ISBN: 0-393-30912-6

W.W. Norton & Company, Inc., 500 Fifth Avenue, New York, N.Y. 10110
W.W. Norton & Company Ltd, 10 Coptic Street, London WC1A 1PU

3 4 5 6 7 8 9 0

To Sue
my colleague, my beloved

Contents

Preface: *Apologia Pro Vita Sua*   9

Acknowledgments   17

One ... Everybody Makes It   23

Two ... How They Do It   42

Three ... The Prince of Pay   51

Four ... All in the Family   85

Five ... High Pay, Low Performance   96

Six ... On the Flying Trapeze   110

Seven ... Share Swappers   133

Eight ... Partners in Profit   138

Nine ... The Taxman Never Cometh   149

Ten ... The Good Guys   159

Eleven ... Ready, Aim, Reload!   174

Twelve ... The Perk Barrel   186

Thirteen ... A Look Across the Waters   204

Contents

Fourteen . . . The Culprits   *214*

Fifteen . . . Reforming the System   *241*

Sixteen . . . Counterattack 1992: The CEOs Respond   *253*

Appendix: CEO Pay and the Investor—
     Cautionary Tales for Stock Pickers   *277*

Sources   *289*

Index   *290*

Preface:

Apologia Pro Vita Sua

For most of my working life, I have been a compensation consultant. Compensation consultants operate in a world that defies the laws of economics: they are given relatively large sums of money by a company's shareholders to increase that company's costs by raising the pay of the company's senior executives.

During more than twenty years I advised major corporations on the two questions that pervade every executive compensation issue: How much, and how? In contrast to many compensation consultants, who involve themselves in the pay of every employee in a company, I concentrated on the pay of that handful of executives comprising the company's senior management. Working at that level, I frequently assessed the degree to which a company's pay levels were competitive—that is to say, how they compared to the

9

pay levels of companies of the same size or companies in the same industry—and I also designed many different types of executive compensation plans, plans intended to get people to work harder, or at least smarter.

When I was working actively as a compensation consultant, I would have defended my every action as being in the shareholders' long-term interests. If the pay levels I helped set enabled the company to recruit the very best senior executive talent, wouldn't that, somehow, help to produce better returns for the shareholders a few years down the road? Or, if I designed a fancy new incentive plan, wouldn't that plan, if it worked, generate extra profits out of all proportion to the extra costs involved and, once again, benefit the shareholders who were ultimately paying my fees? But now, looking back at my behavior, I must confess to having committed a number of sins. Herewith my mea culpas:

In helping a company to decide how much to pay its top executives, I relied too heavily on survey data showing the *current* pay levels of other companies. Trouble was, however, that all the companies were U.S. companies, and so I never saw how American CEOs' pay was outstripping that of CEOs abroad, during a period when foreign companies captured large portions of the American markets. And I never looked back to see how much top executives' pay had been growing in the United States, compared to what ordinary workers were earning.

If a company wanted to pay its top executives above market levels—presumably to assure its ability to attract top talent and to encourage greater performance on the part of the talent the company already had—I generally went along with the CEO's thinking. I never focused very well on the fact that unless other companies were willing to pay their executives *below* market levels, the market would simply explode. And explode it did.

I succumbed more than I should have to the two favorite siren songs of American CEOs. First, if your company has performed brilliantly, then you should pay your top people brilliantly. However, if your company has performed poorly, you can't afford to make people suffer very much, because they will simply leave and go elsewhere; in other words, you have to keep the good people. Simple logic, of course, mandates that there can be very few effective people at the top of a lousy-performing organization. But simple logic was apparently not my forte. As a result, I helped create the phenomenon we see today: huge and surging pay for good performance, and huge and surging pay for bad performance, too. After all, if you are going to pay people highly in good times, because they deserve it, and if you are going to pay people highly in bad times, because you need to keep them with the company, just when is it that you are ever going to cut their pay? There are, so far as I know, only two types of times: good times and bad times.

I also succumbed to the argument that the reason CEOs earn so much today is that there is a scarcity of talent. Most of today's CEOs were so-called Depression babies, people born in the 1930s. That particular cohort, as the demographers term a ten-year span of births, had far fewer births than the cohorts before or after it. Consequently, the supply of potential CEO labor was unnaturally low. Moreover, it was rendered even lower by the fact that until the 1970s, women were systematically excluded from the executive labor force. Hence, so the argument goes, if there is a scarcity of labor, there is naturally going to be an increase in the price of that labor, as company after company fights to obtain and keep scarce talent. The argument seems to hold water, until one thinks about the fact that our major trading partners—Japan, Germany, France, and the United Kingdom—also experienced the Depression of the 1930s and its consequent effect on birth rates. Yet they seem to be able to field a more than adequate supply of CEO talent without paying the moon for it. For my part, I did not think about executive pay in other countries, because I saw it as being irrelevant to the U.S. executive labor market. Technically, it is irrelevant; but the fact that other countries can do the job—and frequently do it better—with lower-priced talent points up that there is something wrong with U.S. executive compensation.

When a company failed on one performance measure, I jumped to help it devise an alternative incentive plan, with the result that, much more often than not, the top executives emerged with a winning hand. In the early 1970s, the stock market underwent a prolonged slump—one from which it did not emerge until 1982. Yet corporate earnings continued to rise, thereby leading a lot of people—myself included—to reason that maybe the stock market was a poor indicator of performance. So I helped clients move away from incentives geared to increases in the market price of their stock. Thus, if a company looked capable of doing well in earnings per share growth, I devised a new long-term incentive plan geared to earnings per share growth. Or, if a company looked capable of doing well in return on equity, I devised a new long-term incentive plan geared to return on equity. It was only later, in the 1980s, that I realized that the stock market in the 1970s was not crazy at all; rather, it was simply applying a steep discount to estimated future earnings because of the huge inflation levels we were then experiencing.

Some years ago, I was quoted in *Fortune* magazine to the effect that there is a fine line between a compensation consultant and a prostitute. That remark earned me a considerable amount of flak from many of my colleagues in the field; one even wrote *Fortune* that a person who discerns a fine line between a compensation consultant and a prostitute must have a considerable amount of difficulty in staying on the right side of that line. For my part, I regretted the remark, because prostitution is a service that has stood the test of time.

Was I a whore during my twenty years as a consultant? I'd like to think not. Although I can now see some errors in retrospect, I don't think I was ever for sale. At least I was not consciously for sale. Indeed, I can recount several times when I resigned as the consultant to a company, because a particular CEO had simply gone too far. But I acted in the full realization that if I didn't please a client, I wouldn't have that client for long. I was, after all, hired by the CEO, and not by the board of directors. Therein lay the problem. If the CEO wanted more money, and I didn't want to recommend to the board that he should get more money, well, there was always a rival compensation consultant who could be hired.

That point was driven home to me a few years ago when I was the consultant to a major pharmaceutical company. Each year, I was asked by the vice president for human resources to write him a letter concerning the pay competitiveness of the company's CEO. At the company's request, the pay being measured was the CEO's base salary and his bonus for annual performance, but it excluded his stock option and other long-term incentive grants. My analyses each year consistently showed that the CEO was being paid at the 75th percentile of the competitive pay distribution—that is, he was being paid more than about three quarters of his peers and less than about one quarter of his peers. That above-average pay positioning was just what the company's board of directors wanted, because it believed the CEO to be superior in his performance. My annual letter was routinely passed on to the CEO, and because it told him what he wanted to hear, he passed it on to the board of directors. Then the year came when I decided to measure the competitiveness, not only of the CEO's base salary and his bonus for annual performance, but also of the value of his long-term incentives and particularly his stock options. I had observed from proxy statements that the CEO had of late been receiving some huge stock option grants, and I felt that a more comprehensive look at his pay package was in order. The vice president of human resources reacted with alarm and counseled me to stick with my usual approach. Nonetheless, I persisted and in due course produced a letter showing that, while the CEO was being paid at about the 75th percentile of the distribution when it came to base salary and annual bonus, he was being paid close to the 100th percentile of the distribution (i.e., higher than everyone else) when it came to the sum of base salary, annual bonus, and long-term incentives.

Months passed after I sent that letter, and I never heard from the company. Finally, I happened to meet the vice president of human resources at a conference at which I was speaking, and I asked him what happened. He told me that he had, as usual, passed on my letter to the CEO. "Well," I asked, "what did he do with it?" The reply: "He threw it in the wastebasket!"

Leaving aside a few bad apples in the field—or should I say a few true hookers—I do not believe that the great majority of compensation consultants are prostitutes. But compensation consultants, like all consultants, want to please their clients, and the system more or less forces them to please their clients if they are to eat. What they need are new clients—not the CEO, but the shareholders.

And that is where I have ended up. To justify my existence as a compensation consultant, I always liked to think that I was ultimately working for the shareholders, using that second-most ancient motive, greed (ontologically speaking, lust had to precede greed; but, though a more ancient motive, it is, on the evidence, not as long-lasting), to help make society more productive and hence improve the lives of everyone, not merely CEOs. But I eventually discovered what many economists have known all along, that CEOs are not perfect agents of their shareholders, that they have their own interests which often diverge considerably from those of their shareholders.

So now I am working a bit more directly for shareholders. Only rarely do I consult with for-profit enterprises any more, and then only for an hour or two. Rather, I write critical articles for publications like *Financial World*, *Fortune*, and the *New York Times*, and I publish a newsletter on executive compensation that singles out CEOs by name for milking their shareholders. And I consult with shareholder rights groups, such as the United Shareholders Association, and giant institutional investors, such as the Council of Institutional Investors and the California Public Employees Retirement System. I also work as an adjunct professor at the University of California at Berkeley. There, I teach a course that is officially titled "Management Reward Systems," but that is known more informally among the Berkeley Business School students as "Greed 259A."

Someone has to take the shareholders' side of the issues involving executive compensation. And that's where I find myself. Although I think that senior U.S. executive pay levels do need to be reduced, I am even more interested in forging a better relationship between pay and performance—in making sure that those who really deliver for their shareholders are rewarded far beyond those who strike out and, by the same token, in making sure that those who strike out are not given a consolation bonus, a lush Golden Parachute, and a ringside seat from which to view their company's journey on to the ash heap of corporate history.

Now that I am working the other side of the street, as some of my former compensation colleagues have said of me, I'm making far less money. But I'm having a lot more fun. I'm only one individual, yet given what's happened to me, I'm beginning to wonder if money is really as motivational as it's cracked up to be.

Berkeley, California
July 1991

Acknowledgments

MANY PEOPLE HELPED ME, directly or indirectly, in writing this book. First, I want to thank several experts in compensation outside the United States who aided me in filling, if only a tiny bit, the gaps in my knowledge of executive compensation practices in other major countries. They are Tatsuaki Kikuchi of NEC Corporation in Tokyo, Peter Domschke of Towers Perrin in Frankfurt, Vincent Regazzacci Stephanopoli of Progress in Paris, John Carney of Towers Perrin in London, and James Matthews of Incomes Data Services, also of London. Their help is much appreciated.

Many others also provided indirect help to me. Sarah Teslik of the Council of Institutional Investors, Dale Hanson and Richard Koppes of the California Public Employees Retirement System, and Ralph Whitworth of the United Shareholders Association have funded various research projects, the results of which can be found throughout this book. But their role as sounding boards and friends has been more important than their checkbooks.

I also wish to thank four people who, in one way or another, have contributed heavily to my general knowledge base, though not specifically to this book. Charles O'Reilly and Baruch Lev, my colleagues at the University of California at Berkeley, have always been available to answer questions. And they graciously masked their pain at my stupidity for asking them. And Stephen O'Byrne and Michael Davis at Towers Perrin have long manned the crash cart whenever my often-limited knowledge of finance threatened to go into cardiac arrest. All these people, too, are my friends, and I could not have proceeded very far without them.

I recently wrapped up a part-time career as a writer for *Fortune*. But though you leave a magazine and go elsewhere, you don't sever long-standing relationships. In that vein, I also wish to thank Geoffrey Colvin, my always patient editor at *Fortune*. He was ever there for me, and if I learned a little bit about writing, he taught it to me.

I now come to my editors at Norton, Donald Lamm and Hilary Hinzmann. I first met Don Lamm at a party many years ago. The party was given by James Kielley, who recently finished a magnificent career at Towers Perrin. I enjoyed being his friend, associate, subordinate. At any rate, I must have said something interesting to Don Lamm, because he remembered my name. The result is this book. I have written three other books, and they were a breeze: I sent in the manuscript, a copy editor made a bunch of changes, I signed off on the changes and, *voilà*, a book appeared. Not so this book. Don Lamm and Hilary Hinzmann pushed me unmercifully. But they rewrote hardly a word; rather, they thoughtfully left the job to me. And rewrite I did—three times, to be exact. The result, I think, was a better manuscript each time, so if you like what you're reading, give a lot of credit to Don and Hilary. Their job wasn't easy; they had to fight me every inch of the way.

Lastly, I come to my long-suffering family. About 90% of the time, I work alone in a bedroom-office in Napa. My wife, Sue, works alone in the adjacent bedroom-office. We see each other about 5,000 times a day. Sue gave up an excellent career as a nursing home administrator to work with me. She likes to joke that she's still running a nursing home, but with only one patient. I don't find that very funny myself. The standard deviation of my temperament is so wide that it has to be expressed in scientific notation, but, fortunately for me, Sue's disposition is as placid as mine is stormy. Without her research help and, more important, without her nursing care, this manuscript would never have been completed. I can recall, for example, the many times when she grabbed my Don Lamm and Hilary Hinzmann dolls out of my hand before I could thrust the pins in. I also want to thank my daughter, Amy, who has been analyzing proxy statements for two years now as a way to earn some money for college. She'd be the first to tell you that working the counter at McDonald's would be an excellent career move compared to what's she been doing.

I hope you can see, gentle reader, that any credit for this book must be shared by many people, and not just me. My heartfelt thanks go to them all.

IN
SEARCH
OF
EXCESS

One

Everybody Makes It

As THE FINANCIAL BOOM of the 1980s went bust in a painful recession in 1990 and 1991, the news media turned a spotlight on CEO Disease. Newspapers, magazines, and television news all depicted the modern American CEO as a cross between the ancient Pharaohs and Louis XIV— an imperial personage who almost never sees what the little people do, who is served by boot-licking lackeys, who rules from posh offices, who travels in limousines that have become so long that, like hook and ladder trucks, a second driver will soon have to be hired to steer the back end of the car around tight corners, and in that modern-day equivalent of Cleopatra's barge, the corporate jet, and who is paid so much more than ordinary workers that he hasn't got the slightest clue as to how the rest of the country lives. The oddest thing about all the fuss is that it was right on target.

Ever since money became the medium of exchange, and perhaps even before that, people have debated how much a man's (or, more recently, a woman's) labor is worth. Plato told Aristotle that no one in a community should earn more than five times the pay of the lowest-paid worker. Aristotle wrote down what Plato said, but, regrettably, he didn't include the rationale for the statement. During the Middle Ages, Catholic philosophers were caught up in debates over the doctrine of just price, which rested on a belief that there was a divine justification for why one type of labor commanded more pay than another. But whatever pronouncements they made were essentially ignored. At the end of the nineteenth century, J. P. Morgan decreed that chief executives of the Morgan enterprises should not be paid more than twenty times the pay of the lowest worker in the enterprise. (Of course, he may have had a method to his madness, because by keeping a lid on executive pay, he successfully lowered costs and increased profits. And guess who owned all the shares?) Most recently, Peter Drucker, the management philosopher from Southern California, taking a page from J. P. Morgan, also opined that a CEO should not earn more than twenty times the pay of his lowest worker.

The notion of some sort of optimum pay ratio has been given concrete expression, from time to time, in government-imposed pay controls. In 1973, President Nixon imposed such controls, not merely on executives but on all workers. The reason? He was alarmed that inflation rate was threatening to push up to as high as 5%—a level that today is all but taken for granted. But pay controls, which are merely price controls under a different name (the pay of a person being the price of his labor), have an abundant history of failure. In 1973, for example, the government at first decreed that no executive could receive more than a 5% increase in a given year, even if the executive was being promoted and moving to a different company. That notion quickly proved unproductive, since hardly anyone was willing to change employers. Then the government decreed that there would be no pay ceiling when someone was moving to another company; rather, the pay ceiling would be reapplied once the move was made. That revised notion also proved unproductive, since now everyone was willing to change employers, and the executive recruiters had a field day.

Experience with direct price controls has been equally dismal. At one point the government of Iran, out of an apparent desire to help its peasants, decreed that the price of wheat be set lower than the price of grains traditionally fed to animals. The result: the peasantry ate the feed grains themselves and fed the wheat to their animals. More recently, the government of the Soviet Union has run aground over the issue of administered prices that distort the use of scarce economic resources.

Frustrated by attempts to control incomes directly, those persuaded that there should be a relatively narrow gap between the pay of top executives and the pay of lowest-paid workers have turned to the tax code. As recently as 1963, an executive who earned taxable income of over $400,000 per year (the equivalent figure today, after correcting for cost of living changes since 1963, would be around $1.7 million) would have been subjected to a marginal tax rate (the rate applicable to any further dollars of taxable income) as high as 91%. And very recently, President Bush became embroiled with the Democratically controlled Congress over the issue of tax fairness and whether or not the rich were paying too little in the way of taxes.

The fact is that every society, whether that of ancient Rome, the United States, or the Soviet Union, has exhibited extreme ambivalence over the issue of pay differentials between the top and bottom of organizations. Consider the Soviets, for example. Until President Gorbachev blew things apart, that country prided itself as a model of egalitarianism. Prices were controlled, and so were pay levels. A person holding a job equivalent to that of a CEO in America might earn only five times the pay of an ordinary worker. But there was no income tax to reduce that differential further in after-tax terms. And Soviet CEOs received lavish perquisites, including large apartments in Moscow at tiny rents—apartments that ordinary citizens could never aspire to; large dachas in the country; chauffeured Zil limousines; and perhaps most important the privilege of shopping in special department stores. There, the elite could not only buy goods from the West—goods that were totally unavailable to the masses—but they could also buy goods available to the ordinary citizen, *at one fifth the regular price.* So much for egalitarianism in the Soviet Union.

It is hard to remember what was going on in the United Kingdom before Margaret Thatcher, since she served as prime minister for so long. But there was a time, not too many years ago, when the U.K. used the tax mechanism with a vengeance to assure that after-tax pay differentials were relatively minimal. Taxes rose to 88% and beyond. But again reflecting the ambivalence that people feel about compensation, the same British government that was imposing an 88% tax rate was permitting its more affluent citizens to deduct their bespoke suits, crafted with loving care in Savile Row, from their tax returns on the basis that they were "uniforms." (U.K. companies today grant fewer perquisites than in the past, but a perennial favorite is the company car. According to *The Economist,* more than half the cars sold in the U.K. each year are bought by companies for their employees.)

Perhaps the gamest attempt to control executive pay occurred in Denmark during the late 1960s. There, if an executive's pay rose beyond $53,000 per year, the marginal tax rose to 105%. Based on my limited research into Danish taxation, few people in Denmark made more than $53,000 per year in the late 1960s. And those who did, of course, kept far less.

As for the United States, from around the globe comes the message, year after year, that we have the most materialistic society going. We also have an abiding faith in individualism and merit. We have been, and still are, worshipful of the person who comes from humble beginnings and with great skill rises to the top. Materialism, when combined with individualism and an appreciation of merit, leads to a willingness to offer an achiever considerable financial rewards. In 1930, when Babe Ruth was the reigning figure in baseball, a reporter challenged Ruth's very high pay. He asked Ruth how a mere ballplayer could justify earning $80,000 per year—$5,000 more than the salary of Herbert Hoover, the president of the United States. The Babe's reply: "I had a better year than he did!"

Today, the president of the United States, the country's CEO, receives a salary of $200,000 per year. We pay some of our entertainers, our athletes, our investment bankers and lawyers and, especially, our corporation CEOs vastly more than that—every month. (Viewed from a more global pay perspective, however, the president doesn't make out all that badly. He has free room and board, and the "room" in this case is a rather impressive, centrally located mansion, replete with God knows how many wood-burning fireplaces. And there are many perks, too, including the use of private helicopters and a private Boeing 747. Among other things, think about how much it would cost to hire the Marine Band to play at one of your dinner parties.) But things have gone too far, I believe. While the pay—in inflation-discounted dollars—of the average American worker has decreased by almost 13% during the past twenty years and by some 5% during the 1980s, the pay of the typical CEO of a major company—in those same inflation-discounted dollars—has risen more than three times. (Although the inflation-adjusted pay of the average worker has declined substantially during the past twenty years, that of the average worker in manufacturing has remained virtually unchanged. It is possible, therefore, that the decrease in real, all-worker pay is illusory and is largely a function of the shift in jobs from higher-paying manufacturing industries to lower-paying service industries that has been occurring for several decades. Nonetheless, a finding that manufacturing pay has been flat for twenty years, while CEO pay has risen more than three times, is plenty damning enough.) Where that typical CEO earned total compensation (excluding perquisites and fringe benefits) that was around 35 times the pay of an average manufacturing worker in 1974, a typical CEO today earns pay that is around 120 times that of an average manufacturing worker and about 150 times that of the average worker in both manufacturing and service industries. And U.S. tax policy during the past twenty years has just made matters worse. The total tax load on highly paid executives has declined substantially at the same time that the total tax load on the average worker has increased—though only by a little. The result is that, during the past twenty years or so, the pay of the average worker, expressed in inflation-discounted dollars and adjusted for taxes, has dropped around 13%, whereas the pay of the average CEO of a major company, also expressed in inflation-discounted dollars and adjusted for taxes, has risen more than four times.

To put things into perspective, a 1991 study I undertook for

Fortune showed that 86% of the CEOs among 200 major companies (the top 100 industrials, the top 50 diversified service companies, and the top 10 from each of the listings for commercial banks, diversified financial institutions, retailers, transportation companies, and utilities) earned $1 million or more per year, while the average CEO earned $1.4 million per year in base salary and annual bonus, and $2.8 million per year when the value of long-term incentives such as stock options was figured in.

And these figures are merely averages. They tell nothing about CEOs whose total compensation is far above the averages—CEOs like J. Peter Grace of W. R. Grace, who in 1973–75 earned about 47 times the pay of an average U.S. manufacturing worker, and in 1987–89 earned about 200 times that worker's pay. Or the late Armand Hammer of Occidental Petroleum, who in the same period went from earning about 41 times the pay of a manufacturing worker to about 138 times. Or Richard Eamer, the CEO of National Medical Enterprises, whose pay ratio rose from about 33 times to about 625 times—a rate of increase that, if applied to the company's nurses, would have guaranteed NME a more than ample supply of professionals in this critically short skill category. And finally, averages say nothing about the person who has most likely earned more compensation than any public-company CEO in history, Steven Ross of Time Warner. His pay rose from about 150 times the pay of an average U.S. manufacturing worker in 1973 to more than 9,000 times the pay of that worker in 1989. Much more will be said of these and other CEOs in succeeding chapters.

These huge gaps at home between the pay of a CEO and the pay of a worker might be less reprehensible if the same huge gaps could be demonstrated in our major competitors—Japan, Germany, France, and the United Kingdom. But my research reveals that only the U.K. shows signs of catching the U.S. executive compensation virus, and it has only a mild case. In contrast to the 160 times by which the pay of an American CEO exceeds the pay of an average American worker, the corresponding differential in Japan is under 20; and even in the U.K., it is under 35.

Throughout this book, I detail case after case of pay abuse. These cases raise a fundamental question: Is the system rotten around the core, or is it rotten to the core? In other words, are we dealing with a handful of abusers, statistical outliers who, in a perverse way, merely demonstrate that the basic system, the system that applies to thousands of CEOs and other senior executives, is fundamentally sound? Hicks Waldron, formerly the CEO of Avon Products, answered that question in the affirmative when he appeared this past May on the ABC program "Nightline."

Until a couple of years ago, I would have agreed with him. But now I have some grave doubts about the entire system. To be sure, if I remove the key outliers from my 202-CEO, 1991, study for *Fortune*—outliers like Steven Ross and Nicholas Nicholas of Time Warner, Paul Fireman of Reebok, Anthony O'Reilly of H. J. Heinz, Michael Eisner of Walt Disney, and Rand Araskog of ITT—the average total direct compensation of the group drops from $2.8 million per year to $2.4 million.

Even so, does a pay package of $2.4 million make any sense? Consider first that the CEO receiving $2.4 million per year is earning some 130 times the pay of an average American worker. And as we have seen, that ratio has been widening at an accelerating rate during the last twenty years or so. Consider also that the direction of that pay ratio has been even more steep when the decrease in income tax rates for highly paid executives is taken into account. And most important, consider what our key trading partners—a better word is fierce competitors—are paying their CEOs and other senior executives. There is little comfort in learning that the average pay of an American CEO drops from $2.8 million to $2.4 million after the outliers are removed, when one is forced to consider that the $2.4 million pay figure is still more than seven times higher than a major Japanese company pays its CEO.

In the compensation world, the issue of whether someone is making too much or too little pay is resolved by conducting a survey. That in turn involves selecting a group of comparator companies, measuring how much they pay for a particular position and then comparing the resulting findings to the pay being offered by the company conducting the survey. A key issue here is just who enters the comparator group. Until now, a GM has doubtless included Ford and Chrysler in its comparator group and probably many other major American companies as well. But has a GM thought to include Toyota in its comparator group? Or Nissan? And until now, an IBM has doubtless included AT&T and Apple Computer in its comparator group. But has it thought to include Fujitsu in its comparator group? Or NEC?

It's hard not to believe that GM or IBM study the selling prices of their Japanese competitors when they decide the prices at which to sell their own products. And it's hard not to believe that GM or IBM study how much Japanese companies are paying their factory workers when they analyze their own cost structures. So if Toyota and Nissan, or if Fujitsu or NEC, are valid comparators for pricing and labor cost determinations, why are they not valid comparators for determining the pay of American executives?

When asked that question on a national television talk show this past spring, one well-known compensation consultant snorted to the effect that "you can't compare the pay of an American CEO to his Japanese counterpart, because the cultures are so different." Granted the cultures are very different, and, unhappily, so are the products. The Japanese make better cars than we do, and they offer them at better prices. The Japanese culture may be different, but that different culture is killing us. So, to dismiss different executive pay levels in other countries against whom we compete every day in the international and domestic marketplaces is plain fatuous. We had better start including the CEOs of Japanese, German, French, and U.K. companies in our comparator groups, and we had better start doing so right now. If we do, then what do you suppose will happen? Average pay will drop, because that's the result when you add below-average paid executives to a comparator group. And if average pay drops, then American companies with high executive pay scales will no longer be able to say with a clear conscience that "we are simply paying the average and meeting the market." Those same companies are going to have to cut the pay of their CEOs and other senior executives.

If we're paying $2.2 million and the Japanese are paying around

$300,000, that gap is going to have to be reduced, if not eliminated entirely. Of course, we can try to persuade the Japanese to pay their executives more. But there's little chance that we'll succeed, because the Japanese are, on the evidence, just too smart to fall into that trap.

Then, too, we need to consider that the bloated pay packages of American CEOs, with very few exceptions, contain hardly any pay risk. Those CEOs get paid hugely in good years and, if not hugely, then merely wonderfully in bad years. So even the defense that high pay is required because of the high risks being taken is shot full of holes.

Is the system rotten around the core or to the core? I'll take Choice B.

Criticize a highly paid CEO about the size of his pay package and he will be apt to respond along these lines: "You think I'm paid too much? Go look at how much Jose Canseco makes! And Joe Montana. And several hundred other sports stars. Go look at how much Bill Cosby makes. And Jack Nicholson. And several hundred other movie stars, directors, and producers. Go look at how much Felix Rohaytn of Lazard Freres makes working on Wall Street. And corporate adviser Bruce Wasserstein. And several thousand other investment bankers. And while you're at it, don't forget about Michael Milken! Heck, go look at how much Samuel Butler makes at that big New York law firm, Cravath, Swaine & Moore. And Arthur Liman at Paul Weiss. And several thousand other big league attorneys."

Earlier that morning, the very same CEO likely had a bruising conversation with his chief human resources officer concerning the so-called doctrine of comparable worth. That doctrine, which has been heartily embraced by most feminist organizations, holds that there is something wrong with a society that pays a truck driver more than a nurse, an electrician more than a schoolteacher—and so forth. The reason advanced for these disparities is that occupations like nursing and teaching are heavily populated by women, who have long been the victims of pay discrimination. The remedy: Look at positions by comparing their true worth to one another in terms of skills and responsibilities, and then pay them accordingly. A nurse will shortly be discovered to be worth as much as, and most likely more than, a truck driver, and a teacher will be discovered to be worth as much as, or most likely more than, an electrician.

A member of President Reagan's cabinet pronounced the doctrine of comparable worth "loonier than Loony Tunes." CEOs—and the CEOs and top executives of our biggest corporations are almost exclusively male—have routinely railed against it on the basis that it contravenes the one principle that underlies free markets everywhere: the law of supply and demand. Hence, electricians supposedly make more than schoolteachers because there are relatively few people who want to be electricians and relatively many people who want to be schoolteachers. Upsetting the law of supply and demand, it is argued, can undermine our entire society. For example, because of union bargaining, New York City's sanitation workers are paid virtually the same as the city's policemen and firemen, yet they are highly unlikely to be shot or burned to death in the line of duty. And like New York's policemen and firemen, they get to retire with generous pensions after only twenty years on the job. Recently, New York City advertised for a very few sanitation workers; even though picking up the garbage is considered one of society's lowest-ranking occupations, some 3,000 candidates showed up to take the Civil Service examination (which, because of the need to demonstrate realism in such examinations, consisted of carrying two garbage cans around an obstacle course in the shortest possible time). Raising the pay of schoolteachers to that of electricians, it is argued, will attract too many candidates to become schoolteachers; meanwhile, other occupations will go begging for candidates, and society will end up footing a heavier bill for labor, with the result that inflation and all sorts of other bad things will happen. Obviously, the doctrine of comparable worth is an emotional topic for most CEOs. Raising it is broadly equivalent to zapping them with those electric-shock paddles used in cases of ventricular fibrillation.

Of course, the CEO who was railing about the doctrine of comparable worth in the morning can turn right around in the afternoon and compare himself to sports stars, movie stars, investment bankers, and lawyers—all without missing a beat, and all without realizing that he is using the very same comparable worth argument that the social critics have been trying to get him to accept for years.

Nonetheless, let's look at how much these players in other fields do get paid. First, we have the pay of sports stars as reported in the *Sporting News,* the *New York Times,* and *Forbes.* Roger Clemens of the Boston Red Sox was arguably the highest-paid baseball player in early 1991. Recently, he signed a four-year contract worth $21.5 million, or $5.4 million per year. Jose Canseco of the Oakland Athletics probably is the second highest paid; he has a five-year contract worth $23.5 million, or $4.7 million per year. Both Clemens and Canseco, of course, will also earn substantial extra monies for endorsing various commercial products. Indeed, Joe Montana, the star quarterback for the San Francisco Forty-Niners, earns more from product endorsements than he does from being a football player—about $4 million for the endorsements, versus a salary of around $3 million from the Forty-Niners. Even sports stars who have gone over the hill can continue to earn a great deal. *Forbes* estimated the 1991 earnings of Jack Nicklaus, perhaps the greatest golfer who ever lived, at $8.5 million, consisting of a scant $500,000 of prize money and $8 million from product endorsements and appearance fees. When F. Ross Johnson was running RJR Nabisco, Nicklaus was hired to play golf with clients of the company. Nicklaus's pay for a two-year contract: $1 million. However, Nicklaus, good as he is and was, trails another golfer, Arnold Palmer, whose 1991 earnings include $9 million in fees for product endorsements and commercials.

The list can go on and on. Suffice it to say that there are plenty of sports stars out there who make as much as or more than the average CEO. But no sports star makes as much as the highest-paid CEOs. The $200 million or so that accrued to Steve Ross's benefit in 1989, following the acquisition of his company, Warner Communications, by Time Inc., or the $40 million that Michael Eisner of Walt Disney earned in 1988 simply doesn't exist in the sports world.

One also has to consider that there is, arguably, more pay-for-performance built into the remuneration packages of sports stars than there is in the case of CEOs. In his doctoral dissertation (which must have been a lot of fun to research and write), Kenneth Lehn, formerly the Chief Economist of the Securities and Exchange Commission, developed mathematical models to predict the pay of 218 major league pitchers and 358 major league non-pitchers. He could explain more than 70% of the variation in pay between these two groups by knowing a number of factors, all of them quite sensible. Several of those factors were directly related to the past performance of the pitchers (their earned run average during the past three seasons, the average number of innings pitched during the past three seasons, and whether or not the pitcher had earned the Cy Young Award), or the non-pitchers (the number of times at bat during the past three seasons, the batting average during the past three seasons, and the number of stolen bases during the past three seasons). Another factor he found to be significant in predicting pay was the number of years the player had been in the major leagues. In the industrial world, people also tend to be paid more for each further year of experience. The only difference is that the limitation on the number of players a team can have dictates that unproductive ballplayers be weeded out quickly; a limitation on the number of purely corporate executives permitted in an industrial company might also prove quite helpful.

Would that the world of industry were as rational as that of major league ballplayers. In my annual surveys for *Fortune,* I can never push the explanation of CEO pay variation beyond about 40%. Compare that to the 70% pay variation Lehn calculates for baseball players. In short, there is a lot more irrational noise in the way CEOs are paid than there is in the way major league ballplayers are paid.

Kenneth Lehn made another important discovery in his doctoral research. It turns out that most ballplayers' compensation comes only in the form of salary. Product endorsements go to the very few. And the world of complicated annual bonus schemes and exotic long-term incentive plans is alien to the ballpark. The absence of such current incentives means that the pay of a ballplayer tends to be related more to his performance in past seasons than to his performance in this season. To be sure, if the player has a great year or, alternatively, screws up, that result will likely have a significant impact on how much he is paid once his current contract expires and he must negotiate a new one. But that event may be several years away. Because this is so, Lehn found that the more a pay package was predicated on past performance and the greater the length of the pay contract, the likelier it was that the ballplayer would sustain a disability and stay out of commission for a lengthy period. In other words, if you have your pay package "locked," the incentive to come to work each day and to do your best is somewhat blunted, compared to having to put your shoulder to the wheel to receive a current incentive payment.

What Lehn demonstrated here was the opposite proposition to "incentives motivate"; rather, he demonstrated that "lack of incentives demotivates." It's too bad that Lehn's research has not found a wider audience among boards of directors, because if it had, perhaps those boards wouldn't now be so busily engaged in restructuring the pay packages of their company's senior executives to remove any real incentives. As it is, today's typical CEO is given a huge base salary, a guaranteed bonus, a slushy award of free stock that pays off even if the stock price falls by half, a pile of perks, and a lush Golden Parachute just in case he can't find his way to the batter's box. The effect in the industrial world ought to be broadly comparable to that in the ballpark—not so much, perhaps, in a diminished incentive to come to work each day, but rather in the will to play at peak form each day.

Perhaps the most important argument undercutting the notion that the pay of CEOs should be compared to that of sports stars concerns the way in which pay is established in the first place. Take Jose Canseco. His agent must have spent a lot of time negotiating with Walter Haas, the owner of the Oakland Athletics. Haas is no mean slouch when it comes to the world of business; among other things, he grew up in the very business-oriented family that has successfully run Levi Strauss for well over a hundred years. One has to presume, therefore, that he would not have agreed to pay Canseco $4.7 million per year unless he thought he could gain something for the Oakland Athletics in the process—increased profit that would flow from the many extra fans who would come to the ballpark to see Canseco play or tune in Athletics' games on television and radio.

Haas's decision to pay Canseco $4.7 million per year resulted from a negotiation remarkably different from the kind CEOs engage in over their own compensation. The paradigm of fair price setting is perhaps the fabled Arabian rug bazaar. The seller begins the negotiations by asking an outlandish price for his merchandise. The buyer responds with a price so low that the seller tears his garments. Much screaming and yelling ensues, punctuated by the buyer's throwing up his hands in disgust and commencing to walk away. Finally, a bargain is struck. The seller is secretly happy, because had he no other recourse, he would have lowered his price even more. The buyer is secretly happy, too, because had he no other recourse, he would have swallowed hard and offered the seller more money. Moreover, when the negotiation between the buyer and seller began, the seller had a pretty good sense of the final prices his competitors were willing to offer. And for his part, the buyer had already been comparison-shopping in the bazaar, as well as learning about the merchandise that was available and its quality. So, all the elements of a good price were present: an informed seller; an informed buyer; and vigorous, indeed, almost violent, arm's-length negotiations.

Probably the negotiations between Jose Canseco and Walter Haas were a bit less colorful than those in the Arabian rug bazaar. But only a bit less. For his part, Canseco was obviously economically interested in the outcome of the bargaining, and his agent presumably had considerable knowledge useful to the negotiations. In turn, Haas was just as obviously economically interested in the outcome of the bargaining, and he also had considerable knowledge useful to the negotiations. After all, Canseco's agent and Haas have access to pretty much the same information, though each will interpret it differently. Salaries of major league ballplayers are available through the players' union, players' performance statistics are printed in the newspapers every day of the season, attendance figures and TV-radio game ratings are probably available to anyone who knows where to look. A savvy agent presumably finds out how much each 30-second commercial on a local A's or Yankees broadcast brings the club in ad revenue. The club, of course, will claim it's just making ends meet, and the agent will claim the club's rolling in dough. Sounds a lot like the Arabian rug bazaar after all, doesn't it? Finally, the bargaining between a Canseco and a Haas is conducted at arm's length, with each party seeking to maximize his own self-interest. On that basis, therefore, I can only conclude that Jose Canseco is worth the $4.7 million he is being paid. Or at least, he is worth $4.7 million to Walter Haas, the man who has committed to pay the sum. So, if Walter Haas thinks Jose Canseco is worth $4.7 million—especially after a series of arduous negotiations—who, honestly, can say he is not?

In the next chapter, we'll be looking at how negotiations are conducted when the CEO is the seller—in this case, of his own services. Suffice it to say, there's a world of difference. Indeed, several of the elements crucial to setting a valid price are missing altogether: compensation committees of boards of directors tend neither to be shrewd negotiators nor to conduct arm's-length negotiations.

Next, we come to pay in the entertainment world as reported in the *New York Times* and *San Francisco Chronicle.* Ever since the time of Louis B. Mayer, Hollywood stars, producers, and, more recently, directors, have been earning fortunes. Bill Cosby is reported to have earned $115 million over a two-year period from his various endeavors. Motion picture director Steven Spielberg earned some $87 million, again over two years. And hiring stars like Tom Cruise can cost a studio $8 to $12 million—for a single picture. Jack Nicholson made not a small fortune but a large fortune from playing the Joker in *Batman.* Besides his huge direct pay from the producers, he also received lots of extra remuneration from merchandising the Joker doll and image. Pop stars, too, are lavishly paid. Michael Jackson earned $100 million over the same period. And Madonna raked in $62 million. Indeed, the pay of the key players in the entertainment world makes the pay of sports stars seem like small change.

Like sports stars, the pay of movie stars and pop musicians is predicated heavily on their box-office drawing power, or at least the box-office appeal of the films in which they act, or their recordings. However, a number of enlightened movie studios are cutting deals under which the star takes less fixed compensation and in return receives, if the studio has the upper hand in the negotiations, a percentage of the picture's net profit, or, if the star has the upper hand, a percentage of the gross revenues accruing to the studio. Taking a percentage of gross revenues guarantees, of course, that the star will receive some additional reward for his or her services—even if the film never makes a nickel or loses money. Taking a percentage of the film's profits is a bit more problematic, however, because it exposes the actor to a world that exhibits far more creativity than the actor himself—Hollywood's system of accounting for film profits. Take a blockbuster like *Batman,* for example. It grossed over $250 million. But by the time the Hollywood bean counters got through levying cost after cost against the picture, the film was reported to have lost more than $35 million.

Whether pay is predicated on past performance or current performance, there is much more pay-for-performance, albeit with very high numbers, among movie stars than there is among CEOs. And there is also a pronounced willingness on the part of studio heads to dump a star the moment that he or she is no longer drawing the crowds—or, to put it more succinctly, the moment that he or she is no longer a star.

Once again, however, we have to remember that the pay of these worthies was established after arm's-length bargaining by economically interested parties who have considerable knowledge of what they are doing. True, someone may hire Tom Cruise to make a movie, pay him, say, $12 million, and then watch the movie bomb. Looking backwards, the decision was utterly dumb. But one can look backwards at a stock one bought for $50 and had to sell for $25 and reach the same conclusion. Making a dumb decision on a stock doesn't prove that the price of stocks is set irrationally. After all, no one has yet perfected a way to predict the future.

That a free market, though perhaps one that is crazed, operates in the world of motion pictures can be seen from the huge publicity recently given to a lengthy memorandum written by Jeffrey Katzenberg, the head of Walt Disney's motion picture units. Katzenberg decried the huge sums being spent on making movies—sums that are for the most part fueled by the high pay of stars. He vowed to fight back and, in a manner reminiscent of Nancy Reagan's anti-drug campaign, to just say no. Perhaps he will not be successful in persuading Hollywood's superstars to cut their pay, but his counterpressure is what free markets are all about.

There is also the princely paid world of investment bankers. According to a front-page article in *The Wall Street Journal,* Bruce Wasserstein's company, Wasserstein Perella & Co., one of the hottest investment banking firms of the 1980s, received a $5.5 million fee from a single client, Interco, for "five months of work by perhaps two dozen people, most of them working on Interco only part-time." And the pay of partners of Goldman, Sachs, perhaps Wall Street's most prestigious investment banking firm, is rumored to be in the many millions per partner in a good year. And Michael Milken, the Beverly Hills investment banker who earned more than $500 million in pay in a single year and who was the driving force behind the now-discredited junk market, is currently earning about 40 cents per hour under what you might think of as a pay contract with a term of up to ten years that he negotiated with the federal government.

The same two arguments crop up again. First, there is a fair amount of pay-for-performance among investment bankers. If you set up and then tout a deal that turns out to be a disaster, there's a good chance that other companies will turn elsewhere for investment advice. There's a certainty that the client you hurt will turn elsewhere. Second, though Wall Street pros are rumored to be brilliant, they still have to negotiate their fees with some pretty smart people on the other side—people like the chief financial officers of major corporations. And in these days when so-called relationship banking (in which a company sticks with its investment banking firm year in, year out, rather than letting various investment banking firms compete for each deal) has fallen on hard times, pay-for-performance is stronger than ever.

There is also a third aspect to consider. If Wasserstein Perrella or Goldman, Sachs loses money, then Bruce Wasserstein and the partners of Goldman, Sachs will also lose money. Not so with most

CEOs. They can make huge amounts of money, but it is hard for them to lose much money. (Outright losses can be generated to the extent the CEO has substantial shareholdings in his company, but most CEOs do not.) No matter how many times I have touted them, negative bonuses—the kind where the CEO writes a check to the company—have just never caught on.

And there is even a fourth aspect to consider. Working on Wall Street is an exceedingly volatile experience. During the 1980s, it seemed that anyone with a big-school MBA could trot down to Wall Street and rake in a million a year before he or she reached the age of thirty. The pay of Wall Streeters had anti-gravity characteristics— high every year, no matter what. All that has changed since the stock market crash of 1987. Thousands upon thousands of jobs in the investment banking world have been lost, and more than a few highly paid investment bankers are currently said to be considering driving taxicabs.

Finally, we come to the lawyers. According to *The American Lawyer,* the sixty-six partners of Cravath, Swaine & Moore earned $1.5 million per partner in 1990. Even at the tenth-most profitable law firm—Fried, Frank, Harris, Shriver & Jacobson—the average pay for each of that firm's 107 partners was $835,000.

Now pay of $1.5 million per year can't hold a candle to the pay of your typical big company CEO. But what is impressive about the pay in law firms is the *sheer number* of people who can earn relatively large sums of money. Or, to put it another way, the pay among law partners is more egalitarian, while the pay among senior executives in major industrial firms is more hierarchical. Even among the highest-paying industrial firms, it would be difficult to find the top sixty-six executives earning an average of $1.5 million per year.

To echo the famous line in *Casablanca,* the usual suspects must be rounded up once again. First, one has to suppose that pay-for-performance exists among law firms. If you're looking for a good attorney, you are highly unlikely to retain one who has a terrible win/loss ratio or one who routinely gets you into hot water with the SEC or the IRS. So it is no accident that the most highly regarded law firm in the United States, Cravath, Swaine & Moore, also produces the most profits for each of its partners. Second, though there may be less arm's-length bargaining over fees between a company and its law firm than there is in the world of sports, movies, and investment banking (mainly because of the imperfect knowledge that the buyers of legal services have about how much work is required to accomplish a given task, and also because of the lack of ability to forecast the direction in which the give-and-take of legal battling will head), a law firm that charges way too much for its services will likely get its comeuppance eventually. Already, a movement is afoot among major companies to seek alternative dispute resolutions (mediation, arbitration, mini-trials, and so forth) as a way of reducing the growing cost of litigation. Finally, lawyers, like investment bankers, can lose real money if their firm sustains a loss in a given year. Recently a well-known, and huge, law firm—Finley, Kumble—self-destructed. One has to suppose that its partners took substantial hits to their personal balance sheets, given that law firms use a partnership form of organization that leaves partners exposed to losses sustained by the partnership.

In summary, there are quite a few people in other fields who are making nearly as much as and sometimes a lot more than your typical big company CEO. But there are lots of good reasons why this is so. And because those reasons don't figure very heavily in the compensation of CEOs, the argument that a CEO should earn what he earns—or even earn more—because of what sports stars or movie stars or investment bankers or top lawyers earn simply doesn't hold much water.

Two

How They Do It

Imagine yourself as the CEO of a large company. Being a red-blooded American who has fought his way to the top of the organization and also being a fan of Adam Smith—the eighteenth-century economist who argued that there was nothing wrong with trying to maximize your own personal gain because an "invisible hand" would operate to regulate the economy for the greatest good—you're always ready to earn more money.

Now you could simply go to your friendly board of directors and rattle your tin cup in their direction. But naked displays of greed can be a bit embarrassing, and there is always the possibility, though you know it is tiny, that the board will say no. As an alternative, you could have your in-house director of compensation perform some sort of study showing conclusively that you are wildly underpaid. But some snide board member or other will needle you about your director of compensation's objectivity; after all, he works for the vice president of human resources, who reports to the senior vice president of administration, who reports to you; with nothing more than an almost imperceptible lifting of your left eyelid, you can send him packing.

So, not knowing quite what to do, you bring up the subject during your regular Saturday afternoon golf game with three other CEOs. One of them immediately responds: Get a compensation consultant. You promptly inquire as to which consultants your golfing buddies use, and perhaps you do a bit more checking. Then you have your head of human resources interview two or three potential consultants before permitting the finalist to be ushered into your presence.

At this point, you have to decide on the line of attack you will be pursuing with your board. You can, for example, argue that the top management of the company is underpaid and needs some sort of raise. Or, if your company is a great performer, you can argue that high performance deserves high pay. Here you may be conceding that you and your top managers are already paid at the average compared to other companies, or even above the average. But you and your top managers are not being paid as high as you should be, given the superior performance of the company. Or, if your company is imbued with canine characteristics, you can argue that unless something is done to "keep our good people," then the good people will soon depart for greener pastures. Lost in this argument, of course, is the fact that if you had that many good people, your company wouldn't be such a dog. Or, if all else fails, you can argue that the pay package of the top managers is not motivational enough. Some new form of incentive compensation is therefore needed to spur the top management to action.

If you decide on the first strategy—namely, that you and your top managers are underpaid—you start the meeting with your newly retained compensation consultant by suggesting that he (or she) perform a survey of what other companies pay. The consultant is uniquely equipped to handle such a task. If your own in-house compensation director tried to call your competitors and find out what they are paying, he would likely hear a click, followed by a dial tone. After all, why would a competitor want to give you the time of day? But a compensation consultant, if he is trusted by all the parties, can obtain data from all your competitors, as well as yourself. Then he can analyze the data statistically and put out a report that will be given not only to you but to every participating company. The report will never disclose what any specific company pays. Even you will never know what Competitor XYZ pays, though you foot the entire bill for conducting the survey. Rather, you and your competitors will receive such information as the survey average, the survey median, what the highest and lowest companies pay (but no names here), and so forth. Thus, you will be able to get a sense of what's going on out there in the marketplace, without knowing what any single company pays. Your competitors will be happy to participate in such a survey, provided it is professionally conducted, because they, too, receive valuable feedback on the market, and they don't have to pay a cent.

If a survey is going to be conducted, two questions immediately crop up. Which companies should we survey? And which forms of compensation should we survey? Ideally, any list of survey companies ought to meet some sort of "smell test." That is to say, an objective observer of the scene ought to be able to look over the list of potential survey companies and comprehend almost instantly why each company is on the list. So, if the company commissioning the survey is an oil company, the objective observer will easily understand why Mobil Oil is on the list and why Exxon is on the list and why Atlantic Richfield is on the list. But Walt Disney? You may sheepishly reply: "Well, they use oil, don't they?" Or: "Well, they're headquartered in Los Angeles and so are we." Of course, an equally plausible reason for including Walt Disney in a survey of oil companies is that Michael Eisner, Disney's CEO, earns a ton of money. When Eisner jumps into a swimming pool of compensation data, half the water flies out; he is singlehandedly capable of raising the survey average by $1 million a year. So an immediate issue here is whether the list of survey companies you have chosen is a reasonable one or a self-serving one. A good compensation consultant will gently pressure you into surveying the right companies. A less-than-good consultant may overlook the addition of a few high-paying ringers.

The second issue—what forms of compensation to survey—can also be critical to your getting a raise. If, for example, you believe that your base salary and annual bonus are on the low side, but you know you are receiving a ton of stock options compared to other CEOs, you ask the compensation consultant to survey only base salary and bonus. If he asks, as he should ask, why he isn't being requested to survey the entire compensation package, he can be told something like: "You're absolutely right. But one thing at a time. First, we'll survey base salary and bonus, and then next year, you'll be asked to survey stock options and all the other forms of long-term incentive compensation that various companies use." Drooling over the prospect of a long-running engagement with this client, the consultant may quickly accede to the CEO's blandishments.

If you structure the assignment right—making sure that some high-paying companies, though possibly not Walt Disney, are included in your consultant's survey group, and limiting the survey to those forms of compensation in which you suspect your company is low—you will, in due course, receive back a fancy report that concludes, as you figured it would, that you and your top subordinates are very much in need of pay relief. Then you march right into the compensation committee meeting and present the findings. Or rather, you push the consultant ahead of you as you march into the meeting. He then reports his own findings, using lots of graphs and arcane statistics, while you sit quietly back and enjoy the show. Predictably, the compensation committee reacts with outrage. "Why, this is ridiculous, Bill. We never understood until now that you and the other boys, one woman, and one black are paid so low. We'll be doing something about the matter right away."

If yours is a great-performing company, you can wring almost anything out of your compensation committee. If you're Michael Eisner of Walt Disney or Anthony J. F. O'Reilly of H. J. Heinz—both legendary performers who seem to bat .900 and rarely hit anything less than a triple—then all you have to do is mutter something about going to another company or even heading to the beach to enjoy the millions you have already made, and your compensation committee will fall all over itself to give you virtually anything you want. After all, if the compensation committee offers you a pile of money, and you continue to lay one golden egg after another, no one will criticize the committee's decision, least of all the shareholders, who are earning outsized returns. Indeed, it would be almost loutish of a shareholder to get up at the annual meeting and ask why you should be paid so much. But if the compensation committee calls your bluff, and it turns out you really aren't bluffing and you do indeed go to work for a competitor or head to the beach, then everyone will heap invective on the committee for being stupid, and a few shareholders may even try to sue the company.

If yours is a great-performing company, then, you only have to mention your performance, followed by the mantra "We want to pay for performance," and your compensation consultant will be on his way. Compensation consultants love to work for high-performing companies, because when their recommendations result in huge raises for the CEO and his top management team, they can nonetheless sleep soundly at night. After all, the consultant is not merely taking money to tell the CEO what he wants to hear; he is taking money for helping the shareholders to keep a great top management team intact and permitting it to continue to perform spectacularly for the company's shareholders.

If yours is a poor-performing company, you have a bit more of an uphill struggle to get a raise. But nothing is impossible if you have the right attitude and the right consultant. First, you should admit to the consultant right off that yours is not what you might a call a great-performing company. He will soon find out anyway once he starts analyzing data, or perhaps he already knows, having prepared for his first meeting with you. So you indicate that the company is having some hard times, and you promptly and predictably blame the hard times on external events. If you are the head of a major automobile company, for example, you point to the fact that every one of the Big Three automakers is in trouble, not just your company, and you excoriate the Japanese for not playing the international trade game fairly. Once you finish laying the blame off onto others, you note that you are starting to lose key people. Performance has been so bad that you haven't been able to pay bonuses, and even salary increases have slowed to a crawl. What's more, all those options that were awarded to you three years ago are underwater; that is, the strike prices of the options—what you have to pay to exercise them—are now a lot higher than the current market price.

That wasn't the way things were supposed to work out. The market price was supposed to rise above the strike price so as to give you a good profit. But all those external, and uncontrollable, events intervened to produce an unintended result. During this part of the discussion, you note to the consultant that an executive in your company can quit, cross the street, and go to work for a competitor whose stock has also fallen. But in so doing, he will be exchanging underwater stock options for new options where the strike price is equal to the current market price, and not higher.

Some years ago, Arthur Taylor, who was then president of CBS and who is now dean of the Fordham University Business School, had an organ installed in the antechamber to his office. The organ may have been a bit of an indulgence, although there was some business justification, because CBS then owned a large organ-manufacturing company. Since I was trained from childhood as a pianist and also play the organ a bit, I suggested to Arthur one day that I should be hired as the corporate organist. That way, I could sit outside his office and play mood music appropriate to the occasion. So, if earnings were up, I could offer a few bars from Sigmund Romberg's stirring "Stouthearted Men." Or if earnings were down, I could play Siegfried's foreboding leitmotif from Wagner's *Ring* cycle. Now if I were the corporate organist to a CEO who was persuading a compensation consultant that, though his company's performance was poor, more had to be done for the top management to "keep our talented people with the company during these difficult times," I would want to play something like Massenet's Meditation from the opera *Thaïs*—a piece of music that, underscoring the CEO's stirring words, would cause the consultant to break out in a flood of tears.

In this situation, the consultant would probably reason that there is no need to do a survey. Whether the company is at the moment high-paying or low-paying is not the issue. The issue is that the company will have to do more, or it will lose its talent. Again, the consultant will rarely ponder the fact that the company simply can't have much talent, or it wouldn't be in the position it is in.

Rather, the consultant, if he has any religious bent, will be reminded of the stirring story of the Prodigal Son, which appears in

47

the fifteenth chapter of the Gospel According to Luke. There, we find a younger son who has left home and engaged in a life of riotous living. Awakening one day to find himself a total mess, he repents, takes himself home, and begs his father for forgiveness. Not only does the father forgive him, he kills the family's fatted calf and throws a big party for the kid. (Today, a fatted calf would never do; it contains far too much cholesterol.) The Prodigal's older brother is not amused. While his kid brother was away living his riotous life, he was working in the fields, obeying his father's every wish and, in short, being a good boy. When he faults his father for not giving him a fatted calf, much less throwing him a bash, his father replies: "Son, thou art ever with me, and all that I have is thine. It was meet that we should make merry, and be glad: for this thy brother was dead, and is alive again; and was lost, and is found."

The Bible is full of the promise of redemption. Turn yourself around, and you will be rewarded—even more so than had you never fallen in the first place. So our consultant will rush out and design a new incentive plan that will reward the CEO and his top management lavishly if they remember to face home plate the next time they take to the field. And he will fix those nasty underwater stock options right away. He'll recommend to the board that they simply erase the old strike price on each executive's option agreement and substitute a new, lower strike price.

The consultant will never stop to ponder a difficult problem of logic. If it makes sense to reward a CEO in good times, because that is only just, and if it makes sense to reward a CEO in bad times because you need to keep him with the company, and if there are only two types of times—good times and bad times—then just when, pray tell, is the CEO ever going to get his pay cut? The answer, distressingly, is never.

Finally, if all else fails, the CEO can tell the consultant that he believes the pay packages of the company's top management are not motivational enough. There needs to be an even greater pay-for-performance emphasis incorporated in each executive's pay package. That is again sweet music to the consultant's ear, because he responds to the words "pay-for-performance" in a manner that makes

Pavlov's dogs look sluggish. So the consultant will again forget about doing a compensation survey. The issue here, he will reason, is not pay competitiveness, but rather executive motivation. He will then design a fancy new incentive plan designed to link executive pay to company performance. And he will then add this new incentive plan on top of everything the company is already offering the CEO. He will rarely stop to think that this additional incentive plan, for all its purported motivational magic, is going to increase the company's compensation costs, unless some other element of the pay package is cut back. Or, if he does stop to think about that fact, he may dismiss it on the grounds that the new incentive plan will produce so much more motivation, and hence so much more performance, that the extra costs will be overwhelmed by the extra results the plan will produce.

No matter how the consulting assignment starts, it will almost always end in the meeting room of the compensation committee of the board. It is here that the consultant will make his recommendations. Up to this point, the CEO is not unlike, say, Jose Canseco. He is an informed seller of his talents, because he has a compensation consultant to advise him. But the compensation committee is not very much like Walter Haas, the owner of the Oakland Athletics. Walter Haas is an informed buyer of talent, while the compensation committee is not. It meets only a few times a year, and then only for an hour or so each time. Its members are not pay experts, and they are not given any independent counsel of their own. So they must of necessity rely heavily on what the company's compensation consultant is telling them.

We now come to a divide. If the consultant is honest, he will, like the manufacturer of a drug, cite not only the advantages of what he is recommending but also its side effects. So, if he is recommending a new incentive plan, he will discuss how much the company's overall executive compensation costs will be increasing. And he will take the committee through many possible scenarios of future performance to show it how much, or how little, the CEO will earn under each scenario. In that way, he will help the committee to understand just how sensitive the new incentive plan is to future performance. Of course, if he does this, he may well lose the bulk of the committee members. They are, for the most part, not very adept at statistics and corporate finance, and they may not be able to follow the consultant's sophisticated reasoning. Further, they have no counsel of their own to tell them that what the consultant is saying is or is not true. So they may either fall asleep or look repeatedly at their watches in such a way that the consultant will not fail to notice.

As an alternative, the consultant can avoid all the numbing scenarios and simply present to the committee the CEO's favorite scenario—the one where redemption occurs and the company rides off into the performance sunset. If the budget for this presentation is big enough, the committee members may hear the faint tones of "Stouthearted Men" wafting through the ceiling music system. The committee is generally stirred into immediate action, not knowing, unfortunately, that other performance scenarios—scenarios that are at once more likely to occur and more gloomy than the one the consultant presented—will produce horrifyingly large payouts.

While you're pondering this process, think also about the fact that many of the compensation committee members may be the personal friends of the CEO. And think about the fact that it is the CEO who suggests to the board members how much they should pay themselves. In saying this, I don't mean to suggest that compensation committee members and board members are dishonest people who are willing to sell themselves for a few bucks. Rather, I am only observing that there is a climate of friendship and trust operating here, rather than the more cautious attitude that one usually presents toward someone who is trying to sell you something that will cost you quite a bit of money.

So that's how they do it. A lot of rationalization goes on, and a lot of high-priced talent is retained to prove a conclusion that the CEO has already made. The compensation committee, because it meets so infrequently and has no independent counsel, becomes a willing accomplice. And everybody wins. The CEO gets a raise, the compensation consultant gets his bills paid, and the compensation committee goes home feeling good that it is paying for performance or keeping good people or both. Or almost everybody wins. Everybody but the shareholders.

Three

The Prince of Pay

W<small>ANT A HOLLYWOOD</small> success story that is actually true? Well, start with a young man who is Hollywood-handsome and charismatic to boot. Our hero, who grew up in Brooklyn in exceedingly humble circumstances and who never advanced beyond an A.A. degree, is first found working, improbably enough, as an undertaker in his then father-in-law's business. But the desire to do more than make money out of other people's misfortune—and not that much money, either—burns in him with the intensity of a laser. Soon, he has convinced his in-laws to enter another mundane business, that of parking lots in Manhattan. The new company, called Kinney National, is successful, but going from a below-ground to an on-the-ground occupation is not enough for our hero. Once again, he takes to the acquisition trail, and this time—it could only happen in Hollywood—he bags Warner Brothers, a motion picture studio that, on the evidence, has seen better days. That acquisition forms the core of what shortly becomes known as Warner Communications.

Thereafter, the story, though seemingly unbelievable, gets better and better. First, our hero works to make Warner Brothers one of the best studios in the land. Among other things, he snatches Robert Daly from his top West Coast entertainment job at CBS and makes him head of the studio. Daly knows just what to do, and he does it. Then our hero enters the record business and quickly builds the revenues to a point where they are usually the equal of and sometimes higher than those of the industry leader, CBS Records (now owned by Sony). He also branches into other entertainment-related businesses, including the electronic-game business. His game subsidiary, Atari, produces astounding profits, and Warner Communications' stock breaks record after record in its never-ending ascent. But, alas, the bottom falls out of the electronic-game business, and what had been record profits become about $1 billion of losses. The stock, predictably, falls and falls.

But don't count our hero out yet. He recovers from Atari and leads Warner Communications on a path of relentless growth—both in profits and stock prices. Along the way, he negotiates some pay contracts for himself that leave every other public company executive in America in his rear-view mirror. While negotiating the pay packages, he ends up in a nasty public row with his company's largest shareholder and most influential board member. Meanwhile, he marries, but later divorces, the stepdaughter of the legendary CBS mogul, William S. Paley. Paley respected few people in his long life, and, arguably, none of them were the people that the CBS board kept grooming as his successor. But Paley is reputed to have respected our hero, probably right up to the end of his life. Our hero also managed to have, and recover from, a heart attack. Drama? You bet. But this is Hollywood, and a little drama—indeed, a lot of drama—is just what the doctor ordered.

Our hero's name is Steven J. Ross—Steve to just about everyone. He overcomes these obstacles and many others to climb to the very top of the entertainment industry pyramid. He is not just a faceless CEO, he is, rather, Mr. Entertainment himself. He forms close personal relationships with the top movie stars and recording artists of the day. He lends them Warner Communications' corporate jet so they can spend a little time at Warner Communications' villa in Acapulco. Some nice perks, you say? You're right, but those top movie stars and recording artists bonded with Steve Ross, and kept producing more and more profits for his company.

By 1989, Ross, who was then sixty-two, had everything—or at least everything but the respectability of the blue-blood establishment. That respectability was denied to all who toiled in the entertainment vineyards. Though it has long been a source of considerable profits to such patrician investors as John Hay Whitney (who through contact with William S. Paley, his brother-in-law, decided to invest in various entertainment ventures), the entertainment business was sniffingly regarded as being more than a bit vulgar. On the other hand, a company like Time Inc. had infinite class. Founded by Henry Luce, the Yale-educated son of a Presbyterian missionary, Time didn't just chronicle the goings on of the establishment; it was the establishment. Time was such a desirable concern that it eventually found itself under attack from profit-maximizing, greed-loving characters on Wall Street, and it soon attracted the unwelcome attention of another major entertainment industry figure, Martin S. Davis, the head of Paramount Communications.

Supposedly, executives at Time Inc. had been having talks with Ross about merging with Warner Communications long before Davis appeared on the scene, but there is no question that Davis's presence acted as an exceedingly strong catalyst. After a considerable amount of further drama—including a lawsuit that reached the Delaware Supreme Court—Time Inc. and Warner Communications had to back down from their plans to merge the two companies. A merger would have required the approval of the Time Inc. shareholders, and their disapproval, in the face of Paramount Communication's $200 per share offer for the company, was widely expected. (Many analysts thought that Davis could be persuaded to up his ante to as high as $225 per share.) Instead, Time Inc. called up its friendly bankers and, in a single quarter, increased its long-term borrowings by $9.9 billion. These monies were then used to buy in most of the shares of Warner Communications. The price: a stunning $70 per share—an amount that exceeded by about 40% the $50 or so price at which Warner Communications' stock had been trading just before the merger announcement. (The remainder of Warner Communications' shares were purchased through the issuance of securities rather than for cash.) Ross then became the co-chief executive of the new entity, Time Warner Inc. He now has establishment status, white-haired good looks, renewed health, and huge amounts of pay; by all evidence, he is having lots of fun.

Considering that the decision to deny Time Inc.'s shareholders $200 or even $225 per share was made by the full board of Time Inc., in consultation with lawyers and investment bankers, one is tempted to label what happened to the company's shareholders as a case of gang rape—sort of a boardroom version of Jodie Foster's highly acclaimed movie, *The Accused.* One of the principal players here was Bruce Wasserstein of Wasserstein Perella & Company. Wasserstein opined that a future Time-Warner combination would be a veritable gold mine. Indeed, he told the board that they could figure on a stock price somewhere between $280 and $402 per share by 1993.

Wasserstein may indeed be a brilliant investment banker—at least as judged by the fees he has reaped—but his ability to predict the future is a bit suspect. Time's board, having rejected Paramount's cash offer of $200 per share, and perhaps even $225 per share, and having gone ahead to buy Warner Communications, saw the combined company's stock promptly slump from its high of $182.75 in June 1989 to $96.13 in January 1990. By October 1990, it had dropped even further, to $66.13 per share. Then it began a rebound to around $120 per share as this book is being written. Perhaps Wasserstein will yet be proven correct, and Time Warner's stock will move into the forecasted range of $280 to $402 by 1993. But relocating Time Warner's corporate headquarters to Lourdes might be a useful way to help his prediction along.

Although Ross is likely the highest-paid CEO of a publicly owned company who ever lived, he would barely make the finals in the contest for greatest executive pay villain. He has done an excellent job for his shareholders. From 1973 (the first year for which compensation statistics on Ross still are readily available) through January 1990, when Time acquired Warner Communications and the latter ceased to function as an independent company, Ross engineered a 23.9% compounded annual total return for his shareholders (counting both stock appreciation and dividends). This figure is based on calculating successive ten-year total returns for the 85 monthly starting points, beginning with January 1973 and ending with January 1980. When this performance record is compared to that of the 500 companies which had the highest market capitalization in 1990 (i.e., the aggregate market value of all their outstanding shares) and whose stock had been publicly traded since at least 1971 (a group of 407 companies), Ross ranks at the 83rd percentile of the distribution. In other words, Warner Communication's performance over seventeen years was better than all but 17% of the 407 companies. (If the comparison is extended for a full twenty years—from January 1971 through January 1990, Ross's total return figure drops to 23.4%, but his performance ranking actually rises—to the 88th percentile.) Moreover, Ross achieved this excellent result without subjecting his long-term shareholders to the high volatility that often accompanies superior performance. Looking at the 107 ten-year total return figures calculated between 1971 and 1990, no shareholder who held his stock for an entire ten-year period would have earned less than a 15.2% compounded annual total return on his investment. Indeed, Ross's performance consistency during the 1973–90 period was exceeded only by 11% of the 407 companies.*

So much for the good news. Now let's see what Ross has been paid since 1973. All statistics cited are drawn from public proxy statements. The dates referred to below are for fiscal years.

Let's start with Ross's base salary. The Securities and Exchange Commission (SEC), an arm of the federal government answerable directly to the president, decrees what publicly traded companies are required to disclose concerning their executive compensation levels and practices. The SEC does not, among other things, require companies to separate out the base salary a senior executive is earning. If

---

*All financial figures cited in this book, including total shareholder return rates, earnings per share figures, and return on equity levels, are drawn from data compiled by Standard & Poor's Compustat service. Standard & Poor's is itself a division of McGraw-Hill, the giant New York-headquartered publishing company. All CEO pay data are from company proxy reports.

the company so desires, and most companies do, it need only report the sum of the executive's base salary and his bonus for annual performance. Warner Communications followed the majority practice by not disclosing Ross's salary in 1973 through 1975, but for 1976 and all future years, a salary figure was disclosed. For 1976, Ross earned a base salary of $260,000. It was then raised to $350,000 in 1977, and it remained at the same level for almost the next eight years, i.e., through 1984. At that time, Ross received a whopping raise to $800,000 per year, and he continues today to receive the same salary.

If Ross were judged only by his base salary, he wouldn't rate even an honorable mention in this book. For the fourteen years between 1976 and 1989, he earned a total of $7.1 million, or a relatively low $500,000 per year. But we are just getting started, so grab a bucket of popcorn, sit back, and enjoy the show.

Virtually every major company offers its executives the opportunity to earn substantial bonuses for their performance in a given fiscal year. There is no way, of course, to tell what sort of bonus Ross received in 1973, 1974, and 1975; but, as we saw earlier, Warner Communications increased its disclosure of executive compensation information starting in 1976. For that year, we learn that Ross received a bonus of $254,000. Then, in 1977, he began to be rewarded under a so-called formula bonus plan.

The vast majority of companies prefer a discretionary approach to establishing executive bonus levels. Within broad limits, therefore, the company's board decides, after the year is over, just how much in the way of a bonus it wishes to give to its CEO. Like few other companies, however, Warner Communications set the CEO's bonus parameters before the fiscal year even began. In Ross's case, he was promised that his bonus would be equal to 0.625% of the company's after-tax profits, provided such after-tax profits were at least $45 million. Hence, if after-tax profits were, say, $100 million, Ross would receive a bonus of $625,000. If they were, however, only $44 million, he would receive no bonus at all—or at least no bonus if the board stood its ground. A separate clause of the bonus plan gave the board the right to ignore this $45 million profit hurdle and pay

Ross a bonus anyway. And in another clause, the board was given a further right, this time the right to eliminate any non-recurring items of profit or loss in determining the profit for the year for bonus purposes.

Happily for Ross, the average annual after-tax profits during the preceding five years were $44 million—an amount just about equal to the $45 million minimum standard set by the board. Is there a coincidence here? Had the after-tax profits averaged only $40 million per year for the past five years, would the board have graciously dropped the profit test to $40 million?

Coincidence or not, the $45 million minimum profit standard was quite vigorous. At the beginning of 1977, Warner Communications' shareholders' equity amounted to $268.4 million. Hence, had the company earned $45 million in after-tax profits in 1977, its after-tax return on beginning equity would have been 16.8%, a level that was equaled or exceeded by only 40% of the 500 companies with the largest market capitalization (i.e., the market value of their outstanding shares) at the beginning of 1977.

Viewed from another perspective, Ross's minimum profit standard was even more vigorous. Most companies with bonus plans also have some sort of minimum profit standard, and though few would couch it in dollar terms, as Warner Communications did, the typical standard represents the equivalent of only a 6% return on beginning shareholders' equity. In 1977, fully 97% of the 500 largest companies earned a return on beginning equity that equaled or exceeded 6%.

Ross drove his new bonus plan around the test track in 1977, and it promptly exhibited superior acceleration characteristics. From a bonus of $254,000 in 1976, his bonuses for the next six years were, approximately, $400,000, $500,000, $700,000, $900,000, $1.4 million, and $1.6 million. Then Warner Communications' profits slammed into a brick wall. The company had made a fortune out of the video-game craze, but like the Hula Hoop and the CB Radio crazes before it, video games suddenly fell out of favor. In 1983, Warner Communications sustained a net loss after extraordinary items of $418 million; in 1984, it lost a further $586 million. Profits rebounded in 1985, however, and so did Ross's annual bonus. That year, his bonus was $2 million; the next year, it was $1.8 million.

In 1987, Warner Communications' board altered Ross's bonus formula. Now when a company grows, as Warner Communication had, it makes sense to lower the percentage of profits given to the CEO as a bonus while simultaneously raising the minimum profit level required to earn a bonus. If the company doubles in size, it is not necessary to double the pay of the CEO; perhaps the challenges are a bit greater, but not that much greater. And if the company doubles in size, it will doubtless require more capital to do its job. Thus, if a $45 million profit level represented a 16.8% return on equity before the company doubled its equity, then it will represent only an 8.4% return on equity now. But the Warner Communications board threw out the rule book by *raising* the percentage of profits granted to Ross as a bonus—from 0.625% to 1.00%—while effectively *lowering* the minimum profit level. Read literally, the minimum profit level was advanced from $45 to $75 million. However, had Warner Communications earned $75 million in 1987, the year the bonus change was made, the company's after-tax return on its beginning equity of $1,173 million would have been a minuscule 6.4%. This compares to an equivalent figure of 16.8% when the first bonus formula was introduced ten years earlier. In 1987, 87% of the 500 companies with the largest market capitalization at the beginning of the year earned a return that equaled or exceeded 6.4%. In a ten-year period, therefore, Ross's minimum profit standard had dropped from a 60th percentile level of performance to a 13th percentile level of performance.

Naturally, when you raise the percentage of profits offered to a CEO as a bonus, while effectively lowering his threshold of profit performance, you do wonderful things to his bonus level. Ross's bonus for 1986 was, as just mentioned, $1.8 million. But that was under the old bonus plan. With the new bonus plan in place, Ross's bonus for 1987 leaped to $3.3 million. His bonuses for 1988 and 1989 performance were, respectively, $4.2 million and $3.6 million.

For the fourteen years 1976 through 1989, Ross received annual bonuses totaling $20.7 million, or an average of $1.5 million per year. Now we're beginning to play in the majors.

In 1989, after Time acquired his company, Ross's bonus formula was changed again. Through 1989, as already indicated, Ross had been receiving an annual bonus equal to 1% of Warner Communications' after-tax net income, provided such net income was at least $75 million per year. Given that the combination of Time and Warner Communications could reasonably be expected to produce a bigger profit stream than Warner Communications alone, Ross's bonus percentage was decreased—from 1% to 0.4%. However, the definition of net income was also changed—from an after-tax basis to a pre-tax basis.

Changing that definition may or may not represent another raise for Ross. Suppose here that after-tax net is $100. Under the old bonus formula and ignoring the profit threshold, Ross would have received a bonus of 1% of the $100, or $1. Next, consider that the median company among the Standard & Poor's 500 companies during 1988 and 1989 earned $1.52 in pre-tax income for each dollar it earned in after-tax income. If Time Warner is like the typical Standard & Poor 500 company, it will therefore have to earn $152 of pre-tax income to produce $100 of after-tax income. If Ross receives 0.4% of the $152.00 in pre-tax profits, his bonus will be $0.608.

That sounds as though Ross has been cheated, since he would have received $1 under the old plan. But remember that the profit stream of the combined Time and Warner Communications will be much larger than before. Indeed, the combined pre-tax profit of the two companies for the years 1985 through 1988, the last full year before Time acquired Warner Communications, was 2.24 times the level of Warner Communications' pre-tax profit alone. However, Warner Communications pre-tax profits for 1986 look to be anomalously low, and if we eliminate that year, the company's average past profit figure rises. Therefore, the ratio of Time's profits to Warner Communications' profits drops to a lower 2.05 times. Even if we assume the future ratio is only 2.00 times, Ross's bonus would double—from $0.624 to $1.248. Hence, the effect of moving from a bonus equal to 1% of after-tax profits to one equal to 0.4% of pre-tax profits could be to give Ross a 25% increase in his bonus compensation.

Another feature in Ross's new bonus formula offers him an incontestable advantage. Human beings have the annoying habit of becoming more and more drug tolerant, no matter what drug they are taking. So, if you start feeding yourself lots of penicillin, you will shortly find that it takes a larger and larger dose to achieve the same effect. And you will also eventually find that no dose at all, no matter what its size, will work any longer. Perhaps human beings can also become tolerant of money. At least, those amateur pharmacologists who sit around the Time Warner boardroom table seemed to think so, because they decided that Ross needed more motivation than a mere 0.4% of the company's pre-tax net income could produce. They thereupon offered him a further 0.2% of any pre-tax net income in excess of 120% of the highest net income earned by the company during the three preceding years. Hence, if the highest net income during those three preceding years was, say, $1 billion, then Ross would receive 0.4% of all pre-tax net income up to $1.2 billion (an amount that is 20% greater than the $1.0 billion), and 0.6% of all further pre-tax net income.

Four other features in the new bonus arrangement also tend to favor Ross. First, in calculating pre-tax profits, the decrease in profits caused by the amortization of the goodwill associated with the acquisition of Warner Communications will be ignored. Second, the profit hurdle of $75 million of after-tax net income that must be earned before any bonus is payable under the formula remains unchanged, notwithstanding that the profit stream may have doubled. Or, to put it another way, if Time Warner had earned an after-tax profit of $75 million in 1989, its return on the $3.15 billion combined beginning equity of Time and Warner Communications would have been a teensy 2.4%—a level that was exceeded by 89% of the 500 companies which in 1989 had the largest market capitalization. Looking back, Ross's minimum profit standard has slid about as fast as his pay has risen. In 1977, when his first formula bonus plan was introduced, the minimum profit standard was exceeded by only 40% of the 500 companies with the largest market capitalization. Then, when the formula was changed in 1987, the minimum profit standard was exceeded by 87% of the largest companies. Now his latest minimum profit standard is exceeded by 89% of the companies. If Ross had been entered in a high-jump contest, he would have had to work out pretty vigorously to clear the bar in 1977. By 1987, he could have ballooned to Hulk Hogan size, taken up cigarettes, and still made it over the bar with not much effort. And by 1989, with not too much of a push, he could have rolled over the bar in a wheelchair.

The third and fourth features of his bonus plan sweeten it even more. Of all things, Ross's bonus will be paid, not on an annual basis, as is the case with virtually every other senior executive in the land, but rather on a quarterly basis. The result is that Ross can put his bonus money to work earlier in the year. To be sure, if his quarterly bonus in one quarter is wiped out by a loss in a succeeding quarter, he will eventually have to repay the money to the company, but he at least gets an interest-free loan for a few months. Finally, if the formula fails to produce a bonus that the board finds reasonable, it can do anything extra it wants to do.

Although Time Warner's board can override Ross's bonus formula and award him a bonus anyway in a year when he would have received no bonus, or award him a bigger bonus in a year when he would have received a smaller bonus, it resisted the temptation during Time Warner's first year as a combined company. In 1990, Ross received his formula bonus, but it was sharply reduced from what he received in 1989. In that earlier year, he received a bonus of $3.6 million; in 1990, his bonus was reduced to $2.075 million, for a reduction of 42%.

Ross executed an employment agreement in 1977 that awarded him substantial amounts of deferred compensation in addition to his base salary and his yearly bonus. For 1977, the amount deferred for him amounted to 25% of the sum of his base salary and annual bonus. For the next five years, his deferred compensation opportunity rose in steady 5-percentage-point increments (30%, 35%, 40%, 45%) to 50% of his combined base salary and annual bonus. To illustrate: in 1982, Ross earned a base salary of $350,000 and an annual bonus of $1.6 million. The sum of his base salary and annual bonus was therefore $1.9 million. By itself, cash compensation of $1.9 million would have ranked Ross among the very highest paid executives in the land. But he also received a deferred compensation award equal to 50% of his $1.9 million cash compensation, or $975,000. His current compensation for that year was thus $2.9 million.

At the beginning of 1984, Ross's deferred compensation award was reduced. From 50% of the sum of his base salary and bonus, it dropped to 50% of his base salary alone. The change made no difference to Ross in 1984, however, since he received no bonus that year. Then at the beginning of 1985, his base salary was increased from $350,000 to $800,000, thereby removing a bit of the sting. Over the thirteen years between 1977, the first year Ross received a deferred compensation award, and 1989, he was given a total of $6.2 million of deferred compensation, or an average of $500,000 per year.

Besides giving him a lot more compensation, Ross's deferred compensation plan offered him two further advantages. The fine print of the plan gave Ross the ability to invest the deferred funds any way he saw fit. Thus, he could use pre-tax dollars to play the market and diversify his portfolio away from what would otherwise be heavy reliance on the success of Warner Communications. Moreover, it promised him another goodie—a payment equal to the monies Warner Communications gained by deducting any profits Ross earned. Suppose that $100,000 were placed in Ross's deferral account and that he was successful in doubling the value to $200,000. In that case, when the $200,000 was finally paid out to Ross, Warner Communications would be entitled to take a tax deduction on the entire $200,000 amount. Assuming a corporate tax rate of 34%, the company would be able to lower its corporate tax bill by $68,000. Alternatively, had Ross invested his $100,000 in a way that produced no appreciation at all, Warner Communications would have been able to deduct only $100,000 on its corporate tax return. Its corporate tax bill in that case would have been lowered by only $34,000. It is this $34,000 difference in company tax savings—$68,000 if Ross defers and his money doubles, or $34,000 if Ross defers and his money doesn't appreciate at all—that would be given to Ross as an extra bonus.

Interestingly, Warner Communications' proxy statements failed to reveal what would have happened were Ross to have labored mightily and turned his $100,000 investment into one worth $50,000. In that case, the company's tax relief would have declined from $34,000 to $17,000. Yet had the company simply paid the $100,000 deferred compensation in cash, it could have deducted the entire amount and realized $34,000 in tax savings. Were there any symmetry here, Ross ought to have been required to whip out his checkbook and reimburse the company for the $17,000 it was out of pocket. Silence in a proxy statement is often deafening.

A stock option gives an executive the right, but not the obligation, to purchase a fixed number of shares of company common stock at a fixed price over a fixed term of years. In almost all cases, the purchase price, generally called the strike price, is the market price per share of the stock on the date of grant. So, if an executive is being granted a 10,000-share stock option at a time when the market price per share of his company's stock is $50, then the price he will have to pay for each of those 10,000 shares (the strike price) will also be $50. The period of time during which the option may be exercised is virtually always ten years in duration. Generally, the option may not be fully exercised during the early years of its ten-year term (typically a period of around four years from the grant date); but thereafter, the executive is free to choose the date of exercise.

The way to make money on a stock option, of course, is to get the stock price to rise above the strike price. And the way to make the most money is to catch the exact point during the ten-year option term when the market price is highest. Most people never hit the exact high, but you can make plenty of money even if you're off a little. Moreover, since key executives receive not one but many stock option grants during their careers, the chances to become seriously rich are multiplied.

Although the executive makes money if his company's stock price rises, he does not lose money if it falls. After all, he has the right, *but not the obligation,* to exercise the option. For example, if the strike price of the option is $50 per share, and if the market price takes it on the chin and drops to $20, a shareholder who bought in at the same time the option was granted would have lost $30 per share. But the executive loses nothing because he simply walks away from the option and never exercises it.

Ross had been given some stock option grants prior to 1973. Then in either 1974 or 1975 he was granted an option on 55,000 shares carrying a strike price of $19.38 per share. The following year, he was granted an option on a further 50,000 shares, this time carrying a strike price of $28 per share. And in 1982, he received a much larger option on 250,000 shares carrying a strike price of $39.56 per share. Finally, in 1990, he received what has to be history's largest stock option, one for 1,800,000 shares carrying a strike price of $150 per share. By way of perspective, the typical company makes option grants totaling about 1% of its shares outstanding each year *to all its executives.* In contrast, Time Warner granted more than 3% of its shares outstanding *to a single executive.* Eventually, these stock options are probably going to cause some dilution in the company's earnings per share and its stock price. But the dilution will take a long time to occur, and given Ross's age, the full impact is not likely to be felt in his lifetime.

All but the 1989 option grant have borne lots of fruit. By 1974, Ross received option profits (i.e., the amount by which the market price per share at the time of exercise exceeds the strike price, multiplied by the number of shares being exercised) of $185,000. And in 1980, his option profits were $12 million. Then, in 1987, he received a further $8.8 million in option profits.

In calculating option profits for Ross, as well as for all other executives cited in this book, I assumed implicitly that the executive sells the shares acquired upon the exercise of stock options on the very day of such exercise. The *Wall Street Journal, Forbes,* and *BusinessWeek* also make the same assumption in their annual articles on CEO pay. The fact is that, for most senior executives, the paper profit at exercise of the option and the actual gain are one and the same, because such executives never actually exercise their options.

Rather, the company gives them a check representing what they would have received by exercising their options and selling the stock on the very same day. However, some executives are required by law to hold on to their option shares for six months before they can sell them. And others hold on to their shares for longer than that, simply because they assume them to be a good investment. In such cases, the pre-tax gain the executive actually realizes upon the eventual sale of the shares is apt to be a figure that is different from the figure reported in this book.

The 1989 stock option grant for 1.8 million shares has, of course, the greatest profit potential of all. Besides shattering all past records for size of grant, Time Warner's board introduced two further goodies into the option grant. First, it extended the term from the usual ten years to twelve. Second, it made the option exercisable for the full twelve-year term under any or all conditions, save Ross quitting during the first three years after the grant date. In almost all other companies, termination of employment—whether because of voluntary resignation, death, disability, or retirement—has the effect of shortening the nominal option term below ten years.

When this option was first announced, the strike price was set to equal the market price of a share of Time Warner stock on the date it was to be granted (with the grant being delayed until all of Warner Communications' shares had been purchased by Time, an event that finally occurred in January 1990). But after the Time Warner stock price slumped, the strike price was reset to equal the greater of the stock price at the time of option grant or $150. This more restrictive provision was implemented at a time when the press was beginning to write some very nasty articles about Ross's gargantuan appetite for money.

As of this writing, Time Warner's stock price is $118 per share, and Ross's option has just about ten and a half years to run before it expires. Let's forget about Bruce Wasserstein's prediction that the stock will trade in the $280 to $402 range by 1993. (If we take the midpoint of that range, or $341 per share, and if we consider the current price of $118, Time Warner's stock price would have to increase at the rate of about 103% per year to wipe the egg off

Wasserstein's face.) Rather, let's assume that Time Warner's stock price will appreciate at the same 10.5% per year rate at which the stock prices of companies comprising the Standard & Poor's 500 Index have appreciated since the end of World War II. On that basis, a starting stock price of $118.00 would increase to $336.66 per share ten and a half years later. Subtracting the $150.00 strike price per share leaves Ross with a profit of $186.66 per share. And multiplying by 1.8 million shares gives him an aggregate profit of $336 million.

Of course, there is no assurance that the Time Warner stock price will rise to $336.66 per share by the year 2002, when Ross's option expires. It may go nowhere or even drop. But there is a good probability that it will rise to a point above $336.66 per share, in which case Ross would make more than $336 million from his stock option.

From personal contact with representatives of Ross, I know that he is capable of speaking with two voices on this option. In private, he seems to be saying that his stock option really isn't worth all that much—especially given that the stock would have to rise more than 25% before he would be in a position to make even a nickel of gain. On the other hand, he has told his shareholders that "I believe those 1.8 million shares of Time Warner's stock at $150 a share are going to make me more money than I've ever made in my life." Indeed, Ross has buttressed his public position by buying some $40 million of Time Warner shares with his own money—an action that almost never occurs to a CEO who is looking for a way to invest surplus funds. So an assumption that Ross will make around $336 million from his stock option grant may be conservative; the more so if he can once again deliver for his shareholders the level of performance he has in the past.

During the seventeen years 1973 through 1989, Ross received option profits of $20.9 million, or an average of $1.2 million per year.

In addition to receiving the several option grants just discussed, Ross also received another form of compensation that closely resembles option grants. Warner Communications called this new form of compensation a Bonus Unit. Devised in 1977, the ink was hardly dry on the new plan before Ross was granted 150,000 Bonus Units. Each Bonus Unit gave Ross the right to collect a cash payment equal to the amount by which the future market value of a share of Warner Communications common stock exceeded $27. Hence, if the stock price eventually rose to $60 per share, and if Ross then chose to exercise his 150,000 Bonus Units, he would receive a cash payment equal to $60 minus $27, or $33 per Bonus Unit, thereby giving him $4.95 million for all 150,000 Bonus Units. The term of the grant was for a maximum of six years.

At first glance, a Bonus Unit would seem to be nothing more or less than a stock option masquerading under a different name. But two differences emerge on closer reading. While the strike price of the Bonus Unit was $27.00, the market price of a Warner Communications common share on the date of grant was $29.50. Hence, Ross already had $2.50 per unit sewed up on each Bonus Unit, or $375,000. Even more important, each Bonus Unit came factory-equipped with dividend equivalents. In other words, until the Bonus Unit was exercised, Ross stood to receive whatever dividends were declared, multiplied, of course, by 150,000.

Over the next four years, Ross collected more than $13 million from that single grant of Bonus Units. In 1980, he exercised some of his Bonus Units, for a profit of $5.1 million. In 1981, he exercised the remainder of the Bonus Units, for a profit of $7.4 million. And over the period 1977 through 1981, he received a total of $634,000 in dividend equivalents.

My mother was indulgent in many ways, but not when it came to eating. When she gave me a few cookies, she admonished me not to eat them too fast, to make them last. When, predictably, I gobbled them up in less than a minute and held out my hand for more, she refused to give me any. Over the ensuing years, I have not slowed my cookie-eating pace one bit, but at least I've never been rewarded for being a gobbler.

Not so Steve Ross. Having gobbled up all his Bonus Units in a space of five years, when he could have hung on to them for a year longer, he held out his hand, figuratively speaking, for more Bonus

Units. And his indulgent board, who on the evidence never had any contact with my mother, promptly gave Ross an even bigger grant than he had before. In 1982, he received 250,000 Bonus Units at one point during the year and a further 325,000 Bonus Units later in the year. This second grant of Bonus Units produced a payout that made that from the first grant look like small change. In 1989, when Time acquired Warner Communications, Ross's 1982 grants of Bonus Units were cashed out to the tune of $57.2 million. Moreover, he received dividends of $3.2 million between 1982 and 1989.

Summarizing, Ross's two grants of Bonus Units—one in 1977, and the second in 1982—produced payouts to him of $69.6 million, together with a further $3.8 million of dividend equivalent payments.

Besides receiving classic stock option grants and optionlike Bonus Unit grants, Ross received a third form of long-term incentive compensation that aped stock options. In 1987, he signed a new ten-year pay contract that was so lush and so controversial that it inspired a revolt in his boardroom, as well as an entire article in *Fortune.* More on the boardroom revolt later.

At the time he signed his employment agreement, Ross was given two new forms of long-term incentive compensation, and both were characterized as "Units." Later, in 1989, when Time acquired Warner, proxy materials attempted to distinguish between the two types of units by unimaginatively referring to one as the "A" and the other as the "B" Units. We'll get to the "A" Units shortly, but first let's look at the "B" Units.

Each "B" Unit contained the equivalent of a strike price, in this case the $30.875 per share value of Warner Communications stock on the grant date. As with a stock option, Ross would eventually be entitled to receive the amount, if any, by which the future market value of a share of Warner Communications stock exceeded $30.875.

But there were two twists: one not necessarily favorable to Ross, the second highly favorable. The not-so-favorable twist mandated that Ross's profit, if any, be measured at fixed time intervals. Hence, if any payments at all were to be made to Ross, they would be made at the beginning of 1990, 1992, 1994, 1996, and 1997. Contrast that approach to a classic stock option, under which the executive has considerable flexibility in the ten-year term during which to raise his hand and call for the profit.

But the favorable twist alleviated most of the pain of the unfavorable one. At the time of payout (beginning of 1990, 1992, 1994, 1996, and 1997), Warner Communications would not simply subtract the strike price of $30.875 from the then market price to determine Ross's profit per share. Rather, the company would first determine the average daily high price during the eight consecutive weeks within the two years preceding the date of payout during which the price of Warner Communications stock was the highest. Take the grant expiring on January 1, 1992, for example. In determining the amount to be paid here, the company would wait until January 1, 1992, and then look in its rear-view mirror to find that eight-week period during the larger period, January 1, 1990, through December 31, 1991, when the company's stock price was the highest. It would subtract the strike price of $30.875 from this high stock price and multiply the remainder (if positive) by the number of units granted. Too bad the shareholders can't sign up for a plan that, when they sell their stock, would give them the stock's highest price during the past two years.

Obviously guided by the belief that nothing succeeds like excess, Warner Communications' board went on to grant Ross 1,500,000 units of "B" compensation. Ordinarily, the final payout on the "B" Units would not have taken place until the beginning of 1997. However, Time's acquisition of Warner Communications threw a monkey wrench into the proceedings, because once the acquisition was completed, there would no longer be any quoted stock price for Warner Communications, and hence no way to value the "B" Units. So the board gave Ross another great deal. It valued all of his "B" Units at the time of the acquisition, using the all-time-high price of $70 per share for Warner Communications stock. Indeed, it might have used a price slightly higher than $70, because of a requirement on the part of Time Inc. to pay interest on the $70 price if the acquisition could not be completed within a specified period.

Want a recipe for a gargantuan amount of compensation? First, place in a saucepan the all-time-high price of $70 per share. Then stir in the lower strike price of $30.875, until the mixture difference of $39.125 separates out. Next, pour $39.125 each into 1.5 million baking cups. Finally, bake in a moderate oven for two to three minutes. *Voilà,* a delectable dessert worth $58.7 million.

Perhaps as a sop to the shareholders, the board didn't pay out the $58.7 million in a lump sum. Rather, Ross will receive payments at the time he would have received them, had Warner Communications' stock continued to trade publicly. So he will not receive his final payment until the beginning of 1997. In the meantime, having cashed out of Warner Communications stock at its all-time high, he can direct the investment of those funds in a way that will presumably give him the one thing most CEOs lack: a diversified portfolio. And he will presumably gain further by the neat feature in his earlier pay packages, which gives him the benefit of the tax deductions available to Time Warner on any appreciation in his deferred compensation portfolio.

As can be seen, Steve Ross received three types of long-term incentive compensation, all of which essentially required that Ross drive up the price of Warner Communications stock before he could receive a reward. (I use the term "essentially" because Ross received dividend equivalents along with his Bonus Units, and the value of these, of course, was not dependent on the price of Warner Communications stock.) From his stock options, he received $21.1 million in gains. From his Bonus Units, he received $69.6 million, along with an extra $1.4 million in dividend equivalents. And from his "B" Units, he received $58.7 million. The grand total: $151 million, or about $9 million per year during the seventeen-year period between 1973 and 1990. Meanwhile, his mammoth 1.8 million share stock option, which contains no profit at the moment, is sitting quietly in Time Warner's basement. However, if you listen closely, you can hear the soft trickling of the compensation world's equivalent of the Love Canal—something that will slowly seep into the shareholders' balance sheets and pollute their net worth.

Now, some will defend Ross's $153 million on the basis of the mighty good works he wrought for his shareholders over the years. But there are three reasons to suggest that such thinking is wrongheaded. First, Ross clearly did hit a home run for his shareholders, but he will not go down in the history books as the Babe Ruth of business, for at least 10% of other big company CEOs have delivered even better performances than Ross. Second, we can pretty safely assume that every one of those CEOs in the top 10% of performance earned less, and in almost every case, considerably less, than Ross. So the notion that shareholders had to pay Ross as much as they did to get the performance they did is utter nonsense. Third, and finally, Ross bore hardly any risk when he was in the process of generating his $153 million of profit. Under the terms of his compensation plans, he was not required to invest his own money in Warner Communications stock. Therefore, if the stock dropped in value, he would not have lost a cent of what he already held. And even if the stock had appreciated no further than what the shareholders would have earned had they invested their funds in safe government bonds, he still would have reaped millions in reward.

Today, restricted stock is nearly as popular a form of long-term incentive compensation as stock options. So let's contrast the two plans for a moment. With an option share, the executive has to pay to exercise it. But with a restricted share, the executive pays nothing at all. In other words, he gets the share absolutely free. Or in still other words, his effective strike price is $0. The only way the executive can fail to profit is if the stock price falls to zero. With an option share, the executive does not receive any dividends declared between the date of option grant and the date of option exercise. But with a restricted share, the executive receives full dividend payments from the date of grant. The only way he can lose is if the dividend is cut to zero right after the grant is made and then remains at zero.

Practically speaking, therefore, a restricted share is simply a share of common stock given free to an executive. The only difference between a restricted share and a normal common share is that the executive is not permitted to sell the share during a so-called restriction period. (Most restrictions lapse within five years from the date of grant; occasionally, however, some restrictions persist all the way to the executive's retirement.) Once the restriction period has ended, there is absolutely no difference between a restricted share and a common share.

You might well ask, what does the executive have to do in return for his company's largesse? In all but the most unusual cases, all he has to do is breathe in and out seventeen times a minute during the restriction period. Once a year, the company physician shines a flashlight into his eyes and is supposed to get a reflection back. However, that requirement seems to have been waived on several occasions, at least judging by the subsequent performance of the company. (If the executive quits the company before the restrictions lapse, or is discharged for cause, he would then stand to forfeit the shares. But he could keep whatever dividends he had already received.) In short, an executive with a typical restricted stock grant doesn't have to perform to earn substantial amounts of money. He has only to stay alive, if not necessarily well, on his company's payroll.

Again demonstrating his credentials as a compensation pioneer, Ross received a restricted stock grant as far back as 1973, when hardly anyone had heard of restricted stock. The grant was for a measly 50,000 shares, a level that today would get lost in the rounding of a CEO's pay package. Still, when the restrictions lapsed, he managed to eke out a, for him, tiny $1 million of pay.

Ross received no more restricted stock until 1987, when he was given something that resembled restricted stock. Earlier, we talked about his "B" Units. Now it is time to give center stage to his "A" Units. These called for Ross to receive the *full* Warner Communications stock price on a grant of 900,000 units. Payments were to be made on essentially the same dates as those involving the "B" Units. And the two-year lookback in determining the stock price was also incorporated here.

When Time acquired Warner Communications in 1989, Ross's "A" Units were valued along with his "B" Units. And a further $63 million was contributed to his deferred compensation account, to be paid at the times the units would have been paid had Warner Communications stock continued to trade publicly. Do you hear some hammering going on? That's coming from the carpenters who are feverishly racing to reinforce the floor in the room holding Steve Ross's deferred compensation account.

In all, Ross has received $64 million from payouts of restricted stock or its close equivalent. Given that his first grant was made in 1973, that works out to around $3.8 million per year for each of the seventeen years involved.

During the long Bear Market of the 1970s and early 1980s, a lot of CEOs lost faith in the ability of the New York Stock Exchange (NYSE) to place the correct value on their companies' shares. In effect, when the Dow Jones was soaring, CEOs believed the NYSE was doing a good job of valuing stock, but when it was plummeting, that simply showed that Wall Street traders were being unduly pessimistic. As a result, many companies adopted alternative long-term incentive plans that offered rewards on the basis of something other than an increase in the market price of the company's stock. Warner Communications was one of them. It came to the game relatively late; indeed, its alternative plan was adopted in March 1982, just five months before the greatest Bull Market in history was launched after a speech predicting lower interest rates was made by Henry Kaufman, Salomon Brothers' former chief economist.

Under its new Equity Unit plan, the board gave Ross a grant of 2,000 units. Here, Ross was permitted to purchase shares at their current book value and, eventually, to resell them to the company at their future book value. Hence, Ross could sidestep the vagaries of the New York Stock Exchange, where Warner Communications stock might sell at two times book value one year and one-half times book value the next. Moreover, he would receive normal dividends on his shares, even though he paid a lot less than the then market price per share for each of them.

In general, the change in book value per share in any particular year is simply the earnings per share for that year less the dividends per share for that year. Now, since Ross stood to receive both the appreciation in book value per share and the dividends per share, his normal economic benefit from each share he purchased would equal the entire earnings per share of the company. Since Ross was already receiving part of the earnings per share in the form of an annual bonus, a question might be raised here as to why he needed a second dip into the till. But somehow the board thought he did. They were most anxious for Ross to purchase these new book-value shares. So anxious, in fact, that they sweetened the deal with a low-interest loan the principal and interest on which would not be payable for some years.

Why should a fuss be made over a new plan that gave Ross the right to purchase a paltry 2,000 shares of company book-value stock? Well, the proxy actually mentioned 2,000 *units,* not 2,000 *shares.* Shares or units, what's the difference? As it turns out, quite a bit, because if you bother to read the fine print, you learn that each unit is worth the equivalent of seventy-five shares. So Steve Ross didn't get to purchase merely 2,000 shares of company book-value stock; he got to purchase 150,000 shares. Ross hadn't lost his touch. As usual, he was at the top of his form. And, for the first time, he demonstrated a flair for packaging. Why disclose in a straightforward way that 150,000 shares are involved in the grant? Instead, why not create 2,000 units, behind each of which lurks 75 shares? Indeed, why not just have one unit, which is worth 150,000 shares? Of course, one is such a small number that the proxy reader might just be tempted to wade into that fine print. (The 150,000 units later became 300,000 when the stock subsequently split 2-for-1.)

Ross's Equity Units were cashed out when Time acquired Warner Communications. He received a check for $17.8 million, or an average of about $2.2 million per year for each of the eight years the plan was in place.

Although Warner Communications seems to have come late to the game of non-stock-market-based long-term incentive plans with its Equity Unit plan, it actually started the game much earlier when in 1977, it adopted its Long-Term Management Incentive Plan. Under that plan, Ross was offered a maximum payout of $250,000 for each of five long-term incentive periods. Each period covered three years of performance, with the first offering payouts predicated on performance during 1977 through 1979, and the last offering payouts predicated on performance during 1981 through 1983. To earn the maximum payout, Warner Communications' earnings per share had to increase at the rate of 15% per year.

Ross earned his maximum payout of $250,000 for each of the first four long-term incentive periods, but he struck out on the fifth because of the Atari debacle (when the sudden collapse of the video-game craze led Warner Communications to take $1 billion of losses over a two-year period). Hence, he received $1 million from this final long-term incentive plan. I am embarrassed here to dwell on an inconsequential $1 million payout, when Ross has received hundreds of millions from other compensation plans, but my compulsion for completeness has gotten the better of me. All told, Steve Ross participated in seven different long-term incentive plans, from stock options to Bonus Units, from "B" Units to restricted stock grants, from "A" Units to Equity Units to units under the Long-Term Management Incentive Plan. His total take from all seven plans was $236 million over a period of effectively seventeen years, or about $14 million per year.

Do long-term incentive plans really motivate long-term performance? After all, that's what they are supposed to do. The evidence here suggests rather strongly that the question has to be answered in the negative. For openers, as will be discussed in more detail later on, neither Japan nor Germany, the two countries with the best long-term track record, offer long-term incentive compensation to their senior executives.

Then there is the evidence from the United States itself. In a 1991 study of 955 CEOs, I found that 28% participated in no long-term incentive plans at all (these companies were mostly small, and mainly power utilities), 46% participated in a single long-term incentive plan (typically, a stock option plan), 22% participated in two long-term incentive plans (typically, a stock option plan and a restricted stock plan), and 4% participated in three long-term incentive plans. Knowing the number of long-term incentive plans in which a CEO participated turned out to be handy predictor of whether the CEO was underpaid or overpaid. If the CEO participated in no long-term incentive plans, his pay was apt to be 32% under the market. If he participated in a single plan, his pay was apt to be at the market. And if he participated in two or three long-term incentive plans, his pay was apt to be, respectively, 32% and 64% above the market. Armed only with these statistics, an observer of the compensation scene would be hardpressed not to conclude that everyone would be better off—everyone except executives, that is—if all long-term incentives were simply canceled.

Being paid over the market might not be so bad if it was accompanied by better-than-average corporate performance. But the relationship between the number of long-term incentive plans in which the CEO participates and the company's ten-year total return to shareholders (counting stock price appreciation and dividends) turned out to be negative. For each long-term incentive plan in which the CEO participates, you can deduct 1.43 percentage points from the company's ten-year, compounded annual return to shareholders. Hence, other things being equal, the ten-year return for a one-plan company was 14.2% per year, but the return for a two-plan company was a lesser 12.8%. So, if there are any long-term shareholders benefits to be derived from piling one form of long-term incentive compensation on top of another, those benefits are simply overwhelmed by the huge increase in extra costs involved.

A number of cute games were played during the process of paying Steve Ross his many hundreds of millions in compensation. Perhaps Ross was the games player, or perhaps his financial advisers played the games for him. It is hard to believe that his board was other than an innocent participant, because each of the games resulted in an identical score: Ross = 1; shareholders = 0. Herewith a brief summary of the games. In 1972, an investment partnership was established, under which Warner Communications, the general partner, put up $3.45 million, while Ross and eleven other executives, as limited partners, put up one tenth as much, or $345,000. Warner Communications, as general partner, was entitled to all the dividends generated by the partnership's investments, as well as all the appreciation on such investments, but only until the general partner's cumulative return equaled 5.5% per year. As for further profits, the general partner was entitled only to a 9.1% share, while the twelve limited partners, including Ross, were entitled to a 90.9%

share. If the partnership were to lose money, Ross and his other limited partners would be required to bear 100% of the losses themselves, until their $345,000 original capital contribution was exhausted. After that, the general partner would absorb any further losses, up to its $3.45 million original investment.

This partnership constitutes a prime example of the "heads I win, tails you lose" mentality that pervades the world of executive compensation. I have no idea as to the sorts of investments the partnership made, but there clearly was a strong incentive to make wildly volatile ones. After all, Ross and his other limited partners stood to made 91% of incremental income above the 5.5% return rate, while having to put up only 9% of the total capital. On the downside, they could, of course, lose all of their own investment, but what's $345,000 to a group of high-rolling executives? Viewed from the perspective of Warner Communications' shareholders, however, the deal was hardly a winner. In return for putting up 91% of the capital, the shareholders stood only to get a 5.5% compounded annual return—at best—and to absorb 91% of the partnership's losses—at worst. For reasons not disclosed in Warner Communications' proxy statement, the fund was called the FI fund. But given how it worked, it might better have been called the FU fund. At least, that's what some of the shareholders thought. Three different stockholder derivative lawsuits were brought against Warner Communications, alleging, among other things, "misappropriation and waste of the assets and resources of the Company." Warner Communications fought the lawsuits at first, but it threw in the towel in February 1975 and reached a court-approved settlement that required it to disband the investment partnership. Ross and his eleven other limited partners lost their entire $345,000 investment. I was unable to find any reference in Warner Communications' proxy statements as to just how much, if any, of the shareholders' $3.45 million investment was also lost. Indeed, I could find no further reference of any sort to this partnership in any succeeding Warner Communications proxy statement.

For many years, as already indicated, Ross has been given additional deferred compensation in the form of a passback of his company's tax deduction on gains in his deferred compensation account. But there is no evidence that he has to write the company a check when his investments lose money and the company's tax deduction is accordingly lowered. In 1987, the company disclosed that the value of this passback had reached $2.3 million. It is quite likely that more millions have been added since then.

In plans like the Long-Term Management Incentive Plan, under which Ross earned $1 million for achieving 15% or better earnings per share growth over a period of years, companies typically measure growth off the earnings per share for the single year preceding the start of the performance measurement period. Warner Communications used a three-year average base period, an approach that, more often than not, makes it easier to achieve any pre-established goal. The typical company also requires that earnings per share growth be compounded growth. Warner Communications required only simple growth, again making the achievement of the goal easier. In a typical company, 15% earnings per share growth is 15% earnings per share growth. But at Warner Communications, if you put these two maneuvers together, 15% earnings per share growth is transformed into what other companies would see as only 6.6% earnings per share growth.

When Ross exercised stock options in 1980 with a $12 million gain, he could have held his shares for three years and then qualified for long-term capital-gains tax treatment. However, Warner Communications would have lost its tax deduction on the $12 million gain. Somehow, the board became convinced that it would be better for Ross to sell his shares right away. That way, the company would get its $12 million tax deduction, though Ross would have to pay more in taxes. To solve that last little problem, the company paid Ross an extra $1.8 million. Now I don't know who proposed this neat gambit, but investigators of murders always tell you to see who had a motive. The shareholders theoretically benefited from the transaction by getting a $12 million tax deduction they otherwise would have lost. But, in the process, they paid Ross $1.8 million to dump his company's stock. A great incentive, wouldn't you say? Would any right-thinking shareholder really engage in such behavior? Ross's motives, on the other hand, were a lot clearer. He paid no more tax than he would have paid had he held the stock for three years. He avoided any downside risk associated with holding Warner Communications stock. And he got to diversify himself three years earlier.

As we have seen, when Ross received his 4,000 Equity Units in 1982, he really received 300,000 Equity Units. It is hard not to conclude that someone deliberately set out to deceive Warner Communications' shareholders. But that was only a minor sin. The really big sin with the Equity Units was to change the rules of the game after the game was over. Ross paid the book value per share for his Equity Units, all right. But by the time he sold them back to the company in 1989, Warner Communications' book value per share had risen only a small percentage, due to the huge losses experienced over Atari. After taking into account the accumulated interest Ross owed on his original purchase price, he actually would have lost money when he resold his Equity Units to the company. But those who believe Ross would ever have permitted himself to lose money on a compensation plan are the same people who prior to August 2, 1990, thought that investing in the bonds of the Iraqi government represented a sound investment strategy. No, when it came to cashing Ross in, his ever indulgent board, using its authority to do whatever it wanted, substituted the market price that Time paid to acquire Warner Communications for Warner Communications' book value. As a result, Ross received $72.13 for each Equity Unit instead of taking a loss. And he was paid $17.8 million when, in reality, he should have received no rewards at all.

In negotiating his munificent employment contracts in 1977 and again in 1987, Ross apparently relied on a secret weapon, the relatively large number of his own senior executives whom he had placed on Warner Communications' board. Considering that voting against a pay contract that is being proposed for your boss is many times more injurious to your health than smoking, it is hard not to imagine Ross's subordinates pushing and shoving each other to be the first to the ballot box with an affirmative vote. Indeed, the machinations in the Warner Communications boardroom came to public light in 1987, when one outside director, Herbert J. Siegel, who had become Ross's bête noire, screamed bloody murder. Siegel was the CEO of Chris-Craft Industries, a mini-conglomerate whose primary interest was in television stations. Chris-Craft had earlier bought a huge number of Warner Communications shares in a so-called White Knight maneuver to help Ross forestall a possible takeover raid by Rupert Murdoch. Moreover, it was Warner Communications' largest single shareholder, with control over 17.4% of the combined voting power of all classes of voting stock. At the meeting in February 1987 when Ross's new employment contract was approved, Siegel, according to the proxy statement, "read a statement setting forth his view that the Company's Board of Directors has frequently acted in bad faith, has failed to exercise prudent and responsible business judgments, has consistently kept itself uninformed as to the most basic of issues and has adopted a policy of 'rubber stamping' all that management requests." Apparently, Siegel is not what you might think of as soft-spoken.

Brushing aside Siegel's charges, the board proceeded to approve the proposed employment contract for Ross. Here's how the voting went: There were sixteen directors on Warner Communications' board on the day Ross's contract was approved. Siegel and the five other outside directors who had been nominated by Chris-Craft predictably voted against Ross's employment contract. Most likely, Ross himself abstained from voting on his own contract. That left nine votes in favor of the contract. But five of those votes came from directors who were officers or employees of the company. And at least four of these individuals worked for Ross and hence were beholden to him. (The fifth was probably the secretary of the company, a lawyer, who because he was engaged in private practice, was likely a non-employee; as such, his status as an insider was more conjectural.) In any event, four of the five outside directors who had not been nominated by Chris-Craft to the Warner Communications board also voted in favor of the contract. If the vote had been restricted only to outside directors, on the theory that the inside directors were in a conflict-of-interest position, Ross's employment contract would have gone down to defeat 6–4. Instead, with the five yes votes from the inside directors, his contract was approved 9–6. In certain cases, the United Nations sends observers to monitor elections in faraway countries. It's a pity the U.N. officials didn't bestir themselves to step in a taxi and journey the short distance from 43rd Street and First Avenue in New York City to 50th Street and Fifth Avenue, where Warner Communications' headquarters were located.

Apparently, Siegel even asked for a legal opinion disqualifying the five company officers from voting on Ross's employment agreement, on the grounds that they were hardly disinterested. The company's counsel thereupon opined that "the directors who are officers or employees other than Mr. Ross would not be deemed to be interested directors under Delaware law solely by reason of their status as officers and employees of the Company and, accordingly, were legally qualified to vote on [Ross's employment agreement]."

Legal opinions like that do not inspire terrific confidence in the law, particularly the Delaware law. But with the Delaware courts acting as though they were a branch of the state's Chamber of Commerce, they surely help to motivate companies to incorporate in Delaware. On the other hand, Mr. Siegel's behavior does inspire confidence that there are at least a few outside directors who are willing to do more than strengthen their arm muscles through the use of a rubber stamp. In opposing Ross's new employment agreement, perhaps Siegel was acting out of less than lofty motives, but the result was the same: he did what should have been done.

Ironically, Siegel, though objecting to Ross's huge pay package, himself became a beneficiary of Ross's thinking. When Time acquired Warner Communications in 1989, Siegel's company, Chris-Craft, reaped hundreds of millions of dollars in profit on its Warner Communications shareholdings. For the year ended December 31, 1989, Chris-Craft reported a net profit of $447 million on the sale of its Warner Communications shares. And for the year ending December 31, 1990—as it informed shareholders in its 1989 annual report—the company expected to report a further $215 million profit on its Warner Communications shares.

Siegel entered into an employment agreement with Chris-Craft on September 1, 1983. Among other things, Siegel's agreement, like Ross's agreement, gave him a personal bonus formula. Siegel was offered a bonus equal to 1% of the pre-tax profits of Chris-Craft in excess of $15 million. When the huge profits from the sale of Warner Communications' stock hit the Chris-Craft income statement, Siegel's bonus rose from $351,000 for his performance in 1988 to $12.9 million for his performance in 1989. Indeed, another Siegel who works for Chris-Craft, Herbert's son, William, earned a bonus of $3.1 million that year. In addition, Chris-Craft's proxy reports that Herb Siegel exercised stock options during the three years ending December 31, 1989, and reaped gains on exercise of $5.9 million (his son had profits of $2.7 million). Finally, Herb Siegel, and perhaps William as well, stand to earn additional large bonuses for their performance in 1990 as the further $215 million of gains on Warner Communications stock jacks up Chris-Craft's income statement for a second year. So, though Herb Siegel properly blasted Steve Ross in 1987, he ought at least to have sent him a thank-you note at the end of 1989, and perhaps a few dozen roses as well.

Ross's experience with his board of directors stands in stark contrast to the pay contracts that two other movie industry luminaries recently negotiated for themselves. The two are Peter Guber and John Peters, the dynamic duo who, among other things, gave the world the sixth-highest-grossing movie in history, *Batman*. By all accounts, Guber and Peters, who were hired by Sony to run its newly acquired subsidiary, Columbia Pictures, may have managed to out-Ross Ross when it comes to being paid. Their base salaries are $2.75 million per year each. In addition, they stand to receive 2.5% of Columbia's profits in excess of $200 million and to share in a $50 million bonus pool at the end of five years. Moreover, Sony paid what many analysts think was a wild premium in buying out Guber and Peters's company, appropriately enough called Guber-Peters Entertainment.

But Guber and Peters obtained their pay deals after long negotiations, and, most important, arm's-length negotiations, with Akio Morita, the highly touted CEO of Sony. It may well turn out that Morita made two of the worst buys of his long career, but that does not take away from the fact that the process was a fair one. He desperately wanted Guber and Peters, or thought he did at the time, and he anteed up a huge amount of money to land them. With Ross's rubber-stamp and insider-stuffed board, it was Ross himself who, for all practical purposes, decided that he desperately wanted Ross. And it was Ross himself who, for all practical purposes, anteed up a huge amount of money to land himself. (Demonstrating that he knows how to negotiate at arm's length when he has to, Ross personally thwarted Guber and Peters when they first announced that they were joining Columbia. It seems that the dynamic duo had forgotten about a five-year agreement they had negotiated with Warner Communications' subsidiary, Warner Brothers. When all the dust settled, a red-faced Sony had to give Warner Communications a mountain of economic benefits to free Guber and Peters from their Warner Brothers contracts. The sort of arm's-length negotiation that went on between Ross and Sony is what ought to go on when the pay contract of a CEO is hammered out.)

When Time acquired Warner Communications in 1989, Ross's latest employment agreement, which commenced in 1987, still had eight years to run. But the board gave him then and there what he would have received over the next eight years. And then they signed Ross up to a new fifteen-year contract—one that will keep him doing something for Time Warner until 2004. During the first five of those years, he is to be co-CEO with one of two Time Inc. executives. During the next five years, he is to be chairman but not CEO. Finally, he was also given a five-year further period in which he will be a non-employee adviser to his former company. In summary, Ross will be half a CEO for five years, not a CEO at all for another five years, and not even an employee for the third five years.

In that last five-year period, Ross, who by then will be in his seventies, will receive $750,000 per year for advising Time Warner, *if called upon,* for not more than forty hours per month, or $1,563 per hour. I wonder whether he really will be called upon. Some years ago, I found myself hitching a ride on the corporate jet of one of my clients. A board meeting had just been held, and the jet was flying to Chicago with a group of outside directors. I was busily reading the *Wall Street Journal* and trying not to eavesdrop on the conversations that were taking place, but I couldn't help overhearing the following exchange:

DIRECTOR 1 to DIRECTOR 2: "Hey, Don, I just read in the paper that you retired as CEO of the XYZ Company. So what are you going to do to keep busy?"

DIRECTOR 2: "Well, I'm still going to be a consultant to my former company."

DIRECTOR 1 (with a trace of sarcasm): "What exactly does that mean?"

DIRECTOR 2: "If you must know, I'm going to be a sexual consultant."

DIRECTOR 1: "A sexual consultant! What's that?"

DIRECTOR 2: "Well, when my former company signed me up as a consultant, they told me: 'If we want any of your f_____ing advice, we'll call you!' "

So Ross will likely either end up as an exceedingly high-priced real consultant or a sexual consultant.

In all, Ross earned around $275 million from 1973 through 1989, or somewhere around $16 million per year. That figure excludes the value of some pretty lavish perquisites, as well as such fringe benefits as life insurance and a pension. And there's likely a lot more to come, what with that huge 1.8 million share option waiting to deliver Ross millions, and a proclivity on the part of Ross's board to give him extra goodies even after it has negotiated a firm employment agreement with him.

The funny thing is that Ross could have made all the millions he made and have been celebrated as a hero in this book had he had sufficient faith in his ability to perform outstandingly. If he had only eschewed all his various pay gimmicks, and if he had only taken a more modest salary, and if he had only relied totally on stock option grants as his long-term incentive of choice, he would also have made several hundred million in pay over the years he has been CEO. And he would have made it a lot more fairly.

There seems to be no possible defense for paying Ross all that money, given the way he went about making it. He or his board—and under the circumstances there would appear to be no practical distinction—simply ripped off the shareholders.

Four

All in the Family

THE WORLD'S top concert artists, such as Jascha Heifetz and Isaac Stern, often cap their careers by teaching master classes; it goes without saying that if you are accepted as a "student," you are probably close to being a world-class musician yourself. Given Jeffrey J. Steiner's ability to extract compensation from Fairchild Corporation (formerly called Banner Industries), he, too, should consider offering master classes—in this case, in executive compensation. If he does, many of the people already discussed in this book will be fighting with each other to sit in the front row—even including Steve Ross of Time Warner. For Ross has at least delivered a huge amount of performance in return for the gargantuan amounts of pay he has received. With Steiner, huge pay has been received without benefit of any tangible performance.

Steiner is the chairman and CEO of Fairchild Corporation. A fifty-three-year-old college dropout who was born in Vienna, he has been CEO of Fairchild since 1985. The company is involved in a variety of manufacturing and distribution businesses (fasteners, bolts, and power-transmission parts), with a particular concentration in the aerospace industry.

Fairchild Corporation, though a public company, has a family feel. First, there is Jeffrey Steiner's son, Eric. In the 1990 proxy statement, Fairchild discloses that Eric, a director of Fairchild but not an employee, is twenty-eight years old and highly educated. He received an M.D. degree in France in 1988 and practiced medicine for a short time. Then he decided to go back to school to get his MBA—again in France. Assuming he completed his studies, he would have received that degree in December 1990. Although his educational credentials are quite impressive, his qualifications to be a board member of Fairchild Corporation, at least when it comes to working business experience, are a little on the thin side.

And there are some other relatives, too. Various proxies released by the company show that, at different times, Fairchild Corporation has employed as a senior vice president and director one of Jeffrey Steiner's nephews, while that nephew's father-in-law also served as a director of the company. If any of these relatives were paid anywhere near the level of Jeffrey Steiner himself, you would certainly be entitled to think of the Steiners as one happy family.

But before we look into Steiner's pay, let's look at his performance. If you judge a company only by its ability to generate revenues, Fairchild would be one of the best companies in the land. In 1986, the first fiscal year after Jeffrey Steiner joined the company, sales were $149 million. By fiscal 1990 (which ended in June 1990), sales had grown to $703 million, for a compounded growth rate of 47% per year.

Alas, shareholders, though impressed by huge sales growth, want to see something on the bottom line. And there is where Steiner seems to be having more than his share of troubles. First, fully diluted earnings per share, including extraordinary items and discontinued operations for the years 1986 through 1990, were, respectively, $0.50, $0.67, minus $0.76, $2.64, and $0.06. Lest you focus unduly on the excellent $2.64 per share earned in 1989, you should know that more than 100% of the profits were generated by a non-recurring item of income, mainly involving the reduction in Fairchild's interest in a subsidiary. Pre-tax income for that year was $83.1 million, but pre-tax income would have been minus $2.4 million were it not for that one-time item. After ignoring both the highest and lowest returns on average ending equity during the five years of Steiner's reign, Fairchild's performance in this critical area has been only about average compared to the 500 other companies with market capitalization in Fairchild's size range as of the end of 1990.

The final vote on performance is, of course, that cast by the shareholders when they buy and sell shares. Fairchild's closing stock price was $5.58 per share the month Steiner became CEO. For a while, things went swimmingly, with the stock price rising steadily until it peaked at $17.13 in December 1989. Had Steiner quit at that time, he'd look like a fine CEO, because the compounded price appreciation between December 1985 and December 1989 was 32.4% per year. But Steiner did stay on, and the stock price dropped and dropped—all the way to $4.88 per share by the end of October 1990. If you took the time to graph Fairchild's stock prices between December 1985, when Steiner became CEO and the stock was trading at $5.58 per share, and October 1990, when the stock price was $4.88 per share, the resulting figure would look very much like St. Louis' famed arch. (By March 1991, the stock price had risen to close at $8.13 per share.) The shareholders could not have consoled themselves with lavish dividends. Dividends per share in the five years ending in fiscal 1990 were, in chronological order, $0.01, $0.03, $0.01, $0.00, and $0.00.

Steiner did do one thing right from a shareholder perspective: he bought a lot of shares, presumably with his own money. In his initial filing with the SEC in October 1985, he reported that he owned 969,999 Fairchild shares, or about 24% of the shares then outstanding. And by the time the 1990 proxy statement was released, he was reported to own or otherwise control 66% of Fairchild's common shares. In other words, Jeffrey Steiner was very much in control of Fairchild Corporation. In more recent years, he has had the votes to elect any slate of directors he desired.

Before we go further, let's talk for a moment about the continuing interest that the Internal Revenue Service has in the size of executive compensation packages. At first glance, you'd think the IRS couldn't care less how much someone earned, because the greater the earnings, the greater the taxes owed to the government. But the IRS *is* concerned, and the concern relates to the double taxation, or potential double taxation, of corporate profits. To illustrate, let's assume that a single individual owns 100% of a company's stock and serves as CEO. And let's assume further that the company is about to close the books on $1 million of profit before paying corporate income taxes. Given a corporate tax rate of 34% (and ignoring that the first slice of corporate income, but a tiny slice, is taxed at a lower rate), the company would have to pay the IRS $340,000; it would then be left with $660,000 of income after taxes. Now assume that the company, for want of a better alternative, paid out the entire $660,000 as a dividend to its CEO-shareholder. And assume further that the shareholder is already at the maximum marginal ordinary tax rate of 31%. In that case, the shareholder would pay the IRS $204,600 in income taxes and would be left with $455,-400 in after-tax income. Hence, after taxes are paid at both the corporate level and the individual level, less than one half of the $1 million of pre-tax income remains to be spent. Meanwhile, the IRS, after collecting the two taxes, is in the black by $544,600.

Now suppose a way could be found to eliminate one of those two income taxes, the one on corporate profits. That tax could, of course, be eliminated if there were no corporate profits. And achieving no corporate profits is not all that hard to do. In the case of our CEO-shareholder, all he has to do is hold the books open at the end of the fiscal year for an extra thirty seconds or so—just long enough to pay himself a special bonus of $1 million. In that case, pre-tax income will decline from $1 million to zero, and there will be no corporate tax to hand over to the IRS. Then the CEO can declare the $1 million special bonus on his personal tax return and pay a single tax of $310,000. At the end of the day, he is left with after-tax income of $690,000, a figure which is 51.5% higher than the $455,400 with which he would have been left had both his corporation and he been required to pay income taxes.

In a situation like this, the IRS is understandably not amused. There is, after all, a zero-sum game operating here, and if the CEO can improve his after-tax income by $234,600, it follows that the IRS must lose the same $234,600 in income to itself. In such cases, the IRS becomes quite zealous and tries to argue that some of the compensation being paid to the CEO is really not compensation at all but rather a so-called disguised dividend. It thereupon disallows some of the deduction taken as compensation expense, which then causes pre-tax income to rise and the IRS's income to increase. If the company wants to fight rather than pay, it has to prove in court that the compensation paid to the CEO (or whoever else is involved) is reasonable considering the size of the company, the industry in which it is involved, its geographic location, its performance, and so forth.

Normally, the IRS only pushes the "disguised dividend" issue when a handful of executives own all, or almost all, the company's shares and are thereby in a position to engage in self-dealing. From a practical standpoint, therefore, the IRS generally does not go after a publicly owned company, because such a company has, by definition, many shareholders, and not all of them are employees. Nonetheless—and here is where Jeffrey Steiner comes in—when a shareholder owns as much as 70% of the shares outstanding, and when that shareholder pays himself monstrous amounts of compensation while performance is poor, and when the very same company pays almost nothing to its other shareholders in the form of dividends, the IRS ought to be concerned. And it especially ought to be concerned when a board member of Fairchild Corporation is a former Commissioner of the IRS, one Mortimer Caplin by name. With this backdrop, let's now see exactly how much Jeffrey Steiner managed to pay himself.

We'll begin the narrative in 1987. Steiner had signed a five-year employment agreement with an evergreen clause, meaning that unless one or the other party to the agreement raises his hand at a particular point in each succeeding year, the agreement is extended for another five years. His base salary was established at $750,000 per year, which itself was outrageously high for a company with only around $350 million in sales. Steiner also established three so-called bonus pools, one for himself, one for his chief operating officer and a senior vice president, and the third for all remaining bonus-eligible employees. Reflecting his apparently democratic instincts, Steiner funded each pool using the same exact formula, 1% of pre-tax profits. His bonus for fiscal 1987 was $245,000, bringing his total current compensation to $1.1 million.

Steiner had also been granted stock options during the three-year period ending on June 30, 1987. On a post-split basis (after the end of fiscal 1987, the stock was subsequently split 3:2 and then 2:1), he was granted 1,353,000 shares at an average strike price of $7.08 per share. However, a decline in the market price of Fairchild's stock prompted Steiner's board to make a retroactive adjustment in the strike price of his option shares—from $7.08 to $5.16. By rights, Steiner ought not to receive any reward for moving the stock from $5.16 to $7.08 per share, or where it was trading when he received his option. But that is not what will happen; he will instead receive a profit of $1.92 per share—or $2.6 million on all 1,353,000 shares.

Steiner was also a participant in a performance share plan. Under its very complicated provisions, Steiner stood to earn a huge number of Fairchild shares free, provided earnings per share grew at the very healthy rate of 15% per year over the 1986 base year level. He had been granted 200,000 units under the plan—units that were supposed to be earned over a five-year period ending with fiscal 1991.

In the 1988 proxy, Steiner's cash compensation decreased from a year earlier, a fact which could easily have fooled the casual observer into thinking that he was a real pay-for-performance nut. His cash compensation decreased from $1.1 million to $960,000. Somewhat ominously, the board informed Fairchild's shareholders that it might have to consider terminating the company's performance unit plan "because it may no longer be serving its function of providing appropriate incentive. . . ." That announcement should have sent a serious danger signal to shareholders, because about the only time a compensation plan is terminated is when it is about to yield its participating executives little or nothing in the way of payouts.

We now come to the 1989 proxy. Possibly angered by the drop

in his cash compensation the year before, Steiner presumably persuaded his indulgent board to increase his base salary from $750,000 to $1 million. And while he was at it, he also persuaded the board to give him some monster bonuses. First of all, 1989 was a great year for Fairchild, if you count that one-time, non-recurring item of income that, alchemically, transformed a loss year into a banner year. And that one-time, non-recurring item of income must have been counted in the calculation of Steiner's bonus, because his "regular" bonus (i.e., the bonus from his 1%-of-profits formula) was $1.1 million. But the board didn't stop there. It also awarded him a "special cash bonus" of $2 million to recognize his "extraordinary efforts" in the acquisition and divestiture area. All told, Steiner's cash compensation was $4.4 million that year. That is, his cash compensation from Fairchild Corporation was $4.4 million that year.

But the company also had a 48.7% interest in another company, one called Banner Investments. On March 24, 1989 (or some three months prior to the end of fiscal 1989), Fairchild Corporation decided to buy the 51.3% of the shares of Banner Investments it did not then own. Because Banner Investments was a wholly owned subsidiary by the end of fiscal 1989, the board of Fairchild Corporation had to make a further disclosure in the company's 1989 proxy statement, and that involved a bit of extra compensation that Steiner had earned while he was doing double duty as CEO of both Fairchild Corporation and Banner Investments. The extra compensation, which was earned for services performed in the approximately nine-month period between July 1, 1988, and March 24, 1989, amounted to a further base salary of $280,000, a further bonus of $3.3 million, and some director's fees of $23,000. All told, this extra cash compensation amounted to $3.6 million. Adding this $3.6 million to the $4.4 million that Steiner received in his position as CEO of Fairchild Corporation brought his total current compensation for the year up to $8 million. Not bad for a company with sales of $433 million and, but for a one-time, non-recurring gain, a pre-tax loss for the year.

In the olden days of royal hunts, if the king proved to be a bad shot, a loyal retainer could always be counted on to lug the animal to within ten feet of his monarch, tie it down, and stand back. The outcome was never much in doubt. In a similar vein, Steiner also received a $1.8 million option gain in fiscal 1989. It seems that Banner Investments had earlier granted him an option on 1 million shares in Banner Investments stock. The option was granted on August 25, 1988, a scant seven months before Fairchild Corporation bought the outstanding shares of Banner Investments that it did not then own. Now, it is hard to buy some 51% of a company's outstanding shares without causing the price of the stock to rise and, in this case, without causing the value of Steiner's options also to rise. The decision to buy in the outstanding shares of Banner Investments was, of course, made by the board of Fairchild Corporation. And who do you think controlled the board of Fairchild Corporation? A great shot was made by the king!

As we've seen in its 1988 proxy statement, the board of Fairchild muttered darkly that it might have to do something about Fairchild's Performance Unit Plan. Well, the date of the proxy statement was October 26, 1988, and the board acted just thirteen days later, on November 8, 1988. It vested—prematurely—all of Steiner's performance units. As a result, he received, shortly after the end of fiscal 1989, 793,338 free shares of Fairchild stock, which then had a value of $8.9 million. Then the board issued Steiner another 200,000 performance units. The fact that 1989 was the only good year Fairchild had, and only because of a one-time, non-recurring gain, probably figured in the board's reasoning. By vesting the units in fiscal 1989 and reissuing 200,000 new units to Steiner, his payout almost assuredly would have been much greater than had the board elected to let the original 200,000 units do their original duty and last until the end of 1991.

All in all, Steiner received $8 million of cash compensation from Fairchild Corporation and Banner Investments during fiscal 1989, garnered another $1.8 million through the exercise of his Banner Investments stock options, and received free shares from the Performance Unit Plan worth a further $8.9 million. His total take for the year was $18.7 million—not as much as Steve Ross has been accustomed to earning in a single year, but not bad for a relatively small company with a generally dismal performance record.

There is one minor item of compensation we omitted, however. Sometime during fiscal 1989, the board gave Steiner some extra life insurance, the first-year premium for which was $244,000. Given the company's track record and the huge amounts of compensation being siphoned off by Jeffrey Steiner, the board should have taken out a policy on the company's life, not Steiner's.

We come now to the 1990 proxy statement. Not content with a salary of a measly $1 million, Steiner has managed to increase his salary to $1,400,000—and this in the face of a year when pre-tax income was minus $5 million. Of course, with pre-tax income of minus $5 million, Steiner would not have been entitled to receive a bonus from his pool calling for 1% of the profits. And he didn't. But his board rode to the rescue one more time, giving him "special cash bonuses" of $4.4 million. His total current compensation was $6 million. Physicists have theorized that for every bit of matter, there is some anti-matter to balance it. That concept may prove useful in this case. Steiner made $6 million; if the physicists are right, other people had to have lost $6 million. Well, the numbers are a bit off, but the shareholders did sustain a pre-tax loss of $5 million. So maybe there's something to that anti-matter theory.

Steiner also exercised some stock options during fiscal 1990—on September 21, 1989, to be exact. In fact, he exercised all 1,353,000 of his previously granted option shares. His average strike price was $5.16, and he received aggregate option gains of $13.3 million (i.e., the amount by which the market price at the time the option was exercised exceeded the option's average strike price, multiplied by the number of shares exercised). Hence, the market price at the time Steiner exercised his options must have been around $15. He didn't quite hit the all-time-high price of the stock, which peaked at $17.13 per share in December 1989. But he came close. And he did remarkably well, considering that the stock price nosedived starting in 1990, and was selling for as low as $4.88 per share in October 1990.

Two weeks before Steiner exercised his 1,353,000-share stock option, Fairchild granted him an option on another 450,000 shares at a strike price of $15.625. That strike price was also near the high of the market, and so Fairchild's board, accustomed by now to lowering strike prices, soon called in the option and lowered the strike price from $15.625 to $10.875. The dirty deed occurred on February 15, 1990. Fairchild's 1990 proxy, which was dated October 12, 1990, fails to say whether or not the board cut the strike price of Steiner's 450,000-share option grant a second time, even though, by October 19, 1990, the stock was trading in the $5 per share range. Does that mean the board finally refused to knuckle under any further? Or does it simply mean that the second markdown in the strike price occurred after October 12, 1990, and will be reported in the October 1991 proxy statement? Someone cynical like me would probably pick Choice B. But maybe I'm too cynical.

Let's review the bidding for a moment. Steiner's original option strike price on 1,353,000 of his 1,828,000 option shares was $7.08, but it was lowered to $5.16 after a decline in the price of Fairchild stock. Then the stock rose to around $15 per share by the time Steiner exercised the 1,353,000 option shares. It was at that point that Steiner received the first of two windfalls, this one being worth $2.6 million, or the difference between Steiner's original strike price of $7.08 and the marked-down strike price of $5.16, multiplied by the 1,353,000 shares Steiner exercised. Then, right around the time of this exercise, Steiner received another option grant for 475,000 shares carrying a strike price of $15.625. But, as with the earlier grant, the strike price was soon lowered, this time to $10.875. So when—or more correctly, if—Fairchild's stock climbs from $10.875 to $15.625, Steiner will receive a second windfall, in this case, the difference between $15.625 and $10.875, multiplied by the 475,000 shares in the grant, or $2.3 million. Achieving a height of 30 feet on the pole vault would shatter by far every record in the book. The normal way to accomplish this feat is to set the bar at 30 feet and jump over it. But there is also the Jeffrey Steiner method of pole vaulting. Here, you set the bar at 15 feet and jump over it twice.

In the 1990 proxy, the board of Fairchild also asked the company's shareholders to approve an Interest Reimbursement Plan. Under this plan, an executive who borrows funds from a bank to exercise a Fairchild stock option can receive full reimbursement from the company for the interest he pays the bank during a two-year period following exercise. Presumably, Jeffrey Steiner will be making use of this provision when he comes to exercise his currently outstanding stock option grants. Although this new plan will cost the shareholders further money, its cost can be controlled by lowering the strike prices of previously granted stock options, thereby causing the executive to have to borrow less money to fund his option exercise. From that perspective, therefore, perhaps the members of the board of Fairchild Corporation should not be castigated for lowering Steiner's option strike prices, but should be praised as serious cost-cutters.

The year 1990 was a bit better for Jeffrey Steiner than 1989. In 1989, his total pay was on the order of $18.7 million. In 1990, he received cash compensation of $6 million and option profits of $13.3 million, for total compensation of $19.3 million. If you assume that the approximately $19 million per year Steiner has been earning will continue into the future, it is not hard to conclude that Steiner, not very many years from now, will have transferred 100% of the value of Fairchild to his own wallet. That wouldn't be all that wrong, if he owned 100% of the stock, and if the IRS weren't denied the extra income taxes it probably should have had. Of course, it's pretty hard to work up any sympathy for the IRS. But how about at least a little compassion for Banner's other shareholders?

Five

High Pay, Low Performance

Unhappily for the U.S. economy, there are too many CEOs who receive especially high pay but whose companies fail to deliver even average performance. Four who fit the bill are Andrew Sigler of Champion International; Rand Araskog of ITT; the late Armand Hammer of Occidental Petroleum; and J. Peter Grace of W. R. Grace.

Go to a conference of institutional investors, and you may well hear Andrew Sigler, the fifty-nine-year-old, Dartmouth-educated ex-Marine who is CEO of Champion International, inveigh against the short-term outlook of most investors. He will tell you that the problem with America is that people aren't willing to take the long-term view—to adopt a viable strategy, to stick with it even if short-term losses must be borne and, eventually, to emerge into the sunlight of outsized profits. That is how the Japanese have done it, and, Sigler contends, that is how all of us should do it.

He is quite the stump preacher. Pity he doesn't seem to be able to practice what he preaches. Oh sure, he has a strategy. And he seems willing enough to stick with it through the dark days. But neither he nor his increasingly impatient investors have seen much in the way of sun.

The ultimate measure of performance, at least as far as shareholders are concerned, is, or should be, long-term total shareholder return, counting both stock price appreciation and dividends. But shareholder returns can be quite volatile, depending on the stock price prevailing at the beginning of the return period and the stock price prevailing at the end of the return period. To minimize this volatility in looking at Champion International, ITT, and many other companies in this book, I went back to March 1971 and calculated the compounded annual total shareholder return for the ensuing ten years and for each of the 500 companies which had the largest market capitalization and whose stock was publicly traded throughout the period 1971–91 (of the 500 companies, the stock of 407 was traded continuously during the 20-year period). Then I moved forward one month—to April 1971—and repeated the exercise for the ensuing ten-year period. Indeed, I kept moving up at one-month intervals until I had calculated the total shareholder return for the period February 1981–February 1991. In all, I ended up with 120 total shareholder return statistics, each covering a ten-year period, and in the aggregate covering a 20-year period. These 120 figures were then averaged, after first omitting the very highest and the very lowest figure. The result was perhaps the most objective picture one could derive of long-term company performance; calculating returns over 120 different periods virtually eliminates the possibility of deriving a spurious statistic (for example, because the stock price at the beginning or end of a particular ten-year period was abnormally low or high).

When the total shareholder return performance of Champion International, a major paper company headquartered in Stamford, Connecticut, is weighed against that of the other 406 companies with the largest market capitalization, and when the timeframe consists of 120 ten-year, total return observations over the past 20 years, Champion barely tips the scales; its performance places it at the 8th percentile of the distribution. And when we concentrate on the most recent 80 of the these 120 observations, the company also ranks at the 8th percentile. Indeed, Champion continues to stay way down in the rankings even for shorter periods of time (7th percentile for the most recent 40 ten-year periods and again for the most recent 20 ten-year periods). With performance as consistently dismal as Champion's, perhaps Sigler ought to step down from his bully pulpit, roll up his sleeves, and get to work. Better yet, perhaps he ought to call Heidrick & Struggles, one of America's leading executive search firms, and ask them to find a new CEO. That would be the sort of selfless act one expects from a preacher.

In my 1991 *Financial World* article, which assessed the pay packages of 459 CEOs, Sigler was reported to be making $3.5 million per year. That level of compensation, after calibrating for company size and performance, placed him 95% above the market. Not bad for a company with 8th percentile performance. Indeed, when we consider that Sigler is earning so much more than he should, and when we consider that his pay package has probably influenced the pay packages of many of his subordinates in an upward direction, we can now understand, at least in part, why Champion International is performing at the 8th percentile level.

Sigler's pay package exhibits a fault found in a number of pay packages: his pay has much more upside than downside elasticity. Back in the early 1980s, Champion International's performance sagged, with earnings per share after taxes but before extraordinary items plunging from $3.28 in 1980 to minus $0.36 in 1984. Sigler's annual bonus also dropped, but not nearly so much. From $221,000 for his performance during 1979, his bonus dropped more or less steadily to $145,000 for his performance during 1983. Then, for reasons that are not readily apparent, his bonus essentially doubled to $300,000 for his performance in 1984. The only problem here was that 1984 was the year that Champion International lost $0.36 per share.

The company's performance started to rebound in 1985, with earnings per share moving back to $1.59. Earnings per share for 1986 through 1989 were, respectively, $2.08, $4.03, $4.80, and $4.56. In the face of this first decent performance trend in a number of years, Sigler's annual bonus really strutted its stuff, moving from $230,000 for 1985 performance to as much as $677,000 for 1988 performance. For 1989 performance, the bonus was cut to $425,000. Then, in 1990, earnings per share plunged again, this time to $2.11 per share, while return on average equity dropped to an abysmal 5.7%. But did Sigler's bonus drop? No, it rose—from $425,000 to $440,000. Note that Sigler never did have a zero-bonus year, even when, in 1984, the shareholders were especially savaged. Looking back, one can see that, when performance was on the upswing, Sigler's bonus exhibited the aerodynamic characteristics of an F-16 in full-powered climb. But when performance was on the downswing, Sigler's bonus exhibited the aerodynamic characteristics of a feather. Such is what passes for symmetrical thinking in America's boardrooms.

Note also needs to be taken of the built-in bias toward growth that so many American companies have. Granted, Champion International's earnings per share increased tremendously during the period 1984 through 1988. But even in the very best of those years— 1988—the company's return on average shareholders' equity (14.5%) was bettered by 62% of the 500 companies which in January 1988 had the largest market capitalization.

Given that bias toward growth, a CEO who wants to maximize his income would do well not to aim for steady growth and solid return levels, but rather to aim for highly erratic growth. On the downside, as already shown, the penalties won't be very severe. And on the upside, the payouts will be terrific. Moreover, you can cover the same ground time after time and, time after time, be rewarded for it. Build up the earnings per share to $3.00, and then let them fall to $0.01. Then build them back to $3 again, all the time proclaiming what great growth you are experiencing. Never mind that your returns on equity are never very good. However, if you are going to follow this strategy, try not to have a loss year, because calculating earnings per share growth off a loss year is something that not even the most astute mathematician has yet figured out how to do.

Sigler also received several payouts under long-term performance unit plans. Given the appallingly low level of Champion International's total shareholder return performance, one has to wonder about the goals Sigler was being asked to achieve. Further, Sigler has received restricted stock grants. Restricted stock is especially valuable for a CEO who can't seem to engineer much growth in his company's stock price.

You don't have to go to a conference to hear Rand Araskog, the CEO of ITT, speak. You can buy his book, *The ITT Wars,* and you'll get sermons aplenty. But, like Andrew Sigler at Champion International, Araskog, who is also fifty-nine, is better at preaching than doing. At least he is starting to improve his company's dismal performance. Using the same analysis referred to for Champion International, ITT achieves a 17th percentile performance level using all 120 observations covering a 20-year period. If we concentrate on the most recent eighty observations, the percentile ranking rises to 20th. Then it rises to the 23rd percentile for the most recent 40 periods and to the 28th percentile for the most 20 periods. Not very good, but at least the trend is in the right direction.

Rand Araskog earns much more than Andrew Sigler. And perhaps he should, because his performance, though poor, is not as poor as Sigler's. Becoming CEO of ITT not long after the tumultuous reign of Harold Geneen, he inherited a board of directors that was used to doling out huge amounts of compensation for almost any reason. We first glimpse Araskog's pay package as CEO in 1980, his first full fiscal year on the job. In that year, his base salary and annual bonus came to $886,000, while his shareholders earned a very respectable return on equity (ROE) of 15%. Then we watch his base and bonus increase the next year to $963,000, at a time when ROE has dropped from 15% to 10.9%. Don't let anyone say there's no relationship between pay and performance at ITT, because there is. The only troubling aspect of the relationship, however, is that it is negative! Or at least it was negative at certain periods of Araskog's tenure.

In 1982, ITT managed to earn an 11.5% return on its equity, and Araskog received a more or less normal pay increase—from a base and bonus of $963,000 to $994,000. He received another normal increase the next year—to $1,023,000—although performance dipped once again. ROE for 1983 was essentially static at 11.0%.

In 1984, the bottom dropped out of ITT's earnings. Earnings per share after taxes and extraordinary items declined from $4.50 in 1983 to $2.97 in 1984, while ROE was a minuscule 7.4%. To its credit, ITT's board finally summoned up the nerve to make Araskog take a pay hit. His bonus was eliminated entirely that year, so he received only his base salary of around $700,000.

The year 1985 was even worse than 1984, with earnings per share declining again, this time to $1.84, and with ROE sagging to 4.7%. Having mandated that Araskog receive no bonus for his performance in 1984, you would think the board would summon up its nerve yet a second time. Wrong! In the face of absolutely dismal performance, the board elevated the sum of Araskog's base salary and bonus from $700,000 to $1 million.

In 1986, ITT finally achieved a profit rebound. Earnings per share increased from $1.84 to $3.23, but ROE was still an anemic 7.3%. Demonstrating again that there is much more upside than downside elasticity to executive pay, ITT's board raised Araskog's base salary and bonus from $1.0 million to $1.7 million. Note here that the $3.23 level of earnings per share was far lower than the $6.12 achieved in 1980—a year when Araskog's salary and bonus was $886,000.

In 1987, earnings per share increased again—this time to $6.76. And Araskog received an increase in his base salary and bonus from $1.7 to $1.9 million. However, the uptrend was broken in 1988 when earnings per share dropped once again—from $6.76 to $5.70. This time, the board forgot all about cutting Araskog's pay in line with ITT's decreased performance; rather, it gave him a hefty raise in base salary and bonus—from $1.9 to $2.2 million. And the uptrend in salary and bonus was continued when in 1989 Araskog's salary and bonus rose to $2.4 million (earnings per share also rose—from $5.90 to $6.52).

In 1990, earnings per share rose to $7.28 per share, and ITT's compensation committee celebrated the increase by piling more compensation on Araskog than he had ever before received. His salary and bonus rose 63%—from $2.4 to $3.9 million, far more than the 11.7% increase in ITT's primary earnings per share after extraordinary items.

ITT has given Araskog, at one time or another, all the three major forms of incentive compensation: stock options, performance unit grants, and restricted stock grants. The performance unit plan, however, was a bust, with Araskog receiving only one payment (in 1980) of a measly $51,000. Still, if you can't meet performance targets you yourself probably devised, you can lower the bar to ground level and move to restricted stock. In 1986, Araskog began to receive annual grants of restricted stock, and the dosage level was very high. The value of shares granted to him during the period 1986 through 1990 was approximately $17 million.

Araskog's huge base salary and bonus, coupled with his lavish restricted stock grants and option grants, have combined to make him one of America's highest-paid CEOs. The value of his base salary, annual bonus, and long-term incentives was reported in my 1991 *Fortune* article on the pay of 202 CEOs to be $11.5 million per year. Compared to the other CEOs, and after taking account of company size and performance, he is being paid 301% above the market.

In April 1991, I chose to criticize ITT's compensation committee for overpaying Rand Araskog. I did so in a special edition of the newsletter I edit, *The Crystal Report*. The impact of my newsletter, which has a tiny circulation, was greatly amplified by the national press and the electronic media. For its part, ITT claimed that I had treated the company unfairly. We met, and the result was still another newsletter on what had by then become "The ITT Affair." In defending itself, ITT paid special attention to what it saw as a dramatic turnaround wrought by Araskog. In a particularly bold move, which he personally negotiated, Araskog created a joint venture with a French company. The resulting new company, Alcatel N.V., is now the largest telecommunications manufacturing company in the world. ITT had owned 37% of the joint venture's stock, but in 1990 it sold 7% of Alcatel's stock for an after-tax gain of almost $200 million. Based on that sale, it is obvious that ITT has a winner here. It is Araskog's work with Alcatel, more than any other single factor, that apparently motivated ITT's board to reward him so hugely.

Unfortunately for Araskog, ITT as a company consists of a great deal more than its interest in Alcatel; among other things, it owns the Sheraton hotel chain and the Hartford insurance companies. These many other areas have not, in total, exhibited the same excellent performance as the Alcatel joint venture.

In its treatment of Araskog, the ITT compensation committee has exhibited the Prodigal Son syndrome. To be sure, Araskog engineered an earnings turnaround; but earlier, he also presided over an earnings decline. Had he been punished, paywise, during the decline phase, the huge rewards he received during the turnaround phase would have been easier to take. But during the decline phase, he had his pay cut only once, even though the company's earnings per share dropped five years in a row. So, by the time the decline phase ended in 1985, he was earning 54% more than he had been earning five years earlier. Then, during the turnaround phase, his pay increased a further 396%.

Oh, and one other thing. In 1980, ITT's board decided that it would be better for Araskog to have a residence nearer the company's New York headquarters, "in order better to meet the requirements of his position as Chief Executive Officer of ITT and ITT's need that he be more accessible to ITT's headquarters during certain periods of each month." Nothing wrong with that sentiment. But there is something wrong with paying the interest costs on the apartment mortgage, as well as the monthly cooperative association dues, when the person in question is making close to $1 million per year and presumably has the wherewithal to finance his own New York City apartment. By 1981, ITT's shareholders were paying a tab of $178,000 in a single year for Araskog's interest and maintenance.

What a deal! We have to figure Araskog was already receiving free lunches—a perquisite given to almost every CEO. And if he arrived at the office early enough, the company was probably throwing in breakfasts as well. There must have been many evenings when Araskog ate dinner at company expense. And besides all that, he was getting free rent to boot. What could he have had left to spend his $1 million a year on? Taking your shirts to the local Manhattan Chinese laundry doesn't cost all that much. In his book *The ITT Wars,* Araskog decried the financial excesses of the 1980s. It's a pity he didn't devote some ink to the executive compensation excesses of the same decade. But that, of course, might have made his book just a bit too autobiographical.

There are people in Wall Street who spend their working lives dreaming up new securities. Recently, Shearson Lehman Hutton invented the Unbundled Stock Unit (USU), a hybrid security that would permit an investor to buy a company's future dividend stream or its future stock price appreciation. The new creature received a great deal of press attention, but it apparently couldn't thrive outside the laboratory, because it died an early death. Back to the drawing board. But as long as someone is at the drawing board, how about a new security that would index an investor's returns, not to the price of the company's stock, but rather to the increase in the pay package of the company's CEO? It's a shame that such a security wasn't available to the shareholders of Champion International and ITT, because it would have been a moneymaker.

Andrew Sigler of Champion International and Rand Araskog of ITT both have held their jobs for a goodly number of years. But when it comes to longevity, almost no CEO can hold a candle to J. Peter Grace, the CEO of W. R. Grace, or the late Armand Hammer, CEO of Occidental Petroleum. In reviewing what has happened to their pay and their companies' performances, one is reminded of the aphorism that not all wines improve with age.

Grace, now seventy-seven, has been CEO of the company bearing his family name since 1945, having worked his way up to the job in a scant nine years. And Hammer for all practical purposes founded Occidental Petroleum in 1957. Grace is still running his company, but Hammer, at age ninety-two, recently went on to a place where whatever rewards he receives will be tax-free. He has left an absolute circus behind—one where heirs are fighting heirs over his considerable wealth, where Occidental's board is fighting its shareholders over a lavish museum that the shareholders involuntarily built to honor the great man, and where his successor, Ray Irani, is systematically, and it seems with a bit of glee to boot, dismantling Hammer's corporate empire.

It is fairly hard to find performance records more dismal than those of these two CEOs. Looking at 120 consecutive ten-year total shareholder return periods, the shareholder return performance of W. R. Grace ranked it at the 28th percentile of the 407-company performance distribution. In other words, 72% of the companies in the analysis performed better than Grace, while only 28% performed worse. The shareholder return performance of Occidental Petroleum ranked it at the 33rd percentile of the 407-company distribution.

These findings depict the performance of the two companies over a twenty-year period, but they don't tell us much about the direction of the performance, which, in the case of both companies, has been decidedly downhill. For all 120 total return periods, Grace, as we saw, weighed in at the 28th percentile. For the most recent 80, 40, and 20 ten-year total return periods, the percentile ranks were, respectively, 20th, 20th, and 16th. Occidental Petroleum, directionally speaking, looks even worse. From a 33rd percentile rank for all 120 total return periods, it drops to the 19th, 16th, and 15th percentile ranks, respectively, for the most recent 80, 40, and 20 ten-year total return periods.

We may have been critical of Rand Araskog of ITT, whose performance, though still poor, is at least improving. But what about performance that is poor and getting poorer? That is the performance profile exhibited both by W. R. Grace and Occidental Petroleum. Put it this way: If company performance were graded on the curve, not only would both Peter Grace and Armand Hammer have flunked, they would both have been tossed out of college. Yet when it comes to pay, these two CEOs are hardly down in the bottom part of the distribution. Is it possible that Grace would long ago have been booted out of W. R. Grace if his name had not been over the front door? And is it possible that the same fate would have befallen Hammer, who was also more or less a company founder, had not a more final fate intervened?

Let's look at Peter Grace first. During the period 1973–75, Grace's average annual total pay (counting base salary, annual bonus, and the annualized present value of long-term incentives) was $432,000. That level of pay worked out to be 47 times that of the average U.S. manufacturing worker. By the period 1987–89, Grace's average annual total pay had risen to $4.3 million, or 200 times that of the average U.S. manufacturing worker. Yet, as we have seen, the company's performance was heading downhill. In my 1990 study for *Fortune,* Grace was reported to be paid 82% above his indicated market value, after taking into account such factors as company size, company performance, and business risk. However, in 1990 his pay package declined 44%—from $4.5 to $2.5 million—and he was reported in my 1991 *Fortune* article to be a lesser 22% over the market.

In 1981, a grateful board of directors decided to give Peter Grace a special bonus of $1 million (on top of his regular annual bonus), "in recognition of his accomplishments during his 36-year tenure as the Company's Chief Executive Officer." As it turns out, the company's performance in the ten years ending in 1981 was not all that bad; it ranked at the 68th percentile in total shareholder return, compared to 406 other major companies.

In the same year it was giving him $1 million extra for his magnificent accomplishments, the board also adopted for the first time a so-called Performance Unit Plan. Such a plan offers an executive free shares or a sum of cash, provided certain performance goals are met over a period of years, usually three to five. In W. R. Grace's case, Peter Grace was promised the sum of $706,000, provided certain unspecified goals were met over the three years 1981 through 1983. Well, he didn't meet the goals and so received no payout from the plan. The board thereupon gave him a second chance. For the performance period covering the years 1983 through 1985, Peter Grace was offered the opportunity to earn $807,000. Once again, Grace stepped up to the plate, and once again, he struck out. And this from an individual who just a few years before had been given a $1 million bonus for his stellar performance.

Many years ago, when I was working as a consultant, I received a frantic call from the vice president of personnel of one of my clients. "Get over here right away, because there's something wrong with our Performance Unit Plan," he wailed. "What's wrong?" I asked. "The plan isn't paying off," he answered. To most executives, a good incentive plan is one that pays off, preferably all the time. Very little thought is given to the proposition that the reason the plan may not have been paying off is that it is correctly matching non-rewards to non-performance. In that same vein, perhaps Peter Grace decided that there was something wrong with his company's Performance Unit Plan, because in 1986, after the second performance unit grant failed to produce a payout and before the third performance unit grant (which was to cover performance during the period 1987 through 1989) had commenced, he received the first of a series of restricted stock grants. Restricted stock, it will be recalled, has the handy virtue of not requiring that an executive deliver any performance; rather, all he has to do is hang around to collect his free shares. And given his by-then extraordinarily long tenure with his company, hanging around was something that Peter Grace was arguably good at. His first award of restricted shares was worth some $700,000.

If you go to a track meet and watch the high jump, you'll notice that each time a contestant clears the bar, it is raised to a higher level. And if a contestant knocks the bar over, he or she is eliminated from competition. Would that the world of executive compensation ran the same way. Instead, we have a different sort of game going on. If you knock the bar over, the bar is simply lowered. And if you still knock the bar over, it is lowered still further. Indeed, should it become necessary, a trench will be dug and the bar buried. Watching this sort of competition is not terribly exciting for the spectators— but the contestants love it.

In Peter Grace's case, the board apparently gave him the very best of both worlds. By giving him grants of restricted stock, they buried the bar. But just in case he should summon up enough talent to clear the bar, they also gave him another grant of performance units.

All this largesse has come home to roost in more recent years. After a tentative start on restricted stock in the form of a $700,000 grant, the board got going in earnest and gave him another grant in 1988, this one worth over $5 million. And what do you know, Grace finally cleared the bar under the Performance Unit Plan, which, for its third cycle, ending in 1989, delivered him a further $1.2 million.

We can again observe here the tendency of companies to pile one form of executive compensation on top of another. Hence, the company that heretofore has granted only stock options to its senior executives starts to grant stock options and restricted stock. And worse, it doesn't cut back on the size of option grants to make room for the new restricted stock plan. The result is ever higher executive compensation. By 1989, Peter Grace was receiving stock option grants, restricted stock grants, and Performance Unit Grants. Yet, given his performance, all that incentive compensation was seemingly not enough to motivate him.

As if all this were not enough, the company has routinely provided Peter Grace with "assistance on personal business and personal use of corporate aircraft. . . ." In several different proxy statements, the company has disclosed that the value of these free services ranged as high as $84,000 per year. On the other hand, Peter Grace has given distinguished service to his country, among other things by heading the so-called Grace Commission between 1982 and 1984. The official name of the Grace Commission was the President's (of the U.S., that is) Private Sector Survey on Cost Control. It is more than a bit ironic that the head of the Grace Commission, who was responsible for assembling a list of thousands of ways the U.S. government could cut its costs, seems incapable of controlling the cost of his own pay package.

Armand Hammer of Occidental Petroleum presents a similar picture of excessive pay for lackluster performance. For the period 1973–75, he earned $377,000 per year, or 41 times the pay of an average U.S. manufacturing worker. By the time we get to 1987–89, his pay had risen to $3 million per year—138 times the pay of an average worker. And in my 1991 *Fortune* study, his pay was reported to be 101% above the market for CEOs generally.

Besides receiving restricted stock grants (as well as stock option grants), Hammer further advanced the state-of-the-art in risk reduction by being an early pioneer of the guaranteed minimum bonus. As far back as 1981, he was promised that his annual bonus would be not less than $240,000 per year. By the time we reach 1990, the guaranteed minimum bonus level had increased to $420,000. Coupled with his 1989 base salary level of $1,534,000, his minimum compensation level—no matter what the company's performance—was just a shade under $2 million per year ($1,954,000). Perhaps it was that assurance of financial security that permitted Dr. Hammer the luxury of flying all over the world in his company's 727 jet to meet with world statesmen, and of spending great amounts of time on the construction of the company art museum that will house his vast collection.

Hammer's final assault on his shareholders occurred upon his death. When he died, he was being paid under an employment contract that was written to cover his services until February 1998, at which point, had he lived, he would have been just about one hundred years old. A little-noticed feature of his contract provided that he was to be paid during the entire term of the contract, even if he died before its expiration. As a result, the shareholders had to ante up a further $18.3 million after his death. The *Los Angeles Times* has labeled the transaction a "Golden Coffin." Given that the monies were willed by Dr. Hammer to his foundation, the shareholders could be argued to have made a charitable contribution. But as with the museum Hammer left behind, the charitable contribution was of the distinctly involuntary variety.

J. Peter Grace and Armand Hammer are two CEOs who might have been useful to shareholders in some distant past. But Grace is no longer pulling his weight, and Hammer has left the scene entirely. Yet their indulgent boards of directors kept them on year after year and offered them pay packages that were clearly excessive in relation to their performance.

The Occidental Petroleum board, at least, has been given a clear picture of what the outside world thought of the performance of the company's CEO. When Dr. Hammer died, the news caused Occidental's share price to rise $1.875, or 9%, in a single day. If you multiply that $1.875 increase per share by the 295 million shares Occidental had outstanding at the time, the aggregate increase in market price was around $550 million. You could argue, therefore, that Hammer's personal contribution to shareholder value amounted to minus $550 million. Oh well, it's not many CEOs who can measure their worth with such precision.

Six

On the Flying Trapeze

IT'S ALWAYS great fun to go to the circus, and especially to watch the men and women on the flying trapeze. As Burt Lancaster showed us years back when he made the movie *Trapeze,* life at the top of the Big Top can be quite exciting, and quite dangerous, too—at least when the performance takes place without benefit of a safety net. The trapeze artists can even make our hearts beat faster when they work with a safety net, because the net is located so far away from the trapeze bars. But how exciting would it be to watch a trapeze act where the safety net was raised within a foot of the trapeze bar?

Erecting safety nets under their magnificent pay packages is the specialty of Richard Eamer of National Medical Enterprises, Martin Davis of Paramount Communications, and Lee Iacocca of Chrysler. Their safety net of choice consists of huge grants of restricted stock.

Some CEOs prove magnificent during the early years of their reign, but then their performance starts to slip. Rarely, however, does the CEO's pay package slip in line with the company's fading performance. Richard Eamer, sixty-three, who has been CEO of National Medical Enterprises (NME), an acute-care hospital operator, for twenty-three years, amply demonstrates the point. Looking at NME's performance over the past 20 years and using my 120-period total shareholder return analysis, NME ranked at the 97th percentile of the 407-company distribution. In other words, only 3% of the 407 companies in the study performed as well as or better than NME, while 97% delivered lower performance. Like W. R. Grace and Occidental Petroleum, however, the direction of NME's performance is poor. Its percentile ranks for the most recent 80, 40, and 20 ten-year total return periods are, respectively, 95th, 68th, and 52nd. It's a pity that National Medical Enterprises' board didn't cut Eamer's pay to recognize his faded glory, instead of piling pay on top of pay at the very time when the company's progress has slowed so dramatically.

During the period 1973–75, Richard Eamer's average annual total compensation (counting base salary, annual bonus, and long-term incentives) was $305,000—about 33 times that of an average industrial worker. Yet by 1987–89, when NME's performance was slowing markedly, his average annual total compensation had risen to some $13.6 million per year—or about 625 times the pay of the average industrial worker.

Eamer managed to increase his compensation so magnificently by adopting a bewildering array of compensation plans—so many that he can rightly be called the poor man's Steve Ross. Until fiscal 1984, his compensation arrangements were relatively straightforward, consisting of a base salary, an annual bonus, and periodic stock option grants. But then all hell broke loose. And, curiously, it broke loose just about the time the stock price had peaked. The closing stock price for fiscal year ending May 1983 was $28.75, and the closing prices for the fiscal years ending in May 1984 through May 1989 were, respectively, $20.63, $29.63, $24.00, $26.13, $23.88, and $30.63. You'd almost have needed a carpenter's level to measure whether the trend was flat or slightly up. Finally, however, the stock began to rise, reaching $36 by May 1990 and $49 by late March 1991. Still, the compounded rate of stock price appreciation between May 1983 and April 1991 amounted only to 7.0% per year, or less than what an investor could have earned investing in Treasury securities during the same period.

In 1984, Eamer agreed to extend his employment agreement for two years. In return, a grateful board of directors in effect crammed a B-52 with compensation goodies and dropped the payload over NME's Beverly Hills headquarters. In fiscal 1984, Eamer was given a stock option on 30,000 shares carrying a strike price equal to the market price of NME stock on the date of grant, or $21.125 per share. Nothing out of the ordinary there. But he was also given a further option on 60,000 shares carrying a strike price equal to only half the market price of NME stock on the date of grant. Hence, the strike price of this second stock option grant was a much lower $10.56 per share. Moreover, he was also given, for the first time, some restricted stock—180,000 shares in all.

If you are granted a stock option with a strike price of $21.125 per share, and if the stock price fails to move upward, your option will eventually prove worthless. But a stock price increase is not required to produce substantial amounts of compensation for you if the strike price of the option is not $21.125 per share but half that, or $10.56. With an option on 60,000 shares, you start the game with a paper option profit of $634,000.

And best of all, if you are granted 180,000 restricted shares, where the strike price, if you will, is effectively zero (since you pay nothing for the shares), you start the game with a paper profit of 180,000 x $21.125, or $3.8 million. So, by adding discounted stock options (a 50% discount from market) and restricted stock grants to his compensation portfolio, Eamer assured himself of earning at least an extra $4.4 million, even if NME's stock price didn't rise a cent in future years. Which, essentially, it didn't.

That was only part of the B-52's payload. For fiscal 1985, Eamer was promised exactly the same set of further long-term incentive grants, i.e., 30,000 more option shares carrying a strike price equal to 100% of the current market price; 60,000 more option shares carrying a strike price equal to 50% of the current market price; and 180,000 restricted shares. For fiscal 1986, Eamer was promised one half of what he received in fiscal 1984 and fiscal 1985, i.e., 15,000 more option shares with a 100%-of-market strike price; 30,000 more option shares with a 50%-of-market strike price; and 90,000 restricted shares. For fiscal years 1987 and 1988, Eamer was again promised the same set of grants as for fiscal 1986.

Not a bad haul for extending your employment agreement for a measly two years, wouldn't you say? One has to suppose that Eamer accepted the board's proffered deal in something less than one nanosecond.

Why, one might ask, would a board be so open-handed? Well, don't rule out hero worship. After all, Eamer had been hitting the ball out of the park with quite some regularity before the stock price peaked at the close of fiscal 1983. No wonder that his board revered him. However, like the baseball star who has had one winning season after another but knows that his advancing age and the laws of probability make it highly unlikely that he can continue to perform in the future as he has in the past, perhaps Eamer sensed that his reputation was probably as high as it was ever going to be, and that now, rather than later, was the time to go for the gold.

Now I don't know for sure whether Eamer dreamed up the details of the aforementioned long-term incentive grants, or whether the board had its own outside advisers. But if he is like many other CEOs, he dreamed up the grants himself, or hired a consultant to do the dreaming for him, and the board merely gave them a once-over with its well-worn rubber stamp. There is one thing that Richard Eamer is not, and that is stupid. By all accounts, this self-made man is just about as smart as they come. So why depart from the past pattern of stock option grants carrying strike prices equal to the market price at the date of grant? Indeed, why not go to the board and ask them for a huge stock option grant on the order of the 4 million option shares that the board of H. J. Heinz recently granted to its CEO, Anthony O'Reilly?

Well, about the only reason—if you rule out stupidity or excessive timidity—is because you aren't very bullish about the future of the stock. To illustrate, let's look at the first of Eamer's new round of long-term incentive grants. And, for the sake of not making a complex topic more complex, let's assume that the total return an NME shareholder earns is derived from stock price appreciation, as opposed to a combination of stock price appreciation and dividends (such an assumption is not far from the truth as far as NME is concerned, inasmuch as the three-year average dividend yield between 1982 and 1984 was a relatively low 1.7%).

He received 30,000 option shares carrying a strike price equal to 100% of the $21.125 market price as of the date of grant. Even though there was no profit in the option shares at the time of their grant, there still was plenty of value in the form of a risk-free call on any future appreciation during the next ten years. There are various ways of assigning a price tag to that ten-year call, the most famous of which involves the use of the Black-Scholes option-pricing model, an elegant mathematical concoction devised by two economists whose surnames, Black and Scholes, have become household words in financial circles. Assuming, for the sake of simplicity, that NME would not be paying dividends to its shareholders during the next ten years, the Black-Scholes model places a value of $14.10 on each of the 30,000 shares in the grant. The aggregate worth of all 30,000 of Eamer's option shares was therefore $423,000.

Eamer also received 60,000 option shares carrying a strike price equal to 50% of the market price as of the date of grant. Using the same option-pricing technique, each of these shares had an economic worth, at the time of its grant, of $17.57 per share. Logic suggests that each share must be worth at least the amount of the difference between the share price on the date of grant and the strike price. But each option share is actually worth more than that difference, since, as just mentioned, it confers on the holder the right to pick up any additional profit during the ensuing ten years. The aggregate worth of all 60,000 discounted option shares was therefore $1,054,200.

Finally, Eamer received 180,000 restricted shares. At the time of their grant, the stock price was presumed to be $21.125 per share, so the value of each share was simply $21.125. Hence, the aggregate worth of all 180,000 shares was $3,802,500. Adding together the aggregate present value of the 30,000 non-discounted option shares, the 60,000 discounted option shares, and the 180,000 restricted shares produces a figure of $5,279,700. Not bad for a single year's round of long-term incentive grants.

Now let's suppose that Eamer, instead of receiving $5,279,700 of aggregate present value from three forms of long-term incentive compensation, had contented himself with receiving the same $5,279,700 of aggregate present value from only one form of long-term incentive compensation, namely, a conventional, non-discounted stock option grant. Given that each such option share has a worth of $14.10, Eamer could have opted for a non-discounted option grant consisting of 374,447 shares carrying a strike price of $21.125 per share, and no non-discounted stock option shares and no restricted shares.

Finally, let's make two further simplifying assumptions: that no option shares are exercised until the end of their ten-year terms, and that the restrictions on the restricted shares do not lapse until the very same date.

The question is, how much NME's stock price has to appreciate per year over the ten-year period so that the two packages of long-term incentives—the package containing only non-discounted option shares, and the package containing the combination of non-discounted option shares, discounted option shares, and restricted shares—have the same future value. The answer: 11.7% per year. If the stock price appreciates at this rate, then both compensation packages will have the same $16 million worth ten years after their grant.

If the stock price appreciates at more than 11.7% per year, then the simple package containing 374,447 conventional option shares will produce a greater value to Eamer than the more complicated package containing 30,000 conventional option shares, 60,000 discounted option shares, and 180,000 restricted shares. Consider here that each additional dollar of stock price appreciation (beyond an 11.7% per year stock price appreciation rate) generates an additional $374,447 of profit for Eamer from his 374,447 option shares. But it generates a lesser $270,000 of profit from the combination of three long-term incentives which, in total, contain 270,000 shares of stock. Conversely, if the stock price appreciates less than 11.7% per year, then the more complicated package containing the three different grants will produce a greater value to Eamer than the simple package.

That being the case, how vigorous a level of performance was implied by an 11.7% per year compounded stock price growth rate? To answer that question, we first have to note that the grants under discussion were made to Eamer in 1984, when interest rates were quite high. Indeed, an investor in 1984 could have purchased a 90-day Treasury bill and earned a risk-free return of 9.9% per year. We also have to consider the hypothetical return that a stock with NME's risk characteristics ought to have earned. After taking account of the fact that investing in common stocks ought to—and usually does—carry a higher return than investing in safe government bonds, and after considering further that NME's stock was unusually risky at that time compared to common stocks in general, that hypothetical return would have been about 11 percentage points higher than the ten-year, risk-free rate of 11.0%, or 20.9% per year. So we now know that the 11.7% breakeven stock price appreciation point between the two compensation packages connoted, not superior performance, or even normal performance, but much less than normal performance—performance that was only a bit higher than what an investor could have received without taking on any risk whatsoever.

Since the breakeven stock price appreciation point was such a low 11.7%, and since the normal expected return on NME's stock was 20.9%, why wouldn't Eamer have persuaded his board to forget about granting him 30,000 conventional option shares, 60,000 discounted option shares, and 180,000 restricted shares? Instead, why wouldn't he have persuaded his board to grant him 374,447 conventional option shares? That way, had NME earned, not an 11.7% return, but rather the expected 20.9% return, the package of 374,447 conventional option shares would have produced a gain for him that was $8.1 million more than he would have received from his actual package of three different types of grants. Why? Well, how about because Eamer, being the very smart person he is reputed to be, wasn't all that bullish on his company's stock? How about the theory that he thought in his heart of hearts that NME's stock price probably wouldn't appreciate even at the rate of 11.7% a year?

Maybe those thoughts didn't go through Eamer's mind. But if they didn't, we still have the nagging question of why his long-term incentive package was structured the way it was. And we also have to contend with the fact that, as already demonstrated, NME's stock price, after the grant was made in 1984, behaved in a manner that vindicated the use of three different, long-term incentive grants. That is to say, NME's stock price was essentially flat for six years; then, in the seventh year, it rose enough to produce a 5.7%-per-year appreciation rate. Indeed, looking backwards, Eamer seemingly would have been even better off had he asked his board for a third package—one where the entire $5,279,700 present value was spent on a single grant of 249,927 restricted shares.

Proxy statements released by NME show that Eamer received restricted stock grants in strict accordance with his employment agreement: 180,000 shares each in both fiscal 1984 and fiscal 1985, and 90,000 shares each in fiscal 1986 and fiscal 1987. And he should have received his last-scheduled grant of 90,000 shares in fiscal 1988. Based on averaging the closing prices for fiscal 1987 and fiscal 1988, the worth of those 90,000 shares, measured at the time of their grant, would have been around $2.3 million. So why is it that the proxy covering fiscal 1988 discloses that Eamer received additional restricted stock grants having a value of approximately $18.4 million? Did the board forget that it had already negotiated the terms of Eamer's restricted stock grants through fiscal 1990? Or did it consciously decide to give him "a double dip"?

Many boards of directors have short memories. Having given a CEO a large grant of something a few years back—a grant designed to last for several ensuing years—they promptly forget what they did. And they thus lay themselves open to the CEO's desire for something new, or for a repeat, and duplicative, grant. Perhaps that is what happened here. On the other hand, perhaps NME's board didn't forget anything it had done and decided, quite deliberately, to give Eamer even more restricted shares.

All in all, Eamer received, over six years, restricted stock having an approximate worth at the time of its grant of some $34 million.

Then, in fiscal 1989, he added yet another weapon to his compensation arsenal. To describe the complications of this new compensation arrangement is beyond the scope of our discussion here, but suffice it to say that NME arranged a financing of a special kind of convertible debentures—convertible debentures that had the effect of conferring on Eamer the equivalent of a monster stock option grant. The only redeeming feature here was that the strike price was higher than the market price of NME stock on the date the implicit option grant was made.

Perhaps NME shareholders, instead of denouncing Eamer, should take heart. After all, at just about the time the stock price peaked, he switched from an all-option diet to a far safer diet that included discounted stock option grants and restricted stock grants. And now he seems to be favoring stock options again—indeed, stock options with a higher than normal strike price. Does this mean he is bullish on the stock price again? Or has he simply wrung as much restricted stock out of his board as he can?

Speaking again of restricted stock, Eamer scored another pay coup in January 1990 when NME spun off its nursing homes into a separate corporation, called Hillhaven, and then distributed approximately 85% of the stock of the new corporation to NME's shareholders. Perhaps that spin-off will someday prove beneficial to NME's shareholders, but it proved immediately beneficial to Eamer. He became the CEO both of NME and the new Hillhaven. And he started to collect pay from Hillhaven as well as NME. His cash compensation from Hillhaven is a modest $150,000 per year (in contrast, his cash compensation from NME is some $1.9 million per year). But he also received a restricted stock grant from Hillhaven for 1,500,000 shares.

Now think about this. Eamer spins off Hillhaven as a separate corporation, possibly because the nursing home business these days isn't very profitable. (In 1989, the last year it was still part of NME,

Hillhaven lost $24 million.) The spin-off increases the future prospects of NME, and perhaps for this reason, Eamer switches from NME restricted stock grants to NME stock options. On the other hand, the new Hillhaven probably has little in the way of future prospects, so, wearing his Hillhaven hat, Eamer arranges to be granted restricted stock. This theory is just that, a theory, and it may be totally fanciful. But if in the next few years the stock of NME takes off, while that of Hillhaven does not, remember where you first read the theory. (In the meantime, the theory is not holding up quite as well as might have been hoped. Between January 1990, when Hillhaven was born, and late March 1991, the stock of NME advanced from $33.13 to $49.00, for an increase of 48%, while in the same period the stock of Hillhaven rose from $1.88 to $3.00, for an increase of 60%.)

Richard Eamer of National Medical Enterprises is far from the only CEO who seemingly spends more time inspecting his safety net than mounting the flying trapeze. Another ardent safety checker is Martin S. Davis, the CEO of Paramount Communications. Paramount, which used to be called Gulf & Western Industries, was one of the early conglomerates. Founded by a terrible-tempered Austrian, Charles Bludhorn, Gulf & Western was literally into everything. It owned Paramount Pictures, the motion picture studio; Simon & Schuster, the book publishing concern; Kayser-Roth, a premier manufacturer of pantyhose; and Associates, a consumer finance organization. Besides that, it also owned zinc mines, auto parts manufacturers, thousand of acres of sugar plantations, and a posh resort in the Dominican Republic. In short, it was totally unmanageable; what management there was was buried deep in the mind of its founder, and it sometimes seemed that his long-range plan was drawn from a table of random numbers.

During the heady days of the conglomerate movement—the days when people actually bought the notion that a good manager could manage anything and didn't need any expertise in the particular industry in which he was working—Gulf & Western thrived. But then investors began to realize that they could diversify their portfolios simply by buying the stock of many companies. That being the case, what was the rationale for buying the stock of one company that, in turn, owned many companies? Clearly, the rationale didn't lie in superior management, because the statistics revealed that buying a diversified portfolio generally produced returns that were superior to those of the typical conglomerate.

You might well ask at this point why conglomerates even existed, given that there was no economic necessity for them to exist, and given further that they were generally incapable of producing superior returns compared to a simple diversified portfolio. As it turned out, there were two very good economic reasons for conglomerates to exist, though neither, unhappily, had anything to do with shareholder welfare.

The first reason concerned the impact of company size on executive pay. If a company doubles in size, it hires more accountants and more engineers and more sales representatives. But it doesn't hire a second CEO; rather, the single CEO it already has simply labors under a heavier burden. And consider also that as a company grows, it tends to add a management level or two. Since it is unthinkable not to pay each management level a sizable premium over the next-lower management level, the effect of increasing corporate size is to trigger an increase in executive pay. Hence, if you can engineer a bigger company, you can earn more money—even if the bigger company is no better-performing, and, indeed, is a bit worse-performing, than before. So indulge yourself: buy that paper company you've always been lusting after; and buy that electronics company you've so long admired. Then give yourself a healthy raise.

There is a second sound reason to have conglomerates—and once again, it is the executives who are the winners. For the ordinary investor, portfolio diversification is only a phone call away; your broker will be happy to achieve for you whatever degree of portfolio diversification you desire. Not so for your typical senior executive. If you examine his balance sheet, you'll probably find only two assets of note. The first is the equity in his house. The second is the value of his company stock, including the potential profit in his as-yet-unexercised stock options.

A senior executive can achieve portfolio diversification of sorts simply by selling every company share that comes his way and investing the proceeds elsewhere. If you exercise an option with a $1 million profit, you can go on to sell all the shares as soon as you can, pay your taxes, and take the net profit to your stockbroker so that it can be safely redeployed. Unfortunately, however, selling company shares is considered poor taste in some circles and an act of treachery in others. Investors regularly pore over columns in the *Wall Street Journal* which detail the purchases and sales of corporate "insiders"—mainly corporate officers. Like patterns of mouse droppings and arrangements of entrails, the purchases and sales of corporate insiders are thought by some to be harbingers of what will shortly happen to stock prices. Hence, a bearish signal is communicated to some investors when an insider sells shares. There is also the ancient matter of loyalty. Selling shares in your own company, even if it doesn't do in the stock price, is considered by many to be a disloyal act.

So, if you want to have a diversified investment portfolio, but it is considered bad form to do so by dumping your company shares, how do you get where you want to go? Well, if you can't buy the shares of twenty-five different companies, how about having your company buy twenty-five other companies? You'll still have most of your net worth tied up in the shares of a single company, but you'll at last be diversified.

This maneuver had a craze in the 1960s and 1970s. But in the 1980s, when investors finally caught on to the fact that conglomerates were not exactly the best place to park their money, conglomerate stocks took it on the chin. Nonetheless, Charles Bludhorn, who was quick to acquire any company that took his fancy, continued to exhibit what Sigmund Freud would have instantly labeled anal retentive behavior, and refused to disgorge his many acquisitions. That disgorging was left to his successor, Martin Davis, now sixty-three, who took over on Bludhorn's sudden death in 1983. Davis, who started his career in the entertainment industry as office boy to Samuel Goldwyn, rose to become chief operating officer of Paramount Pictures, before moving on to become executive vice president of Paramount's parent company, Gulf & Western Industries. He was something of an enigma. He was not an operating man; he was not a lawyer; and he was not a financial man—at least not by formal training. He was terribly shrewd and a good judge of horse-flesh. He quickly surrounded himself with some very smart advisers.

Whether his advisers were the first to suggest that Davis disassemble Bludhorn's empire, or he was the first to come up with the idea, is something I do not know. But whoever it was, the idea was quickly adopted, and a giant asset sell-off began. In a relatively short period of time, Gulf & Western reduced itself to three operating units: Paramount Pictures, Simon & Schuster, and Associates. Then Associates was sold to Ford Motor Company, leaving Gulf & Western with only two basic businesses: entertainment and publishing. It was around that time that the company was renamed Paramount Communications. All of this dismantling was accomplished with very little assistance from investment bankers; it was a source of pride to Davis that he and a few of his executives acted as their own investment bankers.

Besides being in entertainment and publishing, Paramount Communications also had a huge pile of cash, in part because of earlier asset sales but mainly because of the impending sale of Associates. So it was sort of natural for Martin Davis to cast a covetous eye at Time Inc.—a company also engaged in both the entertainment and publishing business—when he began to think of things to do with all that cash. Like a dieter who loses 150 pounds and then celebrates by eating an entire chocolate cream pie, Davis went after Time Inc. with a vengeance. The word "vengeance" is not used loosely here, because it is well known in entertainment industry circles that Martin Davis is not a great fan of Steve Ross, the head of Warner Communications, who was the first to attempt a union with Time Inc.

When the bidding for Time Inc. ended, Davis had upped the ante to $200 per share, and Wall Street insiders were pretty confident that he could be persuaded to sweeten the bid by yet another $25. But Time Inc. was determined to have nothing to do with Davis, and so it bulled ahead with its planned merger with Warner Communications. As it happened, Davis was thereby saved from stepping into a giant hole. The stock of the new combined company, Time Warner, which had traded as high as $182.75 per share, plunged to as low as $66.13 per share in the wake of the junk bond debacle and the horrible hangover of endless debt. As this is being written, Davis is still sitting with his pile of cash and still looking for something useful to do with it.

When he is not shuffling assets, Davis frequently engages in another of his favorite pastimes, shuffling management. He is known to be both tough and brusque; apparently, his toughness and brusqueness persuaded Michael Eisner, Barry Diller, Jeffrey Katzenberg, and Frank Mancuso all to depart Paramount. Eisner joined Walt Disney and captained its dazzling turnaround. Diller became head of Twentieth Century Fox and pioneered a fourth network, Fox Broadcasting. Katzenberg works for Eisner and heads Disney's successful film operations. And Mancuso, as of this writing, was looking for a job after a subordinate of his, Stanley Jaffe, an independent producer who was making films for Mancuso, was named by Davis to be president and chief operating officer of Paramount Communications, the parent company.

By taking an unmanageable conglomerate and cutting it down to two core businesses—entertainment and publishing—Davis produced some excellent results for his company's shareholders. Sales, of course, dropped tremendously: from $5.7 billion in 1981 to a low of $1.7 billion in 1985, before moving up to $3.9 billion in the fiscal year which ended in October 1990. But earnings per share exhibited strong, though not steady, growth, and returns on equity improved smartly. Most important, the stock price took off, producing outsized returns for shareholders. From a close of $8.38 per share in December 1982, the stock soared to a high of $66.38 by October 1989. Since then, it has fallen; it was trading as low as $31.50 in September 1990. And by late March 1991, it had risen only to $39.50.

Even with the decline in stock price, however, Davis still has performed in a superior manner. Looking at a sampling of 120 of Paramount Communications' ten-year total returns between 1971 and 1991, the company ranked at the 80th percentile of the 407-

company study group. If the examination is narrowed to the most recent 80, 40, and 20 ten-year total return periods, the company's percentile ranks are, respectively, 79th, 86th, and 76th.

Davis's pay has more than matched the superior performance of his company. He earns a hefty base salary of $950,000 per year. And his bonuses have been Hollywood-sized, as befits the head of a company that owns one of America's great movie studios. Indeed, he has never had a bad year, even though the same can't be said of his shareholders. For his performance in 1983, he was given a bonus of $525,000. Then the progression went more or less straight uphill until 1990: $900,000 in 1984; $638,000 in 1985; $1.3 million in 1986; $1.5 million in 1987; $2.7 million in 1988; and $3.1 million in 1989. In 1990, his annual bonus dipped to $2.7 million—a reduction of 14%. Unhappily for shareholders, however, the performance of the company has been a bit more uneven. Take 1989, for example. Davis's bonus, as can be seen, rose from $2.7 million in 1988 to $3.1 million in 1989. Yet primary earnings per share before extraordinary items plummeted from $3.21 to $0.09, while cash flow decreased from $976 million to $645 million. To be sure, earnings per share after extraordinary items increased from $3.21 to $12.21, but this much lovelier progression was triggered by the gain on the sale of the company's financing subsidiary to Ford Motor Company. In 1990, earnings per share after extraordinary items dropped from $12.21 to $2.16; but earnings per share before extraordinary items rose from $0.09 to $2.16. Interestingly, the $2.16 per share before extraordinary items earned in 1990 was 25% lower than the equivalent figure for 1987. Yet Davis's annual bonus had risen 80% in the meantime—from $1.5 million in 1987 to $2.7 million in 1990.

Lastly, we come to long-term incentives. Here, Davis has received a progression of restricted stock grants that have been stunning in their size; since he became CEO, he has been granted 1 million free shares. Valued at the closing stock price for 1989, these shares had a pre-tax value of $56 million. And, like his annual bonuses, the size of his grants has become larger: his most recent single grant was for 500,000 shares, with a value at the time of approximately $25 million.

Once again, the question must be raised about how much Davis knows, or thinks he knows, about Paramount Communications' future. Like Richard Eamer of National Medical Enterprises, Davis loves restricted stock. As I have already shown, rational people don't love restricted stock unless they are excessively risk-averse or are bearish on future shareholder returns. Given his last grant of restricted stock worth some $25 million, and given further that Paramount Communications' stock price has been flat to down for some time, perhaps the company's shareholders ought to slip on their coats, leave the house as quietly as they can, and lock the door behind them.

The person whose progress on the flying trapeze has been the most fascinating has been neither Richard Eamer of National Medical Enterprises nor Martin Davis of Paramount Communications. Rather, it has been Lee Iacocca, the legendary CEO of Chrysler. From a person who not only performed without a safety net but waved to the crowd when he was in mid-air, Iacocca has become a person who seemingly won't mount even one step of the ladder that leads to the trapeze without receiving a written warranty from the manufacturer of his safety netting.

In November 1978, shortly after he was publicly fired from his job as president of Ford Motor Company by Henry Ford II, Iacocca joined Chrysler as president and soon became CEO. His starting salary was $360,000 per year, and he was granted an option on 400,000 shares carrying a strike price of $11.07 per share. At the time he joined Chrysler, the company was hemorrhaging cash; without government aid, it looked to be dead within months. Indeed, before he turned himself into a hawker of cars, Iacocca earned a reputation as a premier lobbyist. His work in Washington culminated in the Chrysler Corporation Loan Guarantee Act of 1979, under which the federal government lent Chrysler the tidy sum of $1.5 billion.

Reflecting its precarious position, Chrysler's board adopted a Salary Reduction Program in September 1979. Bonus-eligible executives were required to take a salary cut of up to 10% for up to two years. The amount of the cut was then converted into shares of

Chrysler stock, with the stock to be delivered to the executive two years later (in August 1981). Demonstrating his utter fearlessness, at least at that time, Iacocca asked his board to reduce his $360,000 per year salary, not by $36,000, or 10%; rather, he asked his board to reduce his salary to $1 per year. Since the Salary Reduction Program was to last two years, Iacocca would theoretically have lost $719,998 of salary and would have had it converted at the August 1979 stock price of $8.34 per share into 86,331 shares of company stock. As it turned out, Chrysler's board insisted on rescinding Iacocca's draconian pay cut after only one year. On September 1, 1980, the board raised his salary from $1 per year to $324,000 per year and thereby treated him like all other bonus-eligible executives.

For the second year of the two-year Salary Reduction Program, Iacocca was to sustain the normal 10% pay cut. On that revised basis, he was credited with only 43,166 shares for the first year of the Salary Reduction Program. Then, he would have been credited with $36,-000 of shares (his 10% pay cut) for the second year. Since the price-per-share was frozen at the $8.34 per share value for August 1979, he would have been credited with a further 4,317 shares. When the board informed him that he could no longer receive only $1 per year but instead had to be paid $324,000 per year, Iacocca indicated that he would contribute all but $1 per year of his salary to charity "until such time as he deems it appropriate to retain it." So the decision to cut out the $1-per-year bit was, on the evidence, not Iacocca's decision. Even after a year of subsisting on a diet of water, he was game to go on for a second year and would have done so had not his board intervened. (The time at which he decided to stop contributing all but $1 per year of his salary to charity and to keep the money for himself was never disclosed in subsequent proxy statements.)

As it turned out, the decision to cut the salaries of bonus-eligible executives saved cash for the company's shareholders but didn't do any good for the executives involved. Chrysler's stock price, which had been $8.34 per share in August 1979, declined to $5.25 per share by August 1981 when the Salary Reduction Program ended and the accumulated deferred shares were delivered to the company's executives. Even in August 1982, the stock price had only climbed back to where it was in August 1979. But then it more than tripled between August 1982 and August 1983, reaching a pre-split high of $27.75 per share.

During the lean years, Iacocca not only received only $1 in salary; he also received no bonuses. All he had to keep him warm on those cold winter nights in Detroit were several monster stock option grants. But those grants took on tremendous value as the performance of Chrysler turned around. The statistics can be seen quite vividly in the 407-company study. Looking at all 120 ten-year total return periods stretching between 1971 and 1991, Chrysler ranks only at the 20th percentile of the distribution. But the company's percentile rank for the 80, 40, and 20 most recent ten-year total return periods was, respectively, 51st, 67th, and 65th.

With that sort of performance, and with huge stock option grants to accompany it, Iacocca's lean years turned into fat years. During the period January 1, 1981–March 14, 1986, Iacocca received $15.5 million in option gains, with by far the greatest bulk of the gains occurring near the end of that time. During the period January 1, 1986–December 31, 1986, he received another $9.6 million in option gains. During the period January 1, 1987–December 31, 1987, he received yet another $13.5 million in option gains. During the period January 1–1988-December 31, 1988, he received still another $2.0 million in option gains. Finally, during the period January 1, 1989–December 31, 1989, he received $2.4 million in option gains. All told, in the space of six years, Iacocca received $43 million in option gains.

If ever there was a Babe Ruth of executive compensation, it was Lee Iacocca. In 1979, he cut his pay to $1 per year, he loaded up with stock options, and he pointed to centerfield. Then he hit the ball right over the centerfield fence. His salary was restored, and in the 1991 proxy, it reached a high of $918,000 (which figure includes some "supplemental payments and cash equivalent items" not broken out separately). He began to receive annual bonuses, which peaked at a high of $975,000 for his performance during 1985.

When the newspapers first disclosed the huge amounts Iacocca was earning from his stock option exercises, the public reaction, far from being critical, was wildly enthusiastic. Indeed, many people felt that Iacocca would make a fine candidate for president of the United States. Iacocca's triumph had tapped a deep vein in the American psyche: the belief that a kid with a strange surname who grew up in less than affluent circumstances could, through talent, guts, and a willingness to gamble, rise to the top of his profession and achieve great success. In the 1972 presidential election, George McGovern stumped the country, advocating, among other things, a 100% marginal tax rate on estates above a certain level. He reasoned that leaving huge amounts of money to your kids may not be all that helpful to the economy. Your kids may be dolts, and the wealth they receive becomes unavailable to some smarter participant in the economy. When McGovern trotted his 100%-estate-tax message in front of union audiences, he was stunned when the audiences sat on their hands or even booed him. At one point, he asked some union men why they could possibly object to a 100% estate tax when it would hit the rich and thereby remove some of the burden of taxation from the shoulders of working persons. The answer he received went something like this: "Sure, I'm not going to die and leave a $100 million estate. But my kids might make it, and if they do, I want them to be able to keep what they earn." The American Dream lives!

Somewhere between Lee Iacocca's agreement to take $1 per year and today, the American Dream fell into a deep coma. For today, CEOs have forgotten all about the principle of "The greater the risk, the greater the reward." Instead, they are at once increasing the size of their pay packages and doing everything possible to remove all the risk. Sadly, even Iacocca has become a participant in what passes for current thinking.

In 1983, the dreaded "R" word (for "restricted," as in restricted stock) was first heard in the Chrysler boardroom. In addition to receiving some hefty grants of stock options, Iacocca was also given 200,000 shares of restricted stock; and in 1987, he was granted 255,000 shares of restricted stock. Now once again, why would a rational CEO want shares of restricted stock, instead of a much greater number of stock option shares, unless he was convinced that there wasn't all that much steam left in his company's stock price? Perhaps it is sheer coincidence, but Chrysler's stock price, adjusted for subsequent splits, was $12.28 in December 1983, the year Iacocca received his first restricted stock grant. Then it rose to $14.22 at the end of 1984, to $20.72 at the end of 1985, and to $24.67 at the end of 1986. So far, my theory doesn't seem to be holding much water, because the stock price was advancing. But be patient. At the end of 1987, the year Iacocca received his second restricted stock grant, the stock price declined to $22.13 per share. It advanced modestly in 1988, to $25.75 per share at year end. Following that modest rise, the decline set in once again, with the stock price finishing 1989 and 1990 at, respectively, $19.00 and $12.63 per share.

In the light of what happened to Chrysler's stock price, the grant of restricted shares to Iacocca, instead of a much larger number of stock option shares, made a lot of sense. Or, at least it made a lot sense for Iacocca, if not for Chrysler's hapless shareholders. They saw their stock price decline from $20.72 per share at the end of 1985 to $12.63 per share at the end of 1990. To be sure, Iacocca ended up losing too, in the sense that his restricted shares were worth less. But had he been given no restricted stock and instead a much larger number of stock option shares, those shares would, at the moment, not merely be worth less; they would be worthless.

Although Iacocca is beyond the normal retirement age of sixty-five (he is now sixty-six), he has insisted on staying on until he achieves a second turnaround. In the meantime, some of the people he had groomed as potential candidates to succeed him evidently tired of waiting for him to retire and have left the company. Moreover, Chrysler contends that a number of other key executives left the company in mid-1990 because Chrysler paid no cash bonuses for 1989 performance. That was not exactly one of Chrysler's better years; earnings per share before extraordinary items dropped 71% below the earnings per share reported for 1988. Results were so bad that the company's workers received no profit sharing for 1989.

There's a bit of a story in that loss of profit sharing. Back in the last dark days of the U.S. automobile industry—in the early 1980s—General Motors and Ford persuaded their unionized workers to accept profit sharing in lieu of annual increases in pay, increases that tended to occur whether or not the company was successful. Not long after the profit-sharing plans started at General Motors and Ford, both companies paid their workers no profit sharing. But in the same year, they paid their executives fairly handsome annual bonuses. That seeming inconsistency was not lost on the workers and their union, the United Auto Workers (UAW). In response to a cacophony of criticism, GM and Ford defended their seeming inconsistency by noting that their workers' profit sharing was based on profits from North American operations, whereas their executives' bonuses were predicated on consolidated worldwide profits— profits that included their very successful European operations, as well as those from the companies' financing subsidiaries. Having sustained quite a bit of scar tissue over the issue, the UAW, when it negotiated a similar profit-sharing plan with Chrysler, insisted that the new union contract contain language that prohibited the company from paying bonuses to its executives so long as the workers received no profit sharing. The first time this clause was taken out on the test track was in early 1990, and the test initially appeared to be successful. The workers received no profit sharing, and Chrysler's bonus-eligible executives received no annual bonuses for their performance in 1989.

But then, according to Chrysler, a number of executives started to vote with their feet, to quit and go elsewhere. One wonders where they went, because neither General Motors nor Ford were in the pink, based on their 1989 results. (Neither company took the 71% profit hit that Chrysler did, but GM's earnings per share before extraordinary items dropped 7%, while Ford's dropped 25%.) And the Japanese could hardly need their services. Indeed, one wonders why anyone cared where they went; given that Chrysler had performed so poorly, perhaps the shareholders would have welcomed the opportunity to throw in their old hand and draw again from the deck. And if the bad cards in the deck ended up at GM or Ford, why, that would simply be a case of the Trojan Horse School of Management in operation.

In any event, the top management didn't take the loss of some of its bonus-eligible executives sitting down. On the evidence, it must have expended a fair amount of legal fees in finding a way around the prohibition in the UAW contract concerning the payment of bonuses to executives when the workers were being denied their profit sharing. A careful reading of the contract apparently convinced Chrysler's lawyers that the prohibition applied only to bonuses payable in cash. That being the case, senior people at Chrysler must have began to think about bonuses that might be payable in something other than cash. And since Lee Iacocca had already had something like 25,000 miles of experience with restricted stock, the infamous "R" word once again reared its ugly head. Forthwith, Chrysler's bonus-eligible executives received grants of restricted stock. The grants were made in mid-1990, and, curiously, the restrictions were set to lapse only a few months later, in January 1991. The rationale behind these restricted stock bonuses was that Chrysler would thereby be able to hold on to its key executives during a very difficult period.

Perhaps there is some wisdom in trying to hold on to a highly talented executive even at a time when the company as a whole is performing deplorably. But is there any wisdom in giving restricted stock grants to all, or almost all, of Chrysler's 1,800 bonus-eligible executives, as may have been the case? And is there any logic in giving a restricted stock grant to Lee Iacocca? After all, there was absolutely no danger of his going anywhere; he had already announced publicly that he wasn't going to retire until he had turned around Chrysler for the second time. In short, wild horses couldn't drag him out of Chrysler, although his potential successors, who have been laboring in his shadow for years and hoping he would retire, must be watching reruns of the movie *They Shoot Horses, Don't They?* (As this is written, the Gulf War has ended, and Iacocca has mused aloud that maybe he will step down fairly soon and that maybe General H. Norman Schwarzkopf might make a dandy successor. It is hard to tell how serious his musings really are.)

The grant of restricted stock in the middle of 1990 had a curious twist to it. The restrictions on the share grants were originally set to lapse in January 1991. But not long after the grants were made, a change in the tax law occurred. Previously, the marginal rate structure went like this: the first slice of income was taxed at 0%, the next at 15%, the next at 28%, the next at 33%, and, beyond a certain point, the final slice of income was taxed again at 28%. In short, there was a so-called hump in the tax structure—a 33% hump, to be exact. In 1990, after Chrysler made its restricted stock grants in lieu of bonuses, Congress eliminated the hump. The new marginal rate progression became 0%, 15%, 28%, and 31%. In effect, the top tax rate was raised from 28% to 31%, but many people who might have been paying a marginal rate of 33% received a cut in their rate to 31%. So what did Chrysler do? It accelerated the lapse of restrictions on the mid-1990 grants so that, instead of occurring in January 1991, when the new tax law took effect, they occurred in December 1990, when the old tax law was still in effect. That change saved Iacocca and some other senior executives a bit of tax. Since they were already way into the very highest tax bracket, the change in the date of restriction lapse permitted them to pay taxes at the old rate of 28%, instead of the new rate of 31% effective on January 1, 1991. However, that change in the lapse of restrictions, while saving Iacocca and his senior executives a few bucks of tax, cost most of Chrysler's middle managers a few bucks of tax. Had the lapse occurred in January 1991, as scheduled, they might have been able to pay taxes at a 31% rate. Instead, with a lapse in December 1990, they were required to pay taxes at the former rate of 33%.

In moving from stock options to restricted stock, Lee Iacocca demonstrated that he cared more for his own welfare than that of his shareholders. And in moving the lapse of restrictions from January 1991 to December 1990, he demonstrated again that he cared more for his own welfare than—this time—the welfare of his own subordinates. His behavior is more hurtful than the same behavior might have been on the part of some other CEO, because Lee Iacocca was, once, a genuine business hero who played the pay game fairly.

Seven

Share Swappers

Suppose that, as CEO of XYZ Corporation, you were granted a stock option a few years ago on 10,000 shares carrying a strike price equal to the then fair market value per share of $50. And suppose that the stock price has now dropped to $25 per share. Is your option worthless? No, it still has some worth because, even though the stock price has to rise $25 just to get back to the breakeven point, you still may have seven years left before the option's expiration. Time, in this case, may heal all wounds.

Of course, your option is nowhere near as valuable as a 10,000-share option carrying a strike price of $25—the current market value per share—would be. Now, to keep you happy and doing your motivational best, XYZ's indulgent board invites you to bring in your option agreement. Then, in the spot where the strike price has been filled in as $50 per share, the board does a bit of erasing and substitutes a figure of $25 per share. *Voilà!* You have just swapped a stock option with a strike price of $50 per share for one carrying a strike price of $25 per share. So, if the stock price should rise to, say, $35 per share, you will make a $10 profit per share even though the new stock price of $35 is $15 lower than the price prevailing on the date you originally were granted the option shares.

If a board of directors is willing to engage in option swaps, your chances of becoming rich improve dramatically. After all, if the stock price keeps heading South—say, to $10 per share—the board can swap your option shares once again. Sooner or later, the stock price has to rise, doesn't it? And when it does, you'll come out a big winner. Of course, the shareholder who invested his or her money in the stock on the date you received your original option grant may be way in the hole. But when this fact was noted to a senior executive of a major investment banking firm, his response, aptly enough, was: "Screw the shareholders! Let them apply for jobs, and then they can have their shares swapped, too."

Some famous names in business have had their shares swapped, including John Sculley of Apple Computer, John Gutfreund of Salomon, and the late Dr. Armand Hammer of Occidental Petroleum. But these executives are, in the world of serious option swapping, minor league players. Take a look at Frank Lorenzo—the erstwhile CEO of Texas Air, which is now called Continental Airlines Holdings—if you want to see a big league swapper at work.

Lorenzo, now fifty, founded what became Texas Air in 1966. During a stormy nineteen-year tenure, he expanded by buying Continental Airlines and then letting it fall into bankruptcy so he could cancel Continental's labor contracts and thereby reduce labor costs. Later, he tried the same tactic when he acquired Eastern Airlines, but there he failed. Eastern went into bankruptcy and stayed there, draining the parent company in both time and money. Finally, in early 1991, Eastern was liquidated. By the time of its liquidation, the name of Lorenzo's company had been changed from Texas Air to Continental Airlines Holdings.

In 1990, Lorenzo was persuaded to step down as CEO in favor of a former president of Delta Airlines. Under an agreement with Scandinavian Airlines Systems (SAS), his shareholdings were repurchased at a premium price of around $14 per share. The stock was selling for only around $4 to $5 per share at around the time SAS offered Lorenzo the premium price. Lorenzo may be gone, but he is not forgotten. As of June 1990, he continued to remain on Continental's board.

Here's how Continental's board handled Lorenzo's stock options. On January 7, 1986, he was granted an option on 125,000 shares carrying a strike price of $13 per share. (The market price of Continental stock on the same day was a higher $14.375 per share.) Sometime during the three-year period ending with fiscal 1986, he was also granted a further option on 250,000 shares carrying a strike price of $29.25 per share. As already noted, Continental's stock price went into a free fall after the end of 1987. So on December 7, 1987—another one of those December 7ths that may live in infamy—the board cancelled Lorenzo's 375,000 option shares and reissued them with a new, lower strike price, this time $9.25 per share. What's more, the board also granted him an option on a further 650,000 shares, again carrying a strike price of $9.25 per share. Not long afterwards, the Continental board took a further action designed to enrich Lorenzo even as the company was heading toward total failure. Technically speaking, it did not engage in another option swap. But what it did do was to promise Lorenzo a cash bonus of $4.625 for each option share he later exercised. If you think about it, there is absolutely no difference between reissuing the 1,025,000 option shares with a new strike price that is half the old strike price, or leaving the strike price alone and simply paying a cash bonus of $4.625 per share upon exercise of the option.

In short, Lorenzo, prior to December 1987, had options on 350,000 shares carrying strike prices as high as $29.25 per share. And after December 7, 1987, he had options on 1,025,000 shares carrying strike prices of $4.625 per share. Moreover, sometime between January 1, 1989, and January 31, 1990, the board granted him another 500,000-share option, this one carrying a strike price of $11.875, as well as the by-now routine "you give me a dollar, I'll give you 50 cents" offer. Is it any wonder, then, that Lorenzo made millions when SAS came along and bought out his shares, not at the $4 to $5 at which the shares were trading at the time, but rather at $14?

All during this period, Lorenzo was preaching to anyone who would listen about the need to cut labor costs, and when he wasn't preaching, he was actually cutting costs through wholesale firings of striking workers. Once again, the preacher couldn't, or wouldn't, see that a prime labor cost that needed to be cut was his own pay. Instead, he was rewarded for his managerial incompetence.

Although the treatment accorded John Sculley and his fellow optionees at Apple Computer was not quite as outrageous as that given to Lorenzo, Apple's option swaps were nonetheless awesome, because they involved almost 14 million of the company's shares, a number that represented around 12% of the company's then outstanding shares.

Apple stock is quite volatile. In October 1987, it was trading at its all-time high of $59.75 per share. Then it slowly sank, though even during its decline, it had its ups and downs. In September 1989, when the price had dropped to $44.625, Apple's board invited any employee with an option carrying a strike price of more than $44.625 to turn it in and receive back an option with a strike price of $44.625 per share. Apple's employees turned in 1.4 million shares at that time.

But Apple's stock price took no notice and kept on plunging. By September 1990, one year after the first swap, the stock price had sunk to $29.75. The board then acted a second time, inviting any employee with an option carrying a strike price above $29.75 to turn in his or her shares and receive a new grant carrying a strike price of $29.75 per share. This time, a torrent of shares—12.1 million— were exchanged.

Volatility is the friend of the option holder, because with high volatility, the probability that the stock price will really soar heavenward is much greater. Of course, the dark side of volatility is the probability that the stock price will drop like a stone. But if an executive can benefit from volatility when the price is soaring and then turn in his or her option for one with a lower strike price when the price is plummeting, he or she has absolutely the best of all possible worlds. That is what happened at Apple Computer.

True to its reputation as a volatile stock, Apple's stock bottomed out at $24.25 per share just one month after the swap occurred. Then it shot up. From a low of $24.25 in October 1990, it closed at $36.75 in November, $43.00 in December, $55.50 in January 1991, $57.25 in February, and $70.00 in late March. Had Apple's board done nothing, its executives, who mostly had options carrying strike prices of around $40 per share, would have made huge amounts of compensation in any event. With the second swap, they made about $10 per share more profit than they deserved, at an aggregate cost to the company's shareholders of around $125 million.

In an article published in the *San Jose Mercury-News,* a spokeswoman for Apple defended the swap action by saying that "We wanted to level the playing field." She added that the swap was intended "to give them [the executives] some incentive again." She apparently also trotted out the argument that if Apple hadn't acted, many of its employees would have left for other Silicon Valley firms, where they could receive option grants the strike prices of which would be equal to the then market prices per share.

Where does the rationalization end? In the good times, companies claim—and rightfully so—that they need to pay a lot of money to reward their executives for their superior performance. And in the bad times, companies claim that they need to pay a lot of money to hold on to their executives. When do we get the scenario where executives deserve, and actually get, a pay cut? Is there such a scenario? Or is the name of the game simply to find some convenient measure that is going up and then hang a lot of money on it? It's hard not to become rather cynical when a company like Apple goes out of its way to reward its executives for having given the company's shareholders the back of their hand for the past several years.

Eight

Partners in Profit

O NCE UPON A TIME, all investment banking firms were private partnerships.
Partners invested their own capital in their firms, usually consisting
of an initial contribution and then the forced deferral of much of the
partnership's future earnings. Because they had to defer so much of
their income to provide the capital their firm needed to grow and
prosper, they were often caught in a cash squeeze. And that meant
that they couldn't follow a lifestyle that was commensurate with
their total earnings. If their firm prospered over the years, they became rich. If their firm screwed up, they found themselves without a
job, and with their net worth decimated to boot.

Ostensibly because they needed additional investment capital,
but equally likely because they had become tired of living frugally
and taking so much downside risk with their capital, first one and
then several major investment banking firms hit upon the idea of
going public. By selling equity to the public, they could pull a great
deal of their capital out of their former partnerships. That, in turn,

would permit them live it up now rather than later. And equally as important, should their now publicly owned firm go down the tubes, they would not be mortally wounded, having already removed much of their capital from the business.

The only downside to going public, it seemed, was that publicly owned companies didn't pay their senior executives all that much—at least by the standards of privately owned investment banking firms. But that problem could be overcome basically by ignoring it and continuing to pay, in current cash compensation, what the erstwhile partner had been accustomed to receiving in a combination of cash and forcibly deferred compensation. After all, there was no longer any need to require compensation to be deferred to provide capital for the business; the capital was now being provided by outside investors. If the levels of current cash compensation being offered seemed wildly high to those working in fields other than investment banking, a ready explanation was offered: Being an investment banker was just about the hardest, most complicated job around, and was thereby deserving of stupendous amounts of compensation.

The first two major investment banking firms to put their toes in the public-company water were Merrill Lynch and First Boston; both went public in 1971. (First Boston went private in 1989, at which time it had been fully absorbed by Credit Suisse, the giant Swiss financial institution.) One year later, in 1972, these firms were followed into the public marketplace by E. F. Hutton and Paine Webber. (Hutton was later absorbed by Shearson Lehman Brothers, which changed its name to Shearson Lehman Hutton and became part of American Express.) Next to go public was Salomon Brothers. It achieved its goal in 1981, not by the straightforward sale of shares to the market, but rather by merging with an already public entity, Phillip Brothers. The new firm was called, appropriately enough, Phibro-Salomon; and reflecting the merger of two more or less equal businesses, it sported co-CEOs—David Tendler for the Phillip side of the business and John Gutfreund for the Salomon Brothers side.

After Salomon's public debut came Bear Stearns Companies (1985) and Morgan Stanley (1986). None of the publicly traded investment banking firms has turned out to be what you would call a good investment. To be sure, who could have predicted the market crash of 1987 and its attendant damage to the securities industry? But there is a more fundamental, and longer-lasting, reason why investment banking firms are not a good investment. And that centers on the munificent rewards that the top managers like to give themselves.

The late Rosser Reeves, the legendary head of the Ted Bates advertising agency, once remarked that "95 percent of my inventory goes down the elevator every night." Being in a business like advertising, where there are no shiny factories and no fancy products and no patent protection, he could see that the old saw, "People are our most important asset," was not an old saw for his company. By the same token, investment banking firms are also quick to recognize that what distinguishes them from other investment banking firms is the quality of their people.

There are two things fundamentally wrong with executive compensation in the investment banking industry. First, the key players, most of whom well remember the days when their organization was a partnership, still like to think of themselves as a partnership. As a result, they seem to believe they have a God-given right to the first fruits, if not almost all the fruits, of the business. It is amazing how quickly they forget, and how many times they have to be reminded, that the public is putting up the great bulk of their firm's investment capital.

In deciding how much to reward themselves in a given year, publicly owned investment banking firms tend to divide their workforces into two, decidedly unequal halves: those who would be partners, were the firm still a partnership; and all others. Next, they keep their eyes on a key "compensation ratio," which is determined by dividing total current compensation (base salary and annual bonuses) by the sum of (a) pre-tax net income, and (b) total current compensation itself. (The figure for pre-tax income already includes the costs of cash compensation; hence, by adding cash compensation to pre-tax income, the firm derives a number that represents pre-tax profits before cash compensation payments have been deducted from pre-tax profits.) Some firms have a rule of thumb that

the workforce, counting all employees in the firm, ought to be entitled to a compensation ratio of about 50%. But in practice the ratio
tends to rise, often dramatically, when results are poor, and to shrink
somewhat when results are spectacular. Note that this is exactly the
opposite of how the ratio ought to behave, if money is to play its
proper motivational role and if high reward is to be accompanied by
high risk. No matter what the compensation ratio being aimed at,
you can be sure that the "partner" group will be guaranteed an
outsized proportion of the funds available for compensation.

The second problem with investment banking firm compensation is that pay is more collegial than hierarchical. Take a look at a
publicly owned industrial firm, and you will find that the second-
highest-paid executive earns around 65% of the pay of the CEO and
that the third-highest-paid executive earns around 50% of the CEO's
pay. Then look instead at Morgan Stanley, for example, and you find
that for 1989 the second- and third-highest paid executives earned
the same cash compensation as the CEO, and that the fourth- and
fifth-highest-paid executives earned compensation that was 68% of
the CEO's pay. That wouldn't be so bad if top investment bankers
were paid collegially—as in college, as in lowly paid professors. But
if you overlay a collegial compensation system on a CEO pay level
that would choke a horse, you will find that there simply aren't that
many profit dollars left for the hapless public investors.

Indeed, it almost seems that the top management of most investment banking firms is paid that sum of money which will cause the
stock price to remain more or less flat. A flat stock price doesn't
bother most investment bankers, because they sold the great bulk of
their shares shortly after their firms went public, and they now have
their funds in safe municipal bonds.

Take Merrill Lynch. The company went public in June 1971, at a
price of $18.94 per share. Its December closing prices then fell below
its debut price of $18.94 for the next ten years. Indeed, the stock
closed as low as $5.50 per share in December 1974. Finally, it rose
from $16.56 in December 1981 to $30.00 in December 1982. That
was, of course, the year when the last great Bull Market commenced.
Merrill's stock managed to inch up to $36.50 per share by December

1986, but then it began a decline to $20.75 per share by December of 1990. By late March of 1991, however, it had risen to $34.50 per share. Hence, the stock essentially went nowhere during the more than eight years between December 1982, when the stock was trading at $30.00 per share, and late March 1991, when it was trading at $34.50 per share. Indeed, the compounded rate of price appreciation in Merrill's stock between June 1971, when it went public, and late March 1991 was a scant 3.1% per year. Some investment.

But during the latter part of this period, William Schreyer, the sixty-three-year-old CEO of Merrill Lynch, did quite well. The sum of his base salary and bonus rose from $625,000 in 1984 to a high of $2.9 million in 1986. In a pattern that, unhappily, can be seen in many companies, Schreyer's base salary and bonus rose more rapidly in good times than it fell in poor times. To illustrate, his base salary and bonus rose from $1.6 million in 1985 to $2.9 million in 1986, while earnings per share after taxes but before extraordinary items rose from $2.26 to $4.44, and while return on equity had risen from 10.1% to 17.4%. Three years later, when earnings per share were a negative minus $2.35 and when the company lost 6.4% on its equity, Schreyer's base and bonus was still a hefty $1.6 million.

Schreyer, who has been with Merrill Lynch since 1948 when he graduated from college, has also been the recipient of all sorts of additional forms of executive compensation. He receives stock option and restricted stock grants. And he used to receive performance unit grants. Moreover, he participates in investment partnerships run by Merrill Lynch—partnerships that are not open to the public. The 1990 proxy disclosed that in a single year, he had made $52,900 profit on an investment of $100,000 in one of those partnerships. If you look back on the stock price history of Merrill Lynch and then pause to digest the 53% return on his partnership investment that Schreyer made in a single year, it should be fairly obvious that whoever was running that partnership didn't put any of the partnership's money in Merrill Lynch stock.

Schreyer has also participated in a form of compensation that demonstrates the "heads I win, tails you lose" design of many executive compensation plans. The plan is called an Incentive Equity Purchase Plan, and here is how it works. Suppose the current book value per share is $25. (The book value per share is simply the shareholders' equity of the company, as reported in the balance sheet, divided by the number of shares outstanding.) And suppose an executive is given the opportunity to buy 10,000 shares at the current book value per share. Suppose also that at the time when the book value per share is $25, the market value per share is $50. Note here that had the executive used his $250,000 to buy plain old common stock, he would have been able to buy only 5,000 shares, and not the 10,000 shares just mentioned.

During the ensuing years, the executive receives dividends just like any normal shareholder. However, since he has paid half as much as a normal shareholder ($25 per share instead of the market value of $50 per share), his dividend yield is twice as high. At some point, the shares are sold back to the company. And now we come to the best-of-both-worlds nature of the plan. The executive first measures the gain on 10,000 shares using the increase in book value as the measure of appreciation. Then he measures the gain on 5,000 shares using the increase in market value as the measure of appreciation. Finally, whichever measurement gives him the greatest appreciation is the one he chooses. Hence, if the market price takes it on the chin, he can probably squeeze some compensation out of the transaction by opting for the appreciation on 10,000 book-value shares. On the other hand, if the market price rises tremendously, he can reap the benefit of the 5,000 market-value shares. Either way, it's hard for him to come out of the transaction with no money at all.

Salomon's John Gutfreund is often described as portly; to my eyes, he is not much more portly than the typical bloke who is also 61 years of age. But he is a lot smarter. And he is noted for his ruthlessness, though much of what passes for ruthlessness may merely be his very sarcastic tongue. Part of his reputation derives from the fact that he tired of having to run the company as one of two co-CEOs and presumably set about to convince his board to make him the sole CEO. He soon succeeded. His action, on the evidence, didn't exactly please his co-CEO, David Tendler (who had come to the business from the Phillip side), and the latter left the company. To me, Gutfreund's action does not demonstrate ruthless-ness so much as red-blooded American behavior.

Another part of his reputation derives from the fact that he took Salomon Brothers public soon after he became CEO, thereby de-priving some earlier partners, including the legendary William Salo-mon, of the increment between the book value per share, which is what they presumably received when they cashed in their chips, and the market value per share. Once again, I fail to see how this behav-ior can be described as ruthless. Gutfreund was, after all, merely maximizing his income, as Adam Smith said he had every right to do and indeed should do to make the economy more efficient.

When Phillip Brothers and Salomon Brothers merged in late 1981, the stock price was around $12.50 per share. Thereafter the stock price described a beautiful parabola. It rose to a high of $59.38 in April 1986, then dropped and dropped. By December 1987, not two years later, it had dropped all the way to $16.63. However, by late March 1991, the stock price had begun to move up, reaching a high of $28.25 per share. The company's compounded annual rate of shareholder return between October 1981, when Salomon Broth-ers merged with Phillip Brothers, and the end of March 1991, was a meager 8.6%. Compared to the other 406 companies in the data-base, Salomon's total return performance ranked it only at the 19th percentile of the distribution.

For his part, Gutfreund did quite well, despite what was hap-pening to the stock price. He received a base salary only in the $300,000–$350,000 range, but his bonuses were terrific. Counting both cash and deferred bonuses, it was a rare year when he received less than $3 million in bonus money. There was one year, however, when Salomon's results were so poor that Gutfreund waived his bonus altogether. In place of the bonus, the board gave him an outsized stock option.

The use of a stock option as a sort of consolation prize illustrates yet another problem with the world of executive compensation. If you go to Las Vegas and lose all your chips at roulette, you might as well head up to your hotel room, provided you had the foresight to obtain one and pay for it before you started gambling. In the world of executive compensation, however, if you lose all your chips, the management of the casino, though not so open-handed as to refund your money, gives you another pile of chips so that you can keep on playing. If that happens enough times, you just have to win—unless, of course, you're the owner of the casino. In Gutfreund's case, he lost his current cash bonus, but he was given back his chips in the form of a stock option. To be sure, he has made nothing to date from that option because of Salomon's stock price performance; but the option carries a ten-year term, and Gutfreund has plenty of time left before it expires. In sum, John Gutfreund, like William Schreyer at Merrill Lynch, was rewarded handsomely for what turned out to be poor performance.

I have to confess here that I was the consultant who recommended that Gutfreund receive a large stock option in lieu of a cash bonus. You see I, too, was a great fan of the Prodigal Son story; in other words, if Gutfreund could turn Salomon around, why shouldn't he receive some additional compensation? Clearly, a large stock option in this case was preferable to paying a cash bonus, because the option can never be made to yield cash unless the company's stock price rises. But, as I have noted several times already, when does an executive get his pay cut, period? What seemed right for John Gutfreund is, when viewed in the context of the overall American economy, wrong.

There is yet a third investment banking CEO who fits the same description. Ace Greenberg of Bear Stearns can only be described as "a piece of work." Always in motion, the sixty-four-year-old executive spends much of his time on Bear Stearns's trading floor acting like George Patton in the lead tank. When he is not on the trading floor, he is on the telephone. And if you want to call him, he is thoughtful enough to give you an 800 number that will connect you directly with his office.

Greenberg has kept his base salary very low. When the firm first went public in 1985, his base salary was $150,000. Since then, he has taken a raise to $200,000. His other form of compensation is an annual bonus. And this can be very high. The combination of base salary and annual bonus yielded him $4.1 million in 1986, $5.7 million in 1987, $4.5 million in 1989, and $4.2 million in 1990. The year 1988 was a different story, however. Because of a decline in Bear Stearns's profits, his base salary and bonus in 1988 declined to $2.4 million.

Bear Stearns employs a formula bonus plan for those senior executives who formerly were considered partners. Each of these people earns the same $200,000 base salary. Then a collective bonus fund is determined each year according to a pre-established formula based on the pre-tax profits of the firm. Although that formula has helped to inject some pay-for-performance orientation into the company's executive compensation program, there is mounting evidence that the board of directors is losing its nerve.

Between April 1987 and April 1988, Bear Stearns's pre-tax net income declined by 39% compared to that of the preceding year. And Greenberg's total current compensation declined even more—by 57%. Or, to put it another way, his total current compensation declined 1.5 times faster than the decline in pre-tax profits. Between April 1988 and June 1989 (the company switched from an April fiscal year end to a June year end), the company's pre-tax net income rose 43% over the year earlier period. And Greenberg's total current compensation rose even faster—by 85%. In this case, his total current compensation rose two times faster than the rise in profits. Between June 1989 and June 1990, pre-tax net income once again declined—this time by 31% compared to 1989. And Greenberg's total current compensation also declined, but this time only by 7%. Hence, his total current compensation declined only 0.2 times as fast as the decline in pre-tax profits. In fact, however, there was no decline in Greenberg's pay at all. True, his total current compensation declined by 7%, but, for the first time since the company went public, he received a stock option grant—in this case for 63,668 shares carrying a strike price of $14.38 per share. The estimated present value of this stock option grant, when combined with Greenberg's $4.2 million of total current compensation, gave him a total direct compensation package worth $4.5 million. As a result, his decline in total direct compensation was an almost immeasurable 0.4%.

Two things can be observed here. First, Greenberg's pay seems to rise a lot faster when profits are rising than it drops when profits are dropping. And second, the company's pay-for-performance philosophy seems to be running out of steam. By 1990, the response of Greenberg's cash compensation package to the decline in Bear Stearns's profitability was, to say the least, anemic. Moreover, he also received, for the first time, a stock option grant. The present value of that grant, if added to his total current compensation, would have produced a pay package that, for all practical purposes, was the same as he received a year earlier—a year when Bear Stearns's pre-tax profits had risen 43% in a single year.

These same two criticisms, lamentably, are not unique to Bear Stearns. Working with compensation data from some 150 major companies, I found that when primary earnings per share before extraordinary items rise 10%, the typical CEO's base salary and annual bonus rise 13.4%. But when earnings per share decrease 10%, the typical CEO's base salary and annual bonus *rise* 4.1%. Now that's pay-for-performance American style! Indeed, it would take a 55% decrease in earnings per share before the typical CEO had to endure the pain of earning the same amount he received the year before.

Carried over several years, this asymmetry can cause senior executive compensation to rise tremendously. Just for the fun of it one day, I started a computer spreadsheet by assuming that earnings per share in year 0 (the base year) were $1 and that the CEO's salary and bonus was $1 million. Then in year 1, I pretended that earnings per share increased 10%—from $1.00 to $1.10—and that the CEO's cash compensation increased 13.4%—from $1 million to $1.134 million. In year 2, I went on to pretend that earnings per share decreased 10%—from $1.10 to $0.99—and that the CEO's cash compensation increased 4.1%—from $1.134 million to $1.18 million. I then repeated that one-year-up-one-year-down pattern for the next ninety-eight years. In year 100, I discovered that earnings per share had fallen from $1.00 one hundred years earlier to only $0.61, the reason lying in the fact that the 10% decreases were calculated off relatively higher numbers, while the 10% increases were calculated off relatively lower numbers. The CEO's pay in year 100: just a shade under $4 billion! To be sure, no one is going to be CEO of a company for one hundred years, but the analogy may not be totally overdrawn when one considers that the pay of a new CEO more or less takes off from the pay level earned by his predecessor.

Given its profit track record, it is not surprising that Bear Stearns's stock price has not gone very far. In October 1985, the month the company went public, the stock price (adjusted for subsequent splits) closed at $9.81 per share, and in December 1990, the stock closed at $9.64 per share. By March 1991, it had moved up to $13.93 per share. Even so, its compounded rate of price appreciation since October 1985, when it went public, amounted to only 6.7% per year—a rate of return that is less than what an investor could have received from a stingy bank's certificates of deposit. Even when dividends are added in, Bear Stearns's compounded total shareholder return is a relatively low 10.5% per year. That's better than a bank CD rate, but not when you consider the sickening degree of volatility that is associated with the stocks of investment banking firms.

If you ask the typical CEO of a publicly owned investment banking firm why he has to pay his key people so much money, his reply is almost guaranteed to be: "If I don't pay highly, they will hit the bricks and join one of my competitors." Given the startlingly poor investments that investment banking stocks have turned out to be, would that be such a tragedy?

Nine

The Taxman
Never Cometh

ALL OF US owe a debt of gratitude to people who innovate, who operate at the frontier of knowledge. Consider what we owe to Alexander Graham Bell, Thomas Edison, or the Wright Brothers. There are some frontiersmen in the compensation world, too, but their contributions remain largely unsung. Just think what we owe the person who dreamed up the first pension plan, the first health insurance plan, the merit increase. Why, the list goes on and on. Executives, it seems, spend a lot of their waking hours, and probably not a few of the hours they should be sleeping, worrying. If they have lots of stock options, they worry about whether the market price of their stock will rise. Should they exercise now? Or is there a bigger profit to be had by waiting?

Some unsung frontiersman sought to remedy this pressing problem by inventing restricted stock. No longer was the executive burdened with the possibility that he might make nothing from his option grant. Now, as long as the stock price remained above zero, he could be assured of receiving at least some payout. You'd have thought that would have ended the worrying. But it didn't, for there was still the worry over taxes. With a restricted stock grant, the executive typically pays no taxes until the restrictions finally lapse and he is free to sell the shares. Then, at that time, he takes into his ordinary income an amount equal to the number of shares the restrictions on which have lapsed, multiplied by the market price per share on the date the restrictions lapsed. So, if 5,000 shares lapse today, and the stock price today is $100 per share, then this year's ordinary income must be increased by $500,000. And, of course, taxes must be paid on this $500,000 of ordinary income.

At the moment, executives in the United States are blessed with just about the lowest income tax rates around. At the margin, the maximum federal income tax cannot exceed 31%. There are, of course, state and local income taxes that must be paid, too, and, in states like New York and California, they can add quite a bit to one's total tax bill. But having a marginal federal tax rate of only 31% is a great thing—so long as it stays at 31%. After all, it was just raised from 28% in 1990. Everyone agrees that the possibility of it falling below 31% again is about the same as encountering a politician who says what he means. But what about the possibility that the rate in some future year—like the very year the restrictions on your restricted stock grant lapse—will be *above* 31%? After all, the tax rate used to be 50% until 1987; and as recently as 1968, it used to be 70%; and as recently as 1963, it used to be 91%. So, people who worry that their tax bill could be increased in some future year are right to worry. However, life is full of worries, and we can't be insured against all bad events that might occur in the future.

Enter the first of two frontiersmen—pioneering CEOs who have blazed trails in cutting taxes and transferring the bill to their shareholders. The first is Roberto Goizueta of Coca-Cola. Born fifty-nine years ago in Cuba, he fled with his family to the United States when Fidel Castro took over. A Yale-trained engineer, he joined Coke in

1954 in Havana, and worked his way up the management hierarchy. He speaks softly through a cloud of cigarette smoke, and he is gracious almost to a fault; but one should not confuse his polished manners with management softness. He can be tough as any when he needs to be.

Until Goizueta took over Coke, the company had the reputation of being a sleeping giant in its equally sleepy home city of Atlanta. And the performance statistics show it. Looking at all 120 periods in my 20-year total shareholder return analysis, Coca-Cola weighs in at only the 32nd percentile of the 407-company distribution. But its performance has been weighed down by the first forty or so periods—the periods before Goizueta became CEO. When the examination is confined to the most recent 80, 40, and 20 ten-year total return periods, Coca-Cola's percentile rankings are, respectively, 55th, 77th, and 89th. It took a while for Goizueta to turn his large, sluggish ship into a clear channel and then give it power; but once he did, it took off like a speedboat. He even managed to avoid—but barely—the disaster that would have overtaken the company had he persisted in trying to make the world love his New Coke; instead, he turned rout into victory by reintroducing the old Coke as Classic Coke and garnering thousands of lines of free advertising in the process.

Goizueta's pay has risen even faster than his company's performance. As of 1989, he earned a base salary of $1.2 million, including some deferred compensation that is, for all practical purposes, further base salary. He also receives very handsome annual bonuses. As a result, the sum of his base salary and annual bonus for 1990 was a not inconsiderable $3.1 million. On top of all that, Goizueta also receives some sizable option grants, as well as some performance unit grants. However, the centerpiece of his banquet table is restricted stock. During the year ending in 1986, he received around $11 million of free shares. Then, in 1990, he received another 500,000 shares of restricted stock. Based on the $41.39 average market price of Coca-Cola stock during 1990, these shares had a market value at the time of grant of about $20.7 million. In my 1991 study for *Fortune,* I calculated the value of Goizueta's base salary, annual bonus, and long-term incentives to be worth $10.4 million per year. After calibrating for Coca-Cola's size and performance, he was reported to be earning 113% above the market.

That alone would make Goizueta worthy of our attention. But Goizueta also pioneered a new type of executive compensation, a tax protection feature. When it gave out restricted stock grants, Coca-Cola didn't merely content itself with telling an executive that if his taxes went up by the time the restrictions on his shares lapsed (and with Coca-Cola restricted shares, the lapse generally does not occur until the executive retires—an event that can be many years hence), it would reimburse him for the *increase* in his taxes. No, Coca-Cola didn't do that. It promised the executive a cash payment equal to his entire tax bill, including both federal and state income taxes.

To illustrate: suppose an executive is granted today 10,000 restricted shares, and suppose further that the stock price today is $50 per share. Now assume that the restrictions on the shares do not lapse for ten years and that, by that time, the stock price has risen from $50 per share to $200 per share. The executive is required to take into his ordinary income, and in the year the restrictions lapsed, an amount determined by multiplying the number of shares on which the restrictions have lapsed (in this case 10,000) by the market price on the date the restrictions lapsed (in this case $200 per share). Hence, the executive must increase his Adjusted Gross Income by $2 million.

Now, assuming that the executive is already highly paid from his salary, bonus, and option profits, he will owe the federal government a tax of 31% on the $2 million of additional income, or $620,000. Moreover, let's assume he will owe his state another 6% of the $2 million of added income, or $120,000. Hence, his total tax bill, counting both federal and state income taxes, will be $740,000. At this point, the treasurer of Coca-Cola will step forward and give the executive a check for $740,000. Neat, don't you think? And think what would happen if the federal tax rate reverted to the 50% it used to be. Then the combined amount of the check the treasurer would have to write would be $1,120,000.

Adding a tax reimbursement feature not only increases the cost of a restricted stock transaction for the shareholders of Coca-Cola; it also transfers the liability for increased tax rates from the executive to the shareholders. Any self-respecting CEO would be horrified if his union asked for a tax reimbursement feature in its new contract. He would doubtless sputter that such an idea is unheard of and besides is against public policy. Why, if every company had a tax reimbursement feature for every worker, then how could the Congress take demand out of the economy by raising taxes or, alternatively, stimulate demand by lowering taxes? In such a case, raising taxes would turn out to be highly inflationary, rather than deflationary, as company after company increased the pay of its workers. No, such an idea is ludicrous—or at least it is ludicrous for all but a handful of senior executives.

So Roberto Goizueta is an unsung executive compensation frontiersman. He helped to introduce into an otherwise respectable company the idea of denominating an executive's pay in after-tax dollars. Or I should say Roberto Goizueta *was* an executive compensation frontiersman. For Coke announced in its 1991 proxy statement that the company was abandoning its tax reimbursement feature on new restricted stock grants. It isn't often that a company axes an executive goodie, and Coke should be applauded for making such a move.

Frontiersman or no, Roberto Goizueta does not appear to be as deep a thinker as his fellow Atlantan, T. Marshall Hahn, chairman of Georgia-Pacific, the paper products, lumber, and building-supplies giant. Hahn, sixty-four, a former physics professor and college president, is obviously no slouch when it comes to numbers. Somewhere along the line, and probably very quickly, he must have spotted the flaw in Goizueta's thinking. To illustrate here, let's go back to our example where the combined federal and state tax rates are 37%, and where the executive must pay a combined tax of $740,000 on the $2 million value of his lapsed restricted shares. Now, Hahn must have thought, that's a nice deal for the executive, but by giving him a check for $740,000, doesn't that create additional taxable income of $740,000, which itself is subject to a further tax, in this case 37% of $740,000, or $273,800? A quick check with his tax attorneys would have confirmed his gloomy assessment of the situation. So perhaps he asked them to find a way around the problem, and perhaps they replied that it would be frightfully difficult. To be sure, the tax on $740,000 is $273,800. But if you give the executive a further check for $273,800, that amount also becomes taxable. And so on and so on, like the seventh son of a seventh son.

But Hahn, a Ph.D. physicist from MIT, must have known there would have to be some simple mathematical expression that, at a stroke, could solve the problem. And he probably very quickly deduced that you can handle everything by dividing the original $2 million value of the restricted shares by a number determined by subtracting from "1" the combined federal and state income tax rates. Since the combined rates are 37%, subtracting 0.37 from "1" produces a value of 0.63. Dividing $2 million by 0.63 produces a figure of $3,174,603. Deducting from this figure the original $2 million value of the restricted shares produces a value of $1,174,603: this is the amount of the check the treasurer must write so that the executive can sidestep all taxes on his restricted stock grant.

Given that it might have been a while since Hahn had last played with mathematical formulae, he probably would have wanted to prove out his thinking. He would first note that the executive would owe a tax of $740,000 on the $2 million value of the restricted shares. So he would have deducted the $740,000 from the total tax reimbursement check of $1,174,603, leaving a remainder of $434,603. Then he would have considered that the executive would owe a tax on the $1,174,603 tax reimbursement payment itself. And he would have calculated that tax as equal to 37% of the $1,174,603. He would have concluded that the amount owed, $434,603, exactly equalled the amount the executive had left over from his $1,174,603 tax reimbursement payment. And he probably would have congratulated himself on the fact that his math skills were as sharp as they were in the days when he was teaching college physics.

So Marshall Hahn and Georgia-Pacific took the pioneering work of Coca-Cola and moved it to its logical conclusion: If you're going to help someone out with their taxes, why fool around with halfway measures? If you're going to do the job, do it right.

But look at what has happened in this example. The executive has received $2 million of free stock. But to make him whole on his taxes, he had to be given a check that is worth more than half the value of the stock itself. And suppose we think the unthinkable and determine what the tax reimbursement payment would have to be were the federal rate to revert to the 91% rate of prior to 1964. In that case, if we had a further 6 percentage points for the state income tax, the tax reimbursement payment on $2 million of restricted stock would have to be—hold on to your hat—$64,666,667! Tax rates won't go that high, you say. But they did in the period prior to 1964. And if we get a populist president and a populist Congress, who's to say it might not happen again? Remember, the shareholders have implicitly written a blank check for the company's executives, with the amount of the check to be filled in by the federal and state governments some years hence.

In fairness to Georgia-Pacific, the company at least accompanied its tax largesse with a requirement that the stock price double within a five-year period before an executive could take title to all his restricted shares. Indeed, if the stock price doesn't move up by at least 20% during the five-year period, the executive will end up receiving nothing—no restricted shares and no tax reimbursement payment, either. Moreover, Georgia-Pacific has also placed a cap on how much its shareholders can be tabbed for increased taxes. In no event may the tax reimbursement check be for more than the 100% of the value of the shares themselves.

Although Georgia-Pacific tied the earn-out of restricted shares to something other than the executive's breathing in and out, it still did not create a truly viable long-term incentive plan. In January 1988, when its plan was first inaugurated, Georgia-Pacific gave Marshall Hahn a grant of 140,000 shares. The price during the ten consecutive trading days prior to the date of the grant was $33.47 per share. The new plan provided that unless Georgia-Pacific's stock price rose at least 20% during the five years after the grant, and stayed at that level for at least ten consecutive trading days, Hahn wouldn't receive one share. But if it did, he would be vested in 20% of his restricted shares. Then, once the share price rose another 20%, measured off its base price of $33.47, he would be vested in a second 20% of the shares. And so on until the share price rose to $66.94 or more—a doubling from the initial price of $33.47—and again stayed there for ten consecutive trading days. At that point, Hahn would become vested in all 140,000 of his restricted shares.

Georgia-Pacific's stock is more than usually volatile, given the cyclicality inherent in the paper and lumber businesses. In this case, the volatility was upward, for by September 1989, not two years after the initial grant, the company's stock price had risen to more than $60.25, and Hahn had earned a vested interest in 80% of his 140,000 shares. Hence, during a period of twenty-one months or so, Hahn had become vested in 112,000 shares worth at least $6.7 million. In the paper business, however, where long-term decisions sometimes take five to ten years to come to fruition, twenty-one months can hardly be considered long term.

Very shortly after Hahn became vested in 80% of his initial award of restricted shares, Georgia-Pacific's stock price demonstrated a second kind of volatility—downward volatility. By January 1990, the stock price had slid to around $48 per share. Then the company gave out a second round of restricted shares to Hahn and other senior executives. In making the new round, which occurred in March 1990, the company required Hahn to forfeit the opportunity to earn the 20% of the first round's shares in which he had not yet become vested. Thus, he was required to leave on the table 20% of his initial grant's 140,000 shares, or 28,000 shares. But don't shed any tears for Marshall Hahn, because his new grant was for 100,000 shares.

Although Georgia-Pacific's stock price was just about $48 per share at the time this second grant was made, the board magnanimously raised the base price to $50 per share (i.e., the price from which future appreciation would be measured). Hence, Hahn stood to become vested in 20% of his new round of 100,000 shares as soon as Georgia-Pacific's stock price rose 20%—to $60 per share—and stayed there for twenty consecutive trading days.

But isn't this somewhere around where we came in? Hahn had already earned 20% of his first round's grant of 140,000 shares, or 28,000 shares, for moving Georgia-Pacific's stock price from $53.55

to $60.25. And now he has been given the opportunity to earn 20% of his second round's grant of 100,000 shares, or 20,000 shares, for moving Georgia-Pacific's stock price from $50 to $60. Indeed, if Georgia-Pacific were going to play the game fairly, why didn't the company establish a base price for Hahn's second grant of restricted shares equal to the implicit price of $60.25 per share on which he had already been rewarded once?

As of the end of March 1991—a bit more than three years after Hahn received his initial grant—Georgia-Pacific's stock had dropped to about $42.50 per share. Thus, the increase over the three-year period was only 27%, and should by rights have entitled Hahn to become vested in only 20% of the 140,000 shares in his first grant, or 28,000 shares. Yet Hahn has become vested in 112,000 shares, and stands to earn even more for repeating the performance for which he has already been rewarded. And even three years still cannot be considered very long term in the paper and lumber industry.

Hahn's case demonstrates a point that we will see again—this time involving Stephen Wolf, the head of UAL Corporation, the parent to United Airlines. If you really mean to "incent" long-term behavior, then you must avoid the design of incentive plans that pay off big for what turns out to be normal cyclicality.

Another pioneering company that deserves at least an honorable mention for its inventiveness is Occidental Petroleum. It reimburses up to $300,000 per year in California state income taxes paid by its new CEO, Ray Irani. In this case, the reimbursement is not limited to restricted stock grants. Dr. Irani can use it to pay the California income taxes on such mundane items as his base salary.

Finally, we have Bally Manufacturing, which, under the leadership of its longtime but now former CEO, Robert Mullane (apparently, his board gave him to understand that retirement was an attractive alternative, even though he is today only fifty-eight), also decided to offer full tax reimbursement on restricted stock grants. Unlike Georgia-Pacific, however, Bally's tax reimbursement contains no limit on the amount of taxes that may be reimbursed. Therefore, a surge in federal or state income taxes could do quite a job on Bally's income statement. Moreover, Bally also dispensed with the nicety of having to do something to earn the restricted shares. Breathing in and out seems to be good enough, although Bally's near-bankrupt state seems to suggest otherwise. (Dial Corporation, formerly called Greyhound Dial and before that Greyhound, also offers tax-free grants of restricted stock *à la* Bally.)

Plans and grants of the type extended to Mullane must be approved by that disinterested committee of outside directors called the "compensation committee." It frequently happens that the compensation committee misses some pertinent detail of a complicated new executive compensation plan and unwittingly gives its imprimatur to a giveaway. Not so the Bally compensation committee. It is headed by a trained economist, Pierre Rinfret, who in 1990 was the Republican candidate for governor of New York. If anyone should have known about the potential liabilities involved and the fact that offering tax-free compensation really does undermine public policy, it should have been Dr. Rinfret.

Ten

The Good Guys

APERENNIAL DEBATE in history circles centers on whether great men, like Napoleon, really can change the course of history or, alternatively, whether history unfolds in a mysterious process that is only marginally influenced by the Napoleons of this world. Ask your typical board of directors to jump into the debate among historians, and to a man (plus a token woman and a token black), they will vote with the "great man" camp. To them, it is self-evident that if you put the right person in the CEO's job and make sure he stays in the job, great results will ensue. And to make sure he stays in the job, pay him anything he requires, short of the entire sales volume of the company.

Steve Ross can be considered a great man, when you think what he did over the years for the shareholders of Warner Communications. But his pay package, besides being simply too big to swallow, contains lots of gimmicks and was designed to give him substantial rewards even if Warner Communications' performance had turned out to be below average. Hence, people like Steve Ross, and for that matter, Martin Davis of Paramount Communications, are great men, but they are not good guys. It's okay by me for a good guy to be paid hugely if he performs hugely. But the quid pro quo is that he has to take it solidly on the chin if his company's performance turns south.

Three good guys deserve mention here: Paul Fireman of Reebok; Michael Eisner of the Walt Disney Company; and Anthony O'Reilly of H. J. Heinz.

Fireman, a mischievous-looking forty-seven-year-old, founded Reebok and then took it public in July 1985. Reebok at first made its reputation on the style of the shoes it made; now it has entered the realm of high technology, aided by a prominent ad campaign featuring everyone's favorite jocks. The price (adjusted for subsequent splits) at which the stock closed in the month it went public was $3.52 per share. The stock price then soared to $19.00 by the end of 1989, before dropping back to $11.50 at the end of 1990. But by the end of March 1991, it rose spectacularly to an all-time high of $23.75. During the period between July 1985 and April 1991, an investor who bought and held would have enjoyed (and I mean enjoyed!) a compounded total return of 41.3% per year—a return that was surpassed by only two of the 407 other comparison companies.

Turning to compensation matters, Paul Fireman signed an employment agreement with Reebok as early as November 1981—some four years before the company went public. His salary was pegged at $65,000 per year (when the amount was mentioned to one compensation consultant, he said, "I assume you mean $65,000 per month!"). But he was also promised an annual bonus equal to 10% of the pre-tax profits in excess of $100,000. Hence, if the pre-tax profits were, say, $20 million, the sum of $100,000 would first be deducted, leaving $19,900,000. Then Fireman would receive 10% of the remainder as a bonus, or $1,990,000.

Like the bonus arrangement established for Steven Ross of Time Warner, Fireman had to produce profits for the shareholders before he could begin to generate some bonus money for himself. In both cases, the mandated profit level was relatively small—especially so in the case of Reebok. However, Fireman's salary, unlike Ross's, was also very small, in this case only $65,000 per year.

In August 1985, Fireman renegotiated his employment agreement, in the process upping his base salary from $65,000 to $350,000. The percentage increase he received was huge, but the resulting salary of $350,000 still wasn't all that high—especially considering how large the company had grown. In return for receiving the large salary increase, he gave up two things. First, the threshold profit level he had to produce before being entitled to receive any bonus money was increased dramatically—from a flat $100,000 to $20 million. Second, the percentage of profits he was to receive once he crossed the profit threshold was halved—from 10% to 5%. (An additional provision was incorporated to the effect that if Reebok failed to meet its profit goals for the year, Fireman's bonus could be reduced below the amount called for in the formula. But the amount of the reduction was not specified in the proxy statement.)

Clearly, Fireman stood to lose under his new employment agreement, except in the event that Reebok's pre-tax profits dropped below $2.95 million. In that case, his loss of bonus would be more than offset by the increase in his base salary. However, such an outcome had to be exceedingly unlikely. For 1984, Reebok earned pre-tax profits of $12.2 million. Moreover, when the revised pay arrangement was adopted in August 1985, the company was two thirds of the way toward increasing the yearly pre-tax profit figure from $12.2 million to $78.1 million. With pre-tax profits of $78.1 million, Fireman's annual bonus dropped by $4.9 million compared to what he would have earned had he continued under his old employment agreement, and his total current compensation (counting base salary and the annual bonus) dropped by $4.6 million (again compared to what he would have earned). Still, he was richly rewarded, receiving for 1985 a combination of base salary and annual bonus worth $5.5 million. He did not, however, receive any long-term incentive grants—grants such as stock options, restricted stock, and performance units.

There is a subtle but profound difference between Fireman's 1985 bonus formula and the bonus formulas favored by Steve Ross. When Ross meets his minimum profit standard (say, $75 million), he is then entitled to a stipulated percentage of *all* profits, not merely the profits in excess of $75 million. In Fireman's case, however, his profit threshold of $20 million is deducted from the company's profits before his 5% bonus formula is applied. For 1986, Fireman's base salary was $350,000, and his bonus was a startling $12.7 million. For 1987, the salary continued at $350,000, but the bonus increased to $15.1 million. Then Reebok's pre-tax earnings decreased. But you needn't have worked up any special sympathy for Fireman, because his bonus for 1988, though lower than the year before, was still $11.1 million. In 1989, profits rebounded, and so did his bonus—to $14.2 million.

Perhaps motivated by the critical publicity surrounding his monster bonuses, Fireman, in 1990, renegotiated his compensation yet another time. His salary for 1991 and later years has been increased, to a minimum of $1 million per year. But his target bonus opportunity is now limited to a further $1 million per year. Of course, there is nothing to prevent Fireman from receiving an above-target bonus, but the proxy language suggests that the $15 million-or-so bonuses that he had been accustomed to receiving are a thing of the past. Consequently, his total current compensation levels are likely to drop to those of his more normally paid peers. That's all to the good, though it's a shame his salary is being raised to such a high level.

Even though Fireman's total current compensation is likely to be cut hugely, you don't need to feel too much sympathy for him. As a sort of Styptic pencil for his pay cut, his board of directors threw in an extra goodie: a stock option grant on 2.5 million shares. It's hard to imagine a scenario where a 2.5 million share option can be made to produce pay for Fireman which, in present value terms, exceeds what he would have received by continuing with his 5%-of-profits bonus formula. Indeed, it is terribly easy to imagine multitudes of scenarios in which he will earn a lot less under his new employment agreement than under the one it replaces.

Moreover, Reebok's board took a further action, which is certainly in the right direction. It decreed that the strike prices of the

2.5 million option shares would be, on average, 18% above the market price of a share of Reebok stock on the date the options were first granted. Now, an 18% increase in stock price, when amortized over the ten-year life of a stock option, amounts to only 1.7% per year in appreciation. But that is infinitely more appreciation being demanded than under almost every other company's stock option grants, where the strike price is set to equal the market price of a share of company stock on the date of the grant.

In sum, Paul Fireman is a company founder who, though he is still paid way above the market, has at least recognized that as his company matures, he cannot expect to take out of it the same amount of compensation as he did during its explosive growth years.

Michael Eisner of Walt Disney has one thing in common with Martin Davis of Paramount Communications. He, too, was an employee of Paramount Communications. When Davis took over as CEO, Eisner was the president and number two executive at Paramount Pictures. He was one half of the team that had produced stunning and consistent results in an industry where cyclicality was the order of the day. The other half was Paramount Pictures's CEO, Barry Diller. Diller, who was born in San Francisco in 1942, one month before Eisner was born across the country in New York City, had worked with Eisner earlier when both were involved in programming for ABC. Diller came to Paramount in 1974 and two years later lured Eisner away from ABC. Their successful partnership was to last eight years. In 1984, Eisner left to run Walt Disney, and Diller, after feuding for sometime with Davis, quit to run Twentieth Century Fox.

After the death of its founder, the Walt Disney Company began to languish. The new CEO, Ron Miller, was a former football player with the Los Angeles Rams, and his marriage to Walt Disney's daughter was thought by some to be the principal reason for his having become CEO. Disney was one of the first companies caught up in the takeover/greenmail game, in which a raider threatened to take over the company but was often quite ready to go away if the company bought back his minority interest at a premium price. Its pursuit by Saul Steinberg, the New York financier, galvanized the board of directors to take a hard look at the company's lackluster performance. Ron Miller was sent packing, and in his place, the board hired Michael Eisner.

The rest, as they say in show business, is history. Eisner expanded the Dynamic Duo that existed when he ran Paramount Pictures with Barry Diller into a Dynamic Trio. Eisner was the film buff, the Cre- ative-As CEO, the person who directly approves, or as they say in Hollywood, "green-lights" every script. For the more mundane job of operating the company, he turned to Frank Wells, a brilliant, tough, mountain-climbing lawyer. And as his chief financial officer, he lured Gary Wilson away from Marriott Corporation, where Wil- son had engineered a good part of that company's tremendous suc- cess.

If you liked reading the financial statistics of Paramount Commu- nications, you'd love those of Walt Disney. Earnings per share didn't grow unsteadily. They soared—and steadily. From a low of $0.15 per share (after taxes but before extraordinary items) just before Eisner joined the company, they rose to $6 per share in the fiscal year ending in September 1990. Return on equity, which had plunged to as low as 1.7% in the fiscal year just before Eisner joined Disney, rocketed to 26% in 1989 and was still at an ultra-high 25.2% in fiscal 1990. And total return to shareholders was nothing short of breath- taking. Disney ranked at the 39th percentile in its 120-period, ten- year total return. But those statistics go back to 1971, and Eisner didn't become CEO until 1984. Disney's percentile ranks for the most recent 80, 40, and 20 ten-year total return periods were, respec- tively, 64th, 87th, and 90th. Even this last figure doesn't tell the whole story, because it covers a ten-year period that began three years before Eisner joined Disney. From October 1984, when he came to Disney, through February 1991, Eisner has delivered a compounded total return to shareholders of a magnificent 38.9% per year. Over the same time interval, only six companies among the 406 companies studied managed to beat that return figure.

When he first joined Walt Disney in 1984, Michael Eisner was promised a bonus each year equal to 2% of the net income of the company after taxes, after first deducting from such net income an amount equal to a 9% after-tax return on the company's average shareholders' equity. To illustrate: suppose net income in a given year is $200 million and that average shareholders' equity is $1 billion. In that case, $90 million—or a 9% return on shareholders' equity—is deducted from the $200 million of net income, thereby leaving a remainder of $110 million. Eisner's bonus would then be 2% of this remainder, or $2.2 million. When he negotiated a new ten-year employment agreement at the beginning of 1989, his bonus threshold of 9%-of-shareholders' equity was raised to 11%, commencing with the 1991 fiscal year. Hence, with the same $200 million of after-tax net income and $1 billion of average shareholders' equity, his bonus would have dropped from $2.2 million to $1.8 million.

Eisner's bonus formula can be thought of as a sort of compact between him and the shareholders—a compact that goes something like this: "You already pay me a base salary of $750,000, so I agree that I shouldn't receive a bonus until I do something to earn my salary. And that something is an 11 percent return on equity. However, once I reach that threshold level of performance, you will begin to give me some further reward—in this case two cents for each added dollar of after-tax profit I generate."

A bonus threshold of an 11% return on equity is quite ambitious. It virtually guarantees shareholders that, before bonuses are paid, they will earn a return on their investment which is higher than what they could have earned by investing their funds in safe government bonds. And it is far higher than the comparable thresholds used by other companies. In a study of one hundred major companies I conducted a few years ago, I found that the median company employed a threshold of only a 6% return on equity.

An 11% return on equity cannot be considered a slam dunk. To be sure, Disney earned a 26% return on average equity in 1989. But in earlier periods that was decidedly not the case. In the ten years prior to Eisner's hire, Disney earned less than an 11% return fully half the time. Indeed, in the best of those ten years, the company earned only a 13.3% return.

Eisner's bonus plan has paid off spectacularly. In 1990, he received a bonus of $10.5 million in addition to his $750,000 per year base salary. But the real payoff has come from his stock option grants. When he was hired by Disney in 1984, he was given an option on 2.04 million shares carrying a strike price (adjusted for subsequent splits) of $14.36 per share. And when he signed his latest employment agreement at the beginning of 1989, he was given an option on another 2 million shares. Of these, 1.5 million carried a strike price equal to the $68.56 market price per share on the date of grant, while 500,000 shares carried a strike price that was $10 per share higher.

Eisner did not exercise any of his option shares until fiscal 1988, which ended in September 1988. The proxy released in 1989 disclosed that he realized an option gain of $32.6 million, though it doesn't indicate how many of his 4.04 million option shares he exercised to reap that gain. If we assume, however, that he exercised some of the shares he was granted in 1984—shares that carried a strike price of $14.36 each—and if we assume further that he exercised his option in September 1988, when the average monthly price of $63.38 was the highest of any month during fiscal 1988, Eisner would have had to exercise about 665,000 of his 4.04 million share grant to produce the requisite $32.6 option gain. That would have left him with 1,375,000 shares from his 1984 grant, in addition to the 2 million shares in his 1989 grants. Calculated off a late March 1991 market price of $119.25 per share, his unexercised option gains were likely on the order of $240 million. And as of March 1991, he still had more than three years of time remaining on his 1984 option grants and almost eight years on his 1989 option grants. I once asked one of Eisner's key subordinates why Eisner seemed to be interested in amassing so much money. He said he thought that Eisner wanted to create one of America's great family fortunes, on the order of the Rockefellers, Mellons, and duPonts. He appears to be well on his way.

Compared to most other CEOs, Eisner plays the game fairly by assuming a relatively high degree of pay risk. His salary of $750,000 is on the low side for CEOs of companies the size of Disney. Moreover, he has earned the same salary since 1984, and his new contract provides that it remain unchanged until 1998. His annual bonus contains a threshold of performance (11% return on equity) that is almost double the typical threshold that other companies use. He receives no restricted stock—only stock options. And of his most recent grant of 2 million shares, 25% carried a strike price that was about 15% higher than the market price of Disney stock on the date the options were granted.

Anthony O'Reilly, the CEO of H. J. Heinz, is a true Irishman. He was born in Dublin in 1936 and continues to hold an Irish passport. He owns a magnificent mansion near Dublin, where he spends a substantial portion of each year. He personally controls some of Ireland's largest business enterprises. And, from time to time, he is rumored to be a candidate to become Ireland's prime minister.

He has also been described as the Joe Namath of rugby or, perhaps to update the analogy a bit, the Joe Montana of rugby. Apparently, he is still approached by autograph seekers who remember his exploits on the field these many years ago. Finally, Tony O'Reilly would probably win hands down any contest for the most charismatic CEO. Besides his handsome and commanding physical presence, he is a mesmerizing speaker—almost Churchillean in his oratorical prowess. It is puzzling at first to learn that literally thousands of shareholders attend the Heinz annual meeting in Pittsburgh each year until you hear Tony O'Reilly speak and witness the standing ovations he receives from the crowd. On top of simultaneously running Heinz and tending to his Irish business interests, O'Reilly somehow managed in the last few years to obtain a Ph.D. in marketing from the University of Bradford in England. O'Reilly also holds a law degree in Ireland and has lectured at the university level in applied psychology.

Besides all the above, O'Reilly is one of America's highest-performing CEOs. In my analysis of total shareholder returns among the 407 companies with the largest market capitalization, Heinz ranks at the 87th percentile when all 120 periods covering 20 years are taken into account. If we look at the most recent 80, 40, and 20 ten-year total return periods, Heinz's percentile ranks are, respectively, 90th, 93rd, and 94th. Only 25 of the 407 companies bettered Heinz's total shareholder return record during the most recent 20 ten-year periods, and of these, the great majority were much smaller than Heinz. Moreover, this magnificent performance was achieved with relatively little of the sickening stock price volatility that often accompanies high shareholder returns.

One of the wellsprings of O'Reilly's performance may well be his Irish birth and upbringing. As a native of a small country who has also spent a considerable amount of time working in the United Kingdom, O'Reilly instinctively understands the need for an international, as opposed to a strictly American, viewpoint. Among other things, he has been instrumental in expanding Heinz into Africa and China. His internationalist attitude is just now starting to permeate America's leading business schools, all of which are scrambling to turn out American MBAs who think the way O'Reilly does.

O'Reilly, so far as CEOs of American companies go, is a real risk taker. His 1991 base salary of $514,000, though high by almost anyone's standard, is a pittance when compared to CEOs in other comparably sized companies, many of whose salaries approach or even top $1 million per year. In fact, O'Reilly, who would have been entitled to around a 4% base salary increase for 1991 according to his employment contract, elected to take no increase at all, notwithstanding that his senior subordinates received increases of around 4%. To help make up for this salary deficit, he does receive a larger-than-average annual bonus opportunity. Probably the sum of his base salary and his annual bonus would put him near, but slightly under, the competitive median.

O'Reilly also takes risk in another way: he has huge shareholdings in H. J. Heinz. In 1990, he exercised over 2 million option shares and then sold around 800,000 of the shares to pay his taxes. Nevertheless, he was left holding 2.4 million shares of Heinz stock, a holding worth close to $100 million in March 1991. Hence, if Heinz's stock price should drop in half, O'Reilly won't merely have his pay package reduced. He also will stand to lose about $50 million in real money.

Looking only at O'Reilly's slim base salary and bonus, you might think you'd need to book Carnegie Hall for a Tony O'Reilly benefit concert. But that won't be necessary, because he really gets rolling when it comes to long-term incentives. First, he participates in a Performance Unit Plan that features three-year performance periods and a new grant each year. Hence, he received an opportunity to earn a bonus for Heinz's performance during, say, 1986 through 1988; then for its performance in 1987 through 1989; and then for its performance in 1988 through 1990. Payouts under the plan are determined with reference to Heinz's growth in earnings per share during the three-year performance period, as well as its return on equity during the same time frame. And the performance targets imbedded in the Performance Unit Plan are quite tough. The 1989 proxy disclosed that O'Reilly received a payment of about $2 million for his performance during the three preceding fiscal years.

If you add $2 million per year to an almost-competitive combination of base salary and bonus, you are close to breaking out into the clear. But you need something more. And that something, for Tony O'Reilly, is stock options. Proxy statements disclose that during the five years up to and including fiscal 1985, he received 919,610 option shares carrying a strike price of $35.89 per share. However, subsequent to these grants, Heinz's stock split two-for-one on two different occasions. On a post-split basis, therefore, the grant consisted of 3,678,440 shares carrying a strike price of $8.973 per share. And during fiscal year 1989, he received an option on another 1,269,160 shares, this time carrying a strike price of $22.595 per share.

If you add together O'Reilly's base salary and his annual bonus for 1989, his performance unit payout for the three-year performance period ending in 1989, and then put an annualized price tag on the stock options he has been granted during the three-year period 1987 through 1989, the total is $10.4 million per year. After calibrating for Heinz's size, performance, and other related factors, that total ranks him as tenth-highest-paid in my 1990 *Fortune* study of 200 CEOs.

But that total omits O'Reilly's latest stock option grant, which was given to him in conjunction with his signing of a new five-year employment agreement. Dwarfing anything he has received in the

past, the grant is for 4 million shares, carrying a strike price of
$29.875 per share. The grant contains an odd feature, however.
Once the stock price essentially doubles—that is, once it reaches
$61.125 per share—Heinz's board can (though it doesn't have to)
force O'Reilly to exercise his stock option. In other words, the
option contains a "cap" on the amount of appreciation O'Reilly is
permitted to make. The cap is quite generous, though, given that
a profit of $31.25 on 4 million shares multiplies out to $125 million.

Of course, one can easily get carried away and overglorify the risk
taking of a Paul Fireman, a Michael Eisner, or an Anthony O'Reilly.
Granted, O'Reilly and Eisner earn relatively low base salaries. But try
to convince your average working person that earning a base salary of
$514,000 to $750,000 per year is evidence of risk taking. Granted,
O'Reilly and Eisner won't earn a penny from their stock option
grants unless the stock prices of their respective companies rise. But
how difficult, really, is it to engineer a paltry 5% per increase in your
company's stock price? After all, shareholders could earn a considerably greater return than that simply by investing their funds in Treasury bonds. Yet a 5% rise in the stock prices of Heinz and Disney
would give both O'Reilly and Eisner many millions in option gains.

In that vein, let's reexamine O'Reilly's most recent stock option
grant for a moment. He makes nothing unless he can get Heinz's
stock price above $29.875 per share. Then he makes $4 million for
each further one-point increase in the stock price, until he caps out
at $125 million of gain once the stock price reaches $61.125 per
share. Now, imposing a cap may be considered a prudent action by
a board of directors concerned to make sure O'Reilly doesn't make
too much money. But according to modeling I have run, O'Reilly
is apt to hit the cap about 43% of the time; and that assumes only
normal future stock price appreciation, not the levels of performance
O'Reilly has achieved in the past.

How about a different alternative: Up the strike price from
$29.875 to the current cap point of $61.125, and then remove the
cap altogether. Under this alternative, O'Reilly wouldn't make anything until the stock price had virtually doubled—from $29.875 to

$61.125. But then he would have an unlimited right to any further appreciation. Granting a stock option with a premium strike price (i.e., a strike price that is higher than the market price of the stock on the date of grant, or what Wall Streeters call an "out-of-the-money" stock option) is virtually unheard of in executive compensation circles. One quarter of Michael Eisner's most recently granted stock option shares contain a strike price that is $10 per share higher than the market price on the date of grant. And, as we have seen, Paul Fireman's new option grant at Reebok carries an average strike price that is 18% higher than the market price at grant. But you'd have to look fairly hard to find even two more instances of premium-priced stock option grants.

Imposing a super-premium strike price on O'Reilly's option would seem to be an invitation to economic suicide. But consider that his option term is essentially ten years in duration, and that it takes only 7.4% per year compounded annual appreciation to move from a stock price of $29.875 per share to one of $61.125. Add to that a dividend yield of 2.7%, and the total shareholder return would be 10.1%; not all that much higher than what an investor could receive by putting his money in long-term government bonds.

Of course, an uncapped option share carrying a strike price of $61.125 when the market price was $29.875 would be less valuable to O'Reilly than a capped option share (cap of $61.125) carrying a strike price of $29.875. So, to get him to consider playing the game, Heinz's board would have had to offer him a somewhat larger grant. According to mathematical modeling I have conducted, a grant of 4.4 million shares yields about the same present value as O'Reilly's original grant of 4 million shares. O'Reilly loses, of course, if Heinz's stock price never gets to $61.125 per share. But, if we concentrate on the rosy outcomes, he gains by having no cap. If O'Reilly had received this larger grant of 4.4 million shares, he would have realized an option gain of $125 million (i.e., what he would have realized at maximum from his actual, 4 million share capped stock option), with 11.9% per year stock price appreciation over the 9.75-year term of the grant. At this writing, O'Reilly has been CEO of Heinz almost twelve years. During those eleven-plus years, Heinz has achieved an average annual rate of price appreciation of 24% per year; indeed, there were only two years out of the ten where the price appreciation would have been less than the 11.9% per year rate required to give O'Reilly $125 million in option gains. In one of those years, the stock dropped 5.5%, while in the other year, it rose 5.8%. In the third-worst year, Heinz's stock appreciated by 20.4%.

Had O'Reilly received the above-described 4.4 million share grant, and had Heinz's stock then appreciated at more than 11.9% per year during the life of O'Reilly's option, he would, of course, have earned more than $125 million—something that is impossible with his current capped option grant. O'Reilly is known to be a risk taker, and he might well have been willing to play a high stakes game, so long as he was receiving an uncapped grant of 4.4 million option shares. Perhaps it was his board that dreamed up the option cap, more out of a desire to keep his pay under some semblance of control than to motivate him to deliver another ten years of 24% per year price appreciation.

Paul Fireman of Reebok, Michael Eisner of Walt Disney, and Anthony O'Reilly of H. J. Heinz are all spectacular performers, who have earned millions in pay but who also have played the compensation game fairly by taking more than the average amount of pay risk. Indeed, their performance has been so spectacular that it would be hard to find a long-term shareholder willing to stand up and object to the pay they have received.

Still, it is troubling to consider that there are other CEOs out there who have also performed spectacularly for their shareholders but who don't earn anywhere near as much as Fireman, Eisner, and O'Reilly. They include people such as John Bryan, Jr., of Sara Lee; Hamish Maxwell of Philip Morris; Wayne Calloway of Pepsico; Joseph Canion of Compaq Computer; and Richard Zimmerman of Hershey Foods.

Of course, one might counter with a resounding "So what?" Those extra millions that Eisner and O'Reilly earn can be thought of as small change compared to the $504 million Heinz earned after taxes and before extraordinary items in fiscal 1989, and to the $824 million earned by Disney in fiscal 1990. But we need to consider here that the pay of a CEO is not unlike a 4,000-horsepower vacuum cleaner: it sucks up the pay of anyone else who gets close to the nozzle. In a 1990 study of some two hundred companies, I found that there is a high statistical correlation between the pay of the CEO and the pay of the second-highest-paid executive. For each $1 extra the CEO earns, the second-highest-paid executive is apt to be paid 47 cents more. Probably, the extra compensation for the third-highest-paid executive will be less than 47 cents, and so on until you reach the ordinary worker, at which point an electron microscope may be necessary to gauge the increase. Nonetheless, we have to assume that giving the CEO an extra dollar of compensation has a multiplier effect; perhaps in the end that extra dollar will cost the shareholders $40 or $50 when you consider the effect it has on sucking up the pay of executives on many different management levels. Hence, paying Eisner and O'Reilly those extra millions per year is most likely costing the shareholders of the two companies a bundle.

In the end, it is hard to heap too much abuse on the boards of Reebok, Walt Disney, and H. J. Heinz. They did, after all, buy some spectacular CEO talent. One could only have wished that they had visited at least one other store besides Tiffany's (and Cartier's doesn't count!) before making their selections.

Eleven

Ready, Aim, Reload!

THERE'S SOMETHING WRONG with the title of this chapter. Shouldn't it be "Ready, Aim, Fire!"? Well of course it should be, but it isn't—at least it isn't in the wonderful world of executive compensation.

Ask any economist what financial risk is, and he will tell you that risk equates with volatility. If you buy a Treasury bond promising 8% per year interest, you receive 8% per year interest—no more and no less. And you receive your principal back when the bond matures—no more and no less. The only way those two things don't happen is if the federal government goes belly up. And if that happens, there will doubtless be more pressing matters to think about than the mere loss of your capital. Because the chances of receiving an interest rate different from 8% or the chances of receiving back less than you invested as principal are so low as to be immeasurable, an investment in a Treasury bond is said to be a risk-free investment.

But not so in the case of common stocks. There, the dividend you expected to receive can dry up or be, say, twice what you figured. And the amount you invested can be lost entirely or increase in value, say, ten times. This wide range of outcomes—this *volatility*—is what risk is all about.

Americans seem to have a special love affair with risk, for risk takers are uniformly celebrated—or at least, successful risk takers are. Babe Ruth is remembered for pointing to centerfield. George Patton is remembered for his pearl-handled revolvers and his willingness to ride into the thick of battle in the lead tank. And Douglas MacArthur is remembered for taking a huge risk at Inchon during the Korean War by mounting an amphibious landing in an area which experienced 30-foot tides.

You have read in several places in this book about various risk reduction techniques. Now let's review them all together to see how far the problem has progressed. For a start, we have the bloated base salary, which for a growing number of CEOs today exceeds $1 million per year. Even if the rest of the CEO's pay package were fraught with risk, which it is not, how can a CEO talk about taking risk and at the same time keep a straight face when, if the worst happens, he is down to his last $1 million per year?

Next, we have the annual bonus. By design, the bonus is supposed to fluctuate with the company's performance. But quite a few companies offer their executives a guaranteed bonus. For example, a number of senior managers at Time Warner were promised that their annual bonus would not be less than 125% of their base salaries. In other words, they could receive more than 125% of base salary, but they could never receive less. (The guaranteed feature was recently removed, but the affected Time Warner executives received large increases in base salary to soothe the sting.) Such is the modern American executive's idea of risk taking.

Next, we come to the area of long-term incentive compensation. Let's start with the all-time favorite, the stock option. Here, you might say, is a real risky form of compensation; after all, the CEO can't make a nickel unless the stock price rises.

Uh-uh. Remember Frank Lorenzo of Texas Air? The options he had with strike prices of almost $30.00 per share were, almost alchemically, transformed by his loving board into options with effective strike prices of $4.625 per share.

Suppose a CEO receives a stock option on 10,000 shares at a time when the market price of his company's stock is $50 per share. And suppose that the strike price of the option is also set at $50 per share. Now, if the stock price doubles to $100 per share, the CEO ends up earning $50 per share, or $500,000 for all 10,000 option shares. And an institutional investor, which bought 10,000 shares on the same day the CEO received the stock option, also earns the same $500,000 of profit.

Now suppose that the stock price, instead of rising, drops from $50 per share to as low as $10 per share before rising to $35 per share. Our institutional investor, which paid $50 per share, ends up losing $150,000 on its 10,000-share investment. As for the CEO, he ends up earning nothing if his option shares aren't swapped. Of course, earning nothing is not the same as losing $150,000, is it? But the fun really starts if the CEO's board—as an increasing number of boards are wont to do—has him turn in his option shares and receive in their place a new option for 10,000 shares carrying a strike price of $10 per share. In that case, our CEO, by exercising his option when the stock price has risen to $35 per share, makes a profit of $25 per share, or $250,000, at the very same time when the investor has lost $150,000. Stock options are supposed to put the CEO in the same boat as the investor. It looks from here that there are two boats in the water: a leaky rowboat for the investor and the *QE 2* for the CEO.

Consider also the ability of the CEO to largely determine the date on which he will receive his stock option grant. Remember that his board of directors is almost always reactive, not proactive; it waits for the CEO to bring up the matter of stock option grants. And consider also that the CEO, more than anyone else, is in possession of inside information. While even he cannot control the future, he knows about the company's future plans, its promising products, and so forth. So, if anyone knows when a stock has bottomed out and is about to rise, it will be the CEO.

Next, consider that the CEO, within very broad limits, can call the shots as to when the option will be exercised. Just because the option is exercisable for a ten-year period doesn't mean that the CEO must wait, or will wait, until the end of the ten-year term to exercise it. He can pick the date that looks right to him.

Stephen Wolf of UAL, the parent company to United Airlines, is a case in point here. He joined UAL in December 1987, and three months later he received an option on 250,000 shares of UAL stock carrying a strike price equal to the current market price of around $83 per share. To provide a frame of reference, UAL's stock price had been as high as around $100 per share not three months before Wolf joined UAL.

Once Wolf received his option, the stock started to take off. By the middle of 1989, the stock had risen from $83 per share to around $140 per share. Then Marvin Davis, the huge independent investor whose holdings at one point included Twentieth Century-Fox, entered the scene and made a hostile bid for UAL. The stock promptly doubled in value, to $280 per share. But Davis's effort was unsuccessful, and the stock took a nosedive, leading, in the opinion of many analysts, to a drop of 190 points in a single day in the Dow Jones average and prompting fear that another October 1987 (when the Dow dropped 508 points) was about to happen. Thereafter, a union-led buyout effort commenced; but it, too, was unsuccessful. As of October 1990, UAL's stock had dropped back to as low as $84.25, or within $1 of its $83 per share value when Wolf first received his stock option.

So Wolf could have made a huge amount of money on his stock option shares, given that the stock price rose as high as $280 per share. But he made nothing because the stock price dropped back to around $83 per share. And he should have made nothing, because he had, after all, done nothing to improve total shareholder returns on a long-term, as opposed to a short-term, basis.

Anyone who believes that the scenario unfolded in the way it is portrayed in the preceding paragraph still loves to read fairy tales when no one is around. For Stephen Wolf, far from making nothing, reaped option profits of $14 million. He didn't have the sagacity to exercise his stock options when the stock had risen to as high as $280 per share. But he did have the sagacity to exercise his option when the stock price was still at $150 per share. So, timing the grant of a stock option and timing the exercise of an option can help to ensure that the CEO will make good money even when his share-holders are making no money. And if we add a board of directors willing to engage in option swapping just in case the CEO fails to time his option grant to the low of the market, what was intended to be a risky form of compensation becomes close to shooting fish in a barrel. (In fairness to Wolf, UAL's stock, having dropped to $84.25 in October 1990, rose rapidly to a high of $149.75 by February 1991.)

Today, stock options have been made even less risky through the introduction of the so-called reload option feature. Although the details are numbingly complex, suffice it to say that a reload feature guarantees the CEO that he will receive the highest possible price for his option shares. If he fails to pick the day in the ten years when the stock is at its highest price to exercise his option shares, the company will make up the difference. All we need now is for some imaginative compensation consultant to design a reload strike price feature, such that the strike price, instead of being equal to the market price of the stock on the date of grant, is set to equal the lowest price at which the stock was traded during the option's ten-year term.

A favorite risk-reducing technique, of course, is to forget about stock options, and even reload options, and simply to give the CEO totally free shares. With restricted shares—which is the usual way of conveying free shares to an executive—the CEO is guaranteed a pay-out as long as the stock price doesn't fall all the way to zero. And he also receives the dividends to boot. There is no pretense here about putting the CEO in the same boat as the shareholders. Rather, he boards the *QE2* with his head held high and the band playing his favorite marching song.

Of course, it is troubling to consider that your take from a grant of restricted shares will diminish in the event your company's stock price declines. Not to worry. Just act like the board of AMR, the parent company to American Airlines, and authorize a floor price. That way, if the stock price declines, the company will simply write you a check to make up the amount of the decline. And if the stock price rises, you get to keep all the extra profits.

AMR is run by fifty-five-year-old Robert Crandall, who by all accounts is a fire-breathing tough guy—perhaps in part because he is rarely without a cigarette in hand. He seems to have elevated the goal of beating out all other airlines into something of a *jihad,* or holy war. He not only has spearheaded such revenue-raising measures as taking American overseas, but has been at the forefront of the company's cost reduction efforts, as typified by his personal decision to remove the olives from American's in-flight salads, for a savings of $40,000 per year. Even though their salads are now oliveless, travelers consistently rate American as the very best airline in the United States.

AMR has been pretty good to shareholders—as airline stocks go. In an analysis of 120 ten-year total shareholder returns over the past 20 years, AMR scored only at the 30th percentile of the distribution. However, when the most recent 80, 40, and 20 ten-year total return periods are examined, AMR rises, respectively, to the 50th, 49th, and 63rd percentiles. So Robert Crandall, besides garnering rave reviews from travelers, is also starting to improve the take for shareholders.

Turning to matters of pay, Crandall's pay package at AMR is noteworthy only in two respects. First, the sum of his base salary and annual bonus seems to float free of such mundane matters as the company's performance. Indeed, he has never had a bad year; too bad the same can't be said for his company. For 1985, he earned a base salary of $381,000 and a bonus of like amount. AMR itself earned $5.94 per share after taxes and before extraordinary items and enjoyed a very respectable 17.1% return on average shareholders' equity. In 1986, his base salary rose to $454,000, and his bonus once again equaled his base salary. But earnings per share declined from $5.94 to $4.63, and return on equity dropped from 17.1% to 11.7%. (In fairness to Crandall, he was not the CEO of AMR for the entire twelve months of 1985; during the first two months of the year, he was AMR's chief operating officer. So the increase in his pay between 1985 and 1986 would probably would have been less had he been CEO for the entire year in 1985.) In 1987, Crandall's base salary was raised again, this time to $500,000, and his bonus continued to match his base salary. AMR's performance declined even further, however. Earnings per share for the year were $3.28, while return on equity was a measly 7.4%. Then profits rebounded in 1988 (earnings per share more than doubled, from $3.28 to $7.92, while return on equity increased from 7.4% to 15.6%). But demonstrating once again that there is no essential correlation between what Crandall earns and what AMR achieves, Crandall's compensation stayed the same. His base salary continued at $500,000, and his bonus, for the fourth year in a row, matched his base salary.

In 1989, earnings per share once again declined—from $7.92 to $7.16, and return on equity sank to 12.9%. In that same year, Crandall's salary was increased to $567,000, and for the very first time, his bonus was not equal to his salary. In what must be seen as a vigorous pay-for-performance move by AMR's board of directors, Crandall's bonus was cut from 100% of his base salary down to 95% of salary. However, his bonus, expressed in dollars, rose from $500,000 to $538,000. And for good measure, his base salary was raised to $600,000 in 1990. As of this writing, Crandall's bonus for his performance during 1990 has not been announced, given that AMR reports its bonuses one year late compared to other companies. The year 1990 was a bad one for AMR; the company lost $0.64 per share. But, as we have seen, bad years do hardly any damage to Bob Crandall's bonus. A cynical prediction, based on the fact that Crandall's bonus has been 100% of his salary for four of the last five years, would be another 100% of salary. But that prediction is probably too cynical; after all, AMR lost money in 1990. So how about a prediction of 90% of salary? Naw, better make it 80%.

Crandall's steadily-up-as-she-goes pay pattern, though disappointing from a pay-for-performance viewpoint, is in some ways less burdensome for a company's shareholders than the more familiar pattern we have seen several times earlier in this book. That more frequent pattern reveals that when profits rise sharply, so does the pay of the CEO. But when profits fall sharply, his pay hardly drops at all or actually rises.

In 1988, I looked at the performance and pay of fourteen CEOs whose companies' returns on equity had been highly cyclical over the previous five years. I chose to study return on equity because it is generally regarded as the single most important measure of accounting performance. I found that by 1988, median ROE for the fourteen companies was only 9% higher than it had been in 1984. But median executive pay was 56% higher. It got there through the route just mentioned: big increases when performance went up, coupled with no decreases, or even small increases, when performance went down.

The second reason why Crandall's pay package is noteworthy concerns a lavish restricted stock grant the board gave him in 1988. (Technically speaking, the grant actually consisted of deferred shares, rather than restricted shares, but for all practical purposes, there is no distinction between the two categories, and so I will refer to them as restricted shares.) The grant consisted of 355,000 shares, with restrictions lapsing over an eight-year period. At the time the grant was made, AMR's share price was $33.20 per share, so the value of all 355,000 shares was $11.8 million.

By now, readers should be relatively unfazed when they encounter $12 million of restricted stock. After all, Martin Davis of Paramount Communications received a grant worth around $25 million in a single year. But Crandall's restricted stock contained a neat twist: If AMR's share price was less than $33.20 on the dates the restrictions lapsed, the board would give him a cash payment to make up the difference. In other words, Crandall was guaranteed that he would receive the same $33.20 per share value as existed on the day he received his restricted stock grant.

A while back, we talked about the "heads I win, tails you lose" mentality that is increasingly prevalent in executive compensation circles. And here we find a prime example of it. If AMR's share price rises, Crandall receives all of the increase. But if the share price drops, he suffers none of the decrease.

Crandall's grant raises two questions. First, did the board of directors factor in the added economic value associated with a downside protection feature? Clearly, 355,000 regular restricted shares do not have the same worth as 355,000 shares with a floor stock price. If the board did not consider the extra value, as I suspect, then it simply gave Crandall more money than it had in mind to give him, thereby wasting more of the shareholders' assets. Second, leaving aside questions of extra costs, could the grant be considered a proper incentive for Crandall? One of the ostensible purposes of using stock in an executive's compensation package is to foster a greater identification of his interests with those of the shareholders. But offering a floor protection feature—something the normal shareholder does not have—hardly seems a reasonable way to foster such an interest. Moreover, it could be argued that the stock grant might have the unintended effect of encouraging Crandall to take more business risks than necessary. After all, if the risk pays off and the stock price rises to $100 per share, he will become an even richer man. But if it doesn't pay off and the stock price drops to $10 per share, he will not lose a cent.

It is also troubling to consider that when the restrictions lapse on restricted shares, you will have to ante up some money to pay the tax collector. Not to worry. Just persuade your board to ape the boards of Georgia-Pacific and Bally Manufacturing and promise you a sum of cash that will not only be sufficient to pay all the taxes on your restricted share grant but sufficient to pay the taxes on the sum of cash as well.

Finally, if you're really into worrying, you can think about the fact that, while restricted stock offers a sure payout even if the stock price declines, you might not make as much money if the stock price rises as you might have made had you been granted a larger number of stock option shares. To illustrate here, let's assume that a board is willing to grant a CEO 10,000 restricted shares at a time when the stock price is selling for $50 per share. Ignoring the fact that some restrictions on resale are present, the value of these shares at the time of their grant is just what the New York Stock Exchange says it is, namely, $50 per share, or $500,000 for all 10,000 shares. Now if we apply option-pricing techniques, the value at grant of a stock option, one carrying a strike price of $50.00 per share and a ten-year term, is apt to be around $14.50 per share. Hence, to obtain the same $500,000 of value at the time of grant, the company, alternatively, could grant the executive an option on a rounded 35,000 shares. At $14.50 each, 35,000 option shares would have the same $500,000 total value as 10,000 free shares.

At this point, let's consider the economic trade-off between a 10,000-share restricted stock grant and a 35,000-share stock option grant. If the stock price rises from $50 to $70 per share, both grants will have the same value. The 10,000-share restricted stock grant will be worth 10,000 × $70.00, or $700,000. And as for the 35,000-share option grant, each share will have appreciated by $20, producing the same $700,000 gain on all 35,000 shares. If the future stock price is less than $70 per share, the CEO would have been better off with the 10,000-share restricted stock grant. But if the future stock price is higher than $70 per share, the CEO would have been better off with the 35,000-share stock option grant. Considering here that the option has a term of ten years and that achieving a $70 per share stock price by the end of the tenth year following grant requires stock price appreciation of a scant 3.4% per year, you would think that any CEO with the least amount of American get-up-and-go in his genes would always choose the more risky 35,000-share stock option over the less risky 10,000-share restricted stock grant. But, unhappily for our economy, such is not likely to be the case. And such is not likely to be the case even though the CEO can call the timing of the grant, can choose when to exercise the option shares, and can probably convince his board to offer him an option swap in the event the stock price declines. (Our example is a bit overdrawn, because the restricted stock is likely to generate dividends. But even assuming a normal dividend yield of, say, 3.5% per year, the stock option will produce the same value as the restricted stock grant with total return of 6.9% per year, or only about the same return an investor can receive by putting his money in riskless, ninety-day Treasury bills.)

Recently, this "pay me, no matter what" philosophy has been given further expression in a new form of compensation—the so-called tandem grant of restricted shares and stock option shares. Suppose your employer offered to give you either 1,000 restricted shares having a value of $50 each or 5,000 option shares carrying a strike price of $50 per share. Which would you take? In making your choice, you would know, of course, that if you chose the 5,000 option shares, you would stand to earn an extra $5,000 for each one dollar increase in stock price, whereas if you chose the 1,000 restricted shares, you would earn only an extra $1,000. Hence, you would know that you would make more money from 5,000 option shares than 1,000 restricted shares, provided there was a decent increase in the share price. By the same token, you would know that you would be better off with the restricted shares in the event the stock price dropped rather than rose. There's only one thing you wouldn't know, and that is what will happen in the future. Will the stock price rise, and by how much? Or will it fall, and by how much? Predicting the future, you must have discovered by now, is fraught with problems.

But suppose you weren't required to predict the future. Suppose you could make your choice by waiting a number of years and then looking backward. Now, wouldn't that be a fun compensation plan? International Paper must have thought so, because the board gave its CEO, John Georges, a grant of 40,000 restricted shares, or 200,000 option shares. And it told him that, after a wait of several years, he could look backward and choose which of the grants he wished to keep.

Note here that International Paper offered its CEO 5 times more stock option shares than restricted shares, in contrast to the ratio of 3.5 times used above in our typical company example. The use of a higher ratio, of course, lowers the equilibrium point—the point at which the restricted shares and the option shares produce the same economic value to the executive. Assuming that the market price at grant was $50.00 per share (which it approximately was), the equilibrium point, instead of being $70.00 per share, is only $62.50 per share. In other words, all it takes to make the option worth more than the restricted share is a paltry 2.3% per year compounded rate of stock price appreciation during the ten-year term of the stock option. (Add a normal dividend yield of 3.5%, and the equilibrium point is still an ultra low 5.8%.) That level of price appreciation ought to be achievable even if the CEO was selected to run the company by randomly picking a name out of the Manhattan telephone directory. Nonetheless, if the person selected turns out to have only limited talent, there is always the 40,000-share restricted stock grant on which to fall back. If the stock price should decline from $50 per share to, say, $25 per share, the CEO will still earn

40,000 × $25, or $1 million. Plus dividends.

All we need do now is to attach a reload feature to the 200,000 option shares (which International Paper has done), assure the CEO that his option shares will be swapped in the event the stock price declines, add a floor price to the restricted stock and pile on a tax reimbursement feature, and we will have the greatest compensation plan going. It will have the minor disadvantage of giving the CEO millions in payouts even though the shareholders' leaky rowboat has headed for Davy Jones's locker. But you can't expect perfection every time.

As of this writing, the U.S. economy is in a recession, the depth and the length of which are unknown. It will be during this recession that all the aforementioned moves to reduce the risk in a CEO's pay package will show up in spades. The pay of the typical worker will decline, first because of wage freezes or even rollbacks, and second because of layoffs. But, unless all these risk-reducing mechanism contain some hidden flaw, the pay of your typical CEO will hardly decline at all. And when the stock price has hit bottom, huge numbers of option shares will be granted, thereby guaranteeing that the CEO, who missed the opportunity to participate in the hard times, will not be denied the opportunity to participate in the good times that are ahead.

Everyone on Wall Street dreams about the perfect investment— one that promises high, indeed, almost infinite, reward and virtually no risk. No one has yet found that perfect investment. But that's because Wall Streeters, on the evidence, insist on employing conventional economic reasoning. They don't know enough to talk to the compensation consultants. If they did, they would learn that there is an almost perfect investment—one that promises high, indeed, almost infinite, reward and virtually no risk. And that is a CEO's pay package. Once they acquire this gem of knowledge, they ought to be able quickly to apply their packaging techniques to produce a security that would emulate the beauty of what a CEO gets. The payouts ought to be a lot better than those obtained by investing in the old-fashioned way: putting up your money, taking risk, and hoping there's a reward out there.

Twelve

The Perk Barrel

YEARS AGO, when I was just starting my career, I worked for a division of General Dynamics that was manufacturing the Atlas IBCM. Not long after I joined General Dynamics, our office received a new perquisite—a vending machine that dispensed, according to your choice, black coffee, coffee with cream, coffee with cream and sugar, tea, and chicken soup. It was surely welcomed, and it was used a great deal. It had only one flaw: If you happened to follow an employee who had just caused the machine to dispense chicken soup, you got a good-sized dollop of chicken fat in your cup of coffee.

My first experience with perquisites was a far cry from the perquisite-studded life of the late William S. Paley, the legendary chairman of CBS. Here, reconstructed from my own personal interaction with him as a client, is a typical day in Paley's business life. Paley awakened, was served breakfast in bed while watching the CBS Morning News, was dressed by his valet, and then departed, depending on the day, from his apartment on Fifth Avenue or his home in Southampton, New York. So far he received no perquisites, since the tab was on him.

If he was departing from his New York apartment, he entered his limousine for the short ride to Black Rock, CBS's stark granite headquarters on West 52nd Street. The car and the driver were paid by CBS. If he was departing from his Southampton beach home, he boarded a helicopter. The helicopter and pilots were presumably paid by CBS. After the helicopter landed in New York, his limousine took him to the CBS Building.

When he arrived at CBS's headquarters, he boarded a private elevator, which whisked him to the thirty-fifth floor, where his office was located. During his short trip from the limousine to the elevator, it was unlikely that he had any human contact, save a possible nod to the elevator starter. And, of course, no one but him was allowed in the elevator.

Paley spent the morning working behind closed doors. If he desired anything to eat or drink, it was served by a white-coated waiter. And given his legendary appetite, he was served something to eat or drink quite often. At lunchtime, Paley moved only a very few feet to his private dining room. There he, and any guests he happened to have that day, were served an elegant lunch. After lunch, he might have enjoyed a good cup of coffee—one without any chicken fat floating on top. Better yet, the lunch was on CBS.

After an afternoon of further work, Paley was ready to depart the CBS Building. One of his secretaries signalled the receptionist on the thirty-fifth floor, and she pressed a button at her workstation, which in turn summoned an elevator. Then, with its down button blinking in time with a softly chiming sound, the elevator waited until Paley was ready to board it. If he found it necessary to take a last-minute phone call, the elevator continued to wait. No matter that ordinary CBS employees on lower floors were required to wait even longer for an elevator and, when it finally arrived, to jam themselves into it like sardines. After riding the elevator in blessed silence, Paley once again boarded his limousine for the short trip to his Fifth Avenue apartment or to the heliport.

It's a good bet that during this typical workday, Bill Paley never said a word or rubbed shoulders with other than the high and mighty—excepting, of course, a couple of secretaries and the receptionist on the thirty-fifth floor. Oh, and don't forget the elevator starter.

Perhaps with his helicopter and private elevator and private dining room, Paley had more than the usual number of perquisites, but many CEOs are today becoming increasingly isolated from the troops they lead. No George Patton act for them—what with the danger of riding in the lead tank, pearl-handled revolver at one's side, while duking it out with the Germans during World War II. Or, to update the analogy a bit, no Norman Schwarzkopf act for them. The general, it seems, politely declined a Saudi offer of an elegant villa for his use during the Gulf War; instead, he opted for a single sparely furnished room adjacent to his office. No, today's CEO's idea of leadership is to watch the carnage from a Rolls-Royce command car, while enjoying an elegant lunch catered by the Four Seasons.

Besides costing shareholders a lot of money, perquisites also have the effect of isolating the CEO and perhaps fooling him into thinking that everybody lives like he lives. Let's review some of the wonderful perquisites that are lavished on the denizens of the corner office these days.

Almost everybody has a car and driver. But in a growing number of cases, the car is a stretch Cadillac or Lincoln or a top-of-the-line Mercedes or even a Bentley or Rolls-Royce. And the driver is dressed in high boots and the obligatory chauffeur's cap. But he is not your ordinary driver. He has taken a course in limousine security, learning in the process how to turn the behemoth on a dime. And turning a monster limo on a dime is no easy trick—especially when it has been armor-plated. All of these security arrangements are ostensibly to protect the CEO from terrorists; however, there aren't that many terrorists working in U.S. cities nowadays, so the security arrangements are able to do double duty by insulating—and, depending on the company's performance, perhaps even protecting—the CEO from his shareholders.

If the CEO has to travel out of town, there is a corporate helicopter for short trips and a palatial corporate jet for longer trips. I have been on many such jets during my career as a consultant. They share two characteristics in common. First, though a company may be running ad after ad to polish its corporate image, you will never find any identifying marks on the outside of the corporate jet. The last thing a CEO wants is to note the hostile stare of some shareholder who is crammed in the middle coach seat of a regular commercial airliner that is being held interminably on the runway apron. The second characteristic of corporate jet is their extreme luxury inside the cabin. Top decorators are often retained to ply their craft, with the result that the plane no longer looks like a plane, but rather resembles the atmosphere of a posh private club, replete with dark wood paneling and a lot of brass.

Corporate jets are a joy. I remember some years ago flying from New York to Europe and back on the corporate jet of one of my clients. On the return trip, I got to sit in the chairman's special chair, because he was elsewhere. The chair was really more like a throne. Upon entering the jet, you saw it instantly: it sat all by itself, and was much wider and higher than every other seat. Then, at about 45,000 feet of altitude, I called my wife on the skyphone and informed her that we had just entered U.S. airspace and would be landing at the Westchester County Airport in about an hour. Upon landing, I and the other occupants of the plane kept drinking and listening to good music, while we waited a few moments for the customs inspectors to board the plane. The inspectors had been brought all the way from Kennedy Airport to handle our entry into the United States, with the cost being borne by my client's company. No long lines in front of the customs booth for us; we were cleared while lounging in our seats, drinks still in hand. And no pushing and shoving at the baggage carousel; we merely walked out the door of our jet and stepped into waiting limousines, which were parked ten feet from the jet's door. The luggage was then quickly transferred, and I was off for home. Upon arriving, I suffered a severe case of culture shock, because I had to lug our three garbage cans to the curb for the next day's pickup. Oh well, it was a fun trip.

During my trip from Europe on my client's jet, I also had a chance to chat with a couple of delightful women, both of them spouses of senior executives. A lot of companies permit the spouses of senior executives to use company planes, and having your spouse along surely makes the trip more enjoyable. Indeed, the *New York Times* has reported that F. Ross Johnson, the former chairman of RJR Nabisco and perhaps the world's greatest user of perquisites, ordered that a second private plane be rolled out to transport his dog, whose name on the manifest was carried as G. Shepard. Seems that G. Shephard had "an alleged tendency to bite people."

There is sometimes a bit of perversity surrounding the use of the corporate jet. One time, I was chatting with the chairman of a major motion picture company while he was packing his briefcase for a trip from New York to Los Angeles. I asked him how he was flying, and he told me he was going on the corporate jet. I responded with surprise that the plane could make it non-stop from New York to Los Angeles. He replied that the plane could not make it non-stop, and then he told me about a strange airport located in, I believe, Kansas. He said: "It's something to behold. We roar in out of the night, land and are refueled right at the end of the runway. Then we take off again, and the whole process doesn't take five minutes."

What a great demonstration of American efficiency. Now let's see, if you flew first class from New York to Los Angeles on, say, American Airlines, you might incur a cost of around $2,000 for the round-trip fare, and you would get to Los Angeles in about six hours. On the other hand, if you travel on the corporate jet, the cost to the company—including the pay of the two pilots, operating costs, maintenance, and depreciation—might run to $15,000. On top of that, the trip will take, not six hours, but perhaps close to eight hours, what with the stop in Kansas and the fact that the jet can't travel as fast as a commercial airliner. Oh well, CEOs have to make sacrifices just like the rest of us.

Another sacrifice that internationally minded CEOs are making nowadays is to forsake the Concorde for their corporate jets when traveling to Europe. Here again, we find some interesting trade-offs. Traveling on the Concorde, though quite expensive, is still cheap compared to hauling a corporate jet across an ocean. Moreover, the CEO has to sacrifice a lot of time; the Concorde takes perhaps three and one-half hours, while the corporate jet may take eight to ten hours, depending on whether a refueling stop in Iceland or Ireland is needed. However, within the next few years, we are about to see this time sacrifice eliminated. Enter the Gulfstream supersonic corporate jet, a joint project between Gulfstream and the Soviet Union. This baby will be even faster than the Concorde, traveling at up to 1,800 miles per hour. It is expected to cost $50 million per copy. Will that huge cost, not to mention operating and maintenance costs, stop your typical CEO? Not at all. Being the first on your block to own a supersonic corporate jet is the closest thing to an irresistible impulse that a CEO will ever experience. Of course, buying such a plane when almost all your operations are in the United States may present a bit of a problem. But with a quick phone call, the company's investment bankers can be pressed into finding some international ventures into which the CEO can pour shareholder money— money that might have been better spent on increasing the dividend rate.

Contrary to what you might think, the cost of a new supersonic corporate jet is not apt to attract any objections from the company's board of directors. After all, one of the perks they often are given is the opportunity to attend board meetings held at places away from the company's headquarters—places like London, Paris, Lake Como. And how do they reach these faraway places? You get the idea.

Once the CEO lands somewhere, he doesn't step out of his corporate jet and board a bus from the airport to his hotel. Rather, there is the usual limousine waiting by the steps of the jet. The hotel is the best in town. The room is a suite filled with fresh flowers and tempting delicacies. And the meals are eaten at the very finest of restaurants, with the ever present limousine waiting at the curbside.

Many CEOs lunch in private dining rooms. The dinnerware is the finest Spode, the tableware is sterling silver, the room is filled with flowers changed daily, and the food is prepared by a chef who was probably lured away from one of Manhattan's finest restaurants. No restaurant can even begin to compete in pay with a CEO whose stomach is growling and whose checks are written on the company's bank account. Indeed, one CEO I know was so intent on recruiting the chef of a top Manhattan restaurant that he even offered the candidate a 10,000-share stock option; as it turned out, that clinched the deal. Remember, too, that the CEO, besides getting to eat better than his subordinates, gets to eat free. And if he comes to work early enough, he gets a free breakfast, too.

So far, we've taken care of the CEO's stomach. But he has to sleep somewhere, hence there's another problem to solve. Simple: just get him a company-paid apartment. As noted earlier, ITT (only one among a number of companies) for some years paid most of the costs of an in-town Manhattan apartment for its CEO, Rand Araskog. In other client situations I have experienced, CEOs have been given palatial suites at the Carlyle and the Waldorf-Astoria Towers, two of Manhattan's poshest hotels. I recall that the annual rent on the Waldorf Towers apartment was $135,000 per year, and that was in 1983 dollars.

In the case of CEOs working in Manhattan, the company-paid apartment may also confer an additional perk—avoiding onerous New York State and New York City income taxes. The CEO with the suite in the Carlyle has his principal home (i.e., the one he pays for himself) in Connecticut, a state which has no income tax (but may soon, if the state's new governor, Lowell Weicker, has his way). Now, if the Carlyle apartment were registered in the CEO's name and used exclusively by him, he would be deemed a resident of New York, despite his main residence in Connecticut, and he would end up paying full New York State and New York City income taxes, unless he could find a way to stay out of New York for more than 183 days each year. But in this case, the apartment is registered in the company's name. And the company maintains the fiction that the apartment is not held for the exclusive use of the CEO. Translation: Every so often, when the CEO is out of town, the apartment is deliberately offered for use to some junior executive who is visiting Manhattan on business. One such junior executive I talked to told me that he had a great time living in the lap of luxury during a week in New York. But he did mention one problem: he couldn't find any room in the closets to hang his clothes, because the clothes of the chairman and his wife had taken up every inch of pole space.

Sometimes a company also provides its CEO with a vacation spot. Back in the early 1970s, I was twice invited to spend a weekend at a posh retreat maintained by International Paper. That company owned a forest in the Adirondack Mountains, a few hours' drive from New York City. The forest was logged every thirty years or so, but the loggers never got even close to the executive retreat, which was surrounded on one side by a huge mountain lake and on the other by a nine-hole golf course.

CEOs also belong to country clubs and have memberships at posh in-town eating clubs. The costs here are also borne by the grateful shareholders. And they can be quite steep, considering that a CEO like Ross Johnson (head of RJR Nabisco until its recent takeover) may belong to many clubs, and that the initiation fees for each club may exceed $50,000.

One of the newest perquisites has for the moment been extended only to outside directors. One company I have worked with permits each of its outside directors to will $1 million to a charitable institution, with the company footing the bill. Hence, when the director dies, Harvard or Yale receives enough money to fund a chair. By rights, the chair should be named after the company, since the bill was paid by the company; but, you guessed it, the chair is named after the director. When I expressed some concern over the cost of this beneficence, the head of personnel at this company told me not to worry. He said that the company was funding the $1 million bequests by purchasing so-called corporate-owned life insurance on the director's life, and that, based on the assumptions provided by the insurance company, there would be no cost at all; in effect, the proceeds of the insurance would be sufficient to pay for the $1 million bequest and to return to the company, even with a bit of interest, all the funds it had earlier expended in premiums. When I heard this, I was so excited that I suggested that the company extend this $1 million bequest to every employee and to every shareholder as well. After all, if doing so costs nothing, why not make everybody feel good? And to the extent that other companies didn't follow suit, the $1 million gift to each shareholder surely ought to help raise the price of the stock. I received only stunned silence in reply.

Perks have been carried to excess in a number of situations. Herewith a sampling. J. Walter Thompson, the giant New York advertising agency, used to maintain an executive dining room that was actually excavated from a country farmhouse and moved to New York. The cost of maintaining the dining room, which has since been closed, as well as other executive accommodations, was around $4 million per year. Moreover, one executive had a butler deliver him a peeled orange each day. It seems unbelievable to me, but the august *New York Times* reported that the cost of that orange ran to around $300 per day, or $80,000 per year. Some orange!

Shearson Lehman Hutton, as the huge brokerage and investment banking firm was then called, built a ski lodge in Vail, Colorado, for use by its executives and presumably the company's biggest clients. Surrounding the ski lodge were twelve sumptuous townhouses. Interiors were handled by a top New York decorator. Total cost—around $25 million. And Time Warner maintains a company house in Acapulco. Its use is said to be personally controlled by the two co-CEOs who run the company.

The government is suing Thomas Spiegel, the ex-head of the failed Columbia Savings & Loan Association. Among other things, the government has taken exception to the $1.1 million cost of four company condominiums, two in Jackson Hole, Wyoming, one in Indian Wells, California (near Palm Springs), and one in Deer Valley, Utah; to $463,000 paid to Spiegel for personal expenses, including four trips to Europe for Spiegel and his wife; to $55,000 in gun purchases; to $7,000 in tickets for Michael Jackson and other rock star concerts; to $2,000 for a French wine-tasting course; and to $1,700 for silverware.

Merrill Lynch has spent lavishly on perks at the very time it has been laying off employees. However, its president, Daniel P. Tully, fails to see how the two are related. He was quoted in the *New York Times* as saying: "It's so small in terms of people's thinking—to pick on a trip or attack the use of a helicopter. I hope God will give them a larger perspective and less of a jealous streak."

Perhaps the ultimate perk of all was given to the late Dr. Armand

Hammer. The company, and hence the company's shareholders, picked up the $95 million cost of building a public museum in Los Angeles to house the undistinguished art collection of the late doctor. By rights, the museum should have been named the Occidental Petroleum Museum of Art and Cultural Center; it actually was named the Armand Hammer Museum of Art and Cultural Center.

Lost in all the glitter of limousines and corporate jets is an entirely different, and relatively new, class of executive perks. And these babies can add mightily to corporate compensation costs. First, we have the Supplemental Executive Retirement Plan, or SERP for short. Prior to 1974, the year the Employee Retirement Income Security Act (ERISA—or what Richard Furlaud, long the CEO of Squibb, liked to call "Every Rejected Idea Since Adam!") came into being, an executive who reached retirement age after working for his company for, say, thirty years, might have been given a pension equal to 60% of the base salary he earned in typically the five years preceding his retirement. But ERISA put a lid on how much so-called qualified pension plans would be permitted to pay. The initial cap was a pension of $75,000 per year, with the amount being increased each year according to the Consumer Price Index. The cap eventually rose to around $135,000 per year, before being cut back by the government to $90,000, with the cost-of-living escalation starting all over again.

That pension cap caused quite a few problems. Consider the CEO whose final base salary was $500,000 per year. His pension plan called for him to receive a pension of 60%-of-salary, or $300,000 per year. But now the government, at the eleventh hour, was telling the company it could pay him only $75,000 per year. However, a careful reading of what the government was saying revealed that the cap applied only to payments made from a qualified pension plan—the type of pension plan most people have, where payments are made to an outside trust and invested for the eventual benefit of employees. There was nothing in the law, as it turned out, to bar the company from offering an executive a so-called non-qualified pension plan. There were two drawbacks to such non-qualified plans, however. First, contributions to the plan had to remain on the company's balance sheet and could not be sent to an outside trustee. Hence, if the company later went belly up, the assets standing behind the non-qualified pension plan might be lost and the pension terminated early. Second, the company was not permitted to take a tax deduction for payments under a non-qualified pension plan until the payments were made; in contrast, the company stood to receive an immediate tax deduction when it made contributions to a qualified pension plan, even though those contributions wouldn't be paid out in pensions for many years.

Problems notwithstanding, companies rushed to adopt SERPs. So, using the above example, our retiring CEO received, not one pension check for $300,000 per year, but rather two pension checks, one for $75,000 from the qualified plan and the second for $225,000 from the SERP.

So far the CEO would not seem to have gained anything from the passage of ERISA, the SERP notwithstanding. He still ended up getting the same $300,000 per year in pension income. What's more, he now had to take greater risk, given that $225,000 of the income could be lost if his company later failed. But we haven't finished our story, because once SERPs came into being, imaginative pension consultants started to hang lots of bright shiny ornaments on them.

The first ornament was to change the definition of pensionable pay, from base salary to the sum of base salary and annual bonus. Hence, if our hypothetical CEO had been earning a base salary of $500,000 and had been receiving an annual bonus of $300,000, his pension increased from 60% of $500,000 to 60% of $800,000. A neat idea like that doesn't just get adopted by one company; rather, it spreads like a Southern California brushfire fanned by a Santa Ana wind. Soon, the great majority of companies began to offer this new definition of pensionable income to their senior executives. When asked by some critics why, if the company was going to base the pension of the CEO on his total current income, it didn't do the same for the ordinary worker and therefore include the worker's earnings from overtime work, the public relations department responded that overtime was transitory income. Unwittingly, the PR department implicitly conceded that the CEO's bonus income was other than transitory—something that could, of course, have been discerned by a careful reading of past company proxy statements, given that the CEO's bonus seemed to float serenely free of the company's wildly swinging profits.

However, the change in the definition of pensionable pay from base salary only to base salary plus annual bonus went for the most part unremarked. It was too obscure to attract anyone's attention, although the issue did flare up briefly in 1990 when the General Motors proxy disclosed that Roger Smith, who was then retiring as the company's CEO, was going to have his pension approximately doubled because of a change in the definition of pensionable pay. (His new pension would be $1.2 million per year. After adding Social Security on top, the likelihood that Smith would have to worry about his next meal became pretty remote.)

Some companies have not been content merely to make the CEO's bonus pensionable. They have gone on to make payments under long-term incentive plans—even including stock option gains—pensionable. And they have reduced, but only for senior executives, the number of years required to earn any given level of pension. And they have provided, but again only for senior executives, that retirement can occur earlier than age sixty-five—as early as age fifty-five—with no actuarial reduction in the amount of pension income being received.

All of these insidious trends combined in 1990 to produce a monster pension for David Maxwell, the CEO of the Federal National Mortgage Association, popularly known as Fannie Mae, who retired in January 1991. Fannie Mae had been formed by the federal government forty-three years before Maxwell came in as CEO in 1981, but it had been performing poorly.

Fannie Mae's principal business involves home mortgages. It typically buys mortgages written by commercial banks and other lending institutions, securitizes them, and then sells the resulting securities. As a result, the U.S. home mortgage market becomes more liquid, and commercial banks receive funds from Fannie Mae that permit them to make even more home mortgages. The company enjoys two advantages that commercial banks do not enjoy.

First, it borrows money with the implicit guarantee of the federal government. Some experts opine that its borrowing costs are lowered by about 30 basis points (0.3%). Now a 30-basis-point reduction in borrowing costs doesn't sound like much, but when you are borrowing in the tens of billions, those savings add up. Second, Fannie Mae is not required to have the same amount of equity supporting each dollar of borrowings as a normal commercial bank. Hence, it can stretch each of its shareholders' investment dollars further and thereby earn a higher return on equity.

Maxwell proceeded to turn Fannie Mae around smartly. By the end of his ten-year tenure, investors who had bought the company's stock when he joined the company had received a 26% compounded annual return on their investment. When he retired at age sixty, Maxwell was entitled to a pension of $1.4 million per year. However, he opted to take his pension in the form of a lump-sum payment, instead of a series of payments for the remainder of his life and that of his spouse, assuming she survived him. The lump sum was a staggering $20 million, and there will likely be a bit more coming in early 1992 after the company calculates Maxwell's performance unit award for the three-year period ending in 1991.

How in the world did Maxwell end up receiving a pension for ten years of service that was more than twice his final base salary of $650,000 per year? Well, for openers, his pension was not predicated merely on his base salary. Fannie Mae had adopted a definition of pensionable pay that included not only Maxwell's base salary but also his annual bonus and, most important, his payments earned under the company's long-term Performance Unit Plan. Remember that Fannie Mae performed spectacularly under Maxwell. Thus, he earned big annual bonuses and big performance unit payouts, and those payments went straight into his pension base. Second, Maxwell's pension was predicated on his pay during the last three years of his service. At other companies, a pension would normally be predicated on earnings during the last five years of service. Since Maxwell's pay rose explosively at the end of his tenure, predicating his pension on his pay during the last three years of service gave him some additional monies. Third, Maxwell's pension consisted of 60%

of his final pay. At most companies, a pension of 60% of final pay would not be payable until the executive had served around thirty years with the company. In Maxwell's case, the length of service was only ten years, thereby requiring the awesome cost of his pension to be amortized over a shorter period of service. Fourth, and finally, Maxwell's pension arrangement entitled him to retire at age sixty, with no actuarial reduction in his pension. At most companies, if you retire before age sixty-five, the pension you receive is smaller than the one you would have received had you waited to retire until age sixty-five. After all, by retiring earlier, you are likely to be receiving your pension for more years before you die.

An executive of Fannie Mae with whom I spoke shortly after David Maxwell's pension amount was disclosed told me that the company had never intended to give him such a large pension. As he explained it, no one foresaw that the company's performance would be so magnificent and Maxwell's incentive payments so great. His explanation seems a bit lame, especially considering that Fannie Mae's business centers on numbers. Couldn't someone have run a few scenarios before Maxwell was given his pension promise and discovered what was going to happen, with mathematical certainty, if Maxwell hit the ball out of the park?

In short, costs for senior executive pensions have skyrocketed in recent years, in large part because ERISA started people thinking about the subject. If ever a piece of government legislation had unintended consequences, ERISA surely did.

Companies also routinely supplement the life and medical insurance they give to their senior executives. So, if the beneficiaries of an ordinary employee who dies are entitled to, say, two times his final base salary, the CEO's beneficiaries may be entitled to eight times his base salary. And though the ordinary employee has to pay a medical insurance deductible out of his own pocket and go on to foot 20% of all additional bills for medical procedures, and 50% of all bills for dental and psychiatric services, the CEO gets 100% of his medical, dental, and psychiatric bills reimbursed, with no deductible whatsoever. Reimbursing an otherwise small deductible doesn't give the CEO much of a benefit. But forgiving the payment of 20% to 50%

of constantly escalating medical bills makes the deal considerably more interesting. And if the CEO has six neurotic children with bad bites, the savings can be terrific.

Almost all companies offer their senior executives something called personal financial counseling. The executive, within wide limits, can choose his own financial adviser, and the company foots the entire bill. The rationale: If the company pays for the executive's professional financial advice, the executive will not need to spend as much time worrying about his own financial affairs and will thereby be able to devote the time saved to worrying about his company's financial affairs.

Many companies also pay bills to have their outside auditors prepare the CEO's tax return. And they go on to pay legal bills as well, including the preparation of wills, divorce settlements, and the like.

No self-respecting executive joining a company from the outside these days does so without a front-end, or signing, bonus. And in many cases, the bonus is in the seven figures. At the same time, the entering executive may be given a bonus guarantee; hence, he does not have to worry that if the company's fortunes sag right after he joins, he will lose some or all of his normal bonus. Typically, the bonus guarantee lasts for two or three years, although in cases like that of Dr. Armand Hammer at Occidental Petroleum, the guarantee turns out to be for life.

Sometimes, an executive entering the company is also successful in obtaining other guarantees. For example, Joseph Graziano who came to Apple Computer as chief financial officer was given a 200,000-share stock option grant. He was told, with respect to 100,000 of the 200,000 shares, that if Apple's stock price didn't increase at least $12 per share during the first year after grant, the company would give him a cash bonus to make up the difference; as to the second 100,000 option shares, if the stock price did not increase at least $15 per share during the first two years after grant, he would again be given a cash make-up.

Sears, Roebuck recently pioneered what it calls a Tax Benefit Right (TBR). When attached to an option share, a restricted share, or a performance unit, for example, the TBR confers on the executive a payment equal to the maximum federal individual tax rate on the underlying value of the compensation received. Suppose a TBR is attached to a stock option: if the gain on that option is $1 million, and if the maximum federal individual tax rate is 31%, then Sears cuts a check for the executive in the amount of $310,000. To reassure its shareholders that it hasn't given away the farm, Sears declared in its proxy that the $310,000 payment "would itself be deductible by the Company . . . for federal income tax purposes, and the Company . . . will receive the benefit, if any, from such deductions." It's terribly nice of Sears to think of its shareholders. Now if Sears's management could only find a way to revitalize a retailing business that used to be the biggest and best in the United States. . . . Judging from Sears's profit problems, it is no longer the best. And last year, it lost its biggest label to Wal-Mart.

Other companies have innovated, too. They have given their executives Stock Depreciation Rights (SDRs). Because of insider trading laws that applied until very recently, an executive who exercised a stock option usually was prohibited from selling the shares for six months. During that period, of course, the stock price might decline, thereby robbing the executive of some or all of his option profits. An SDR protects against this eventuality. If the stock price declines $10 per share between the date the option was exercised and the first date the option shares can be freely sold, the company gives the executive a check for $10 per share. Why the shareholders should want to incur additional cost in the face of a stock price decline is never mentioned. Nor is the fact that the executive gets to keep any extra gains that occur because the stock price rises, rather than falls, in the six months after the option's exercise. As bad as SDRs are, I haven't yet seen a company attach a Tax Benefit Right to a Stock Depreciation Right, but stay tuned

Finally, we have one of the most egregious perks of all, the Golden Parachute. A Golden Parachute can pay the executive millions (I have seen Golden Parachutes with payouts of up to $30 million) in the event his company is taken over and he is turned out. The nagging thing here is that companies rarely get taken over if they are high-performing; it is the ones with canine characteristics that attract raiders. Hence, the CEO ends up getting paid lots of money for abysmal performance.

The public became so incensed about Golden Parachutes that, a few years back, Congress passed legislation imposing stiff tax penalties on Golden Parachute plans the present value of which equaled or exceeded three times the executive's average total compensation in the five years preceding the takeover. The penalties included loss of the company's tax deduction on the extra compensation involved and a surcharge of 20 percentage points on the executive's personal income tax. Notwithstanding these heavy penalties, a number of companies attached what Sears would call a Tax Benefit Right to the executive's Golden Parachute; hence, if the executive had to pay extra tax, the company would ante up enough extra money to pay the tax and the added tax on the extra money.

A few companies, reasoning that ordinary workers might be in at least as much peril as senior executives in the face of a takeover, offered less, but at least some, severance benefits to all workers. In an interview with the *Detroit Free Press,* I jokingly referred to these arrangements as "Tin Parachutes," and the name stuck. But the great majority of companies did not offer Tin Parachutes because of the huge extra costs involved. The cost argument, of course, was never raised when it came to senior executives' own lavish Golden Parachutes. In effect, if your average CEO were captain of the *Titanic,* he would have beaten the women and children to the lifeboats—and by a good margin, too.

For the most part, Golden Parachutes are misnamed. They really ought to be called Golden Condoms, because, at once, they protect the executive and screw the shareholders.

Perquisites are terribly corrosive. Not only do they cost the shareholders a bundle whether or not the company performs well, but their very presence may go a long way toward assuring that the company will not perform well. Senior executives become increasingly isolated from what is really happening in their own companies. And as they move from palatial office to stretch limousine to corporate jet, they may come to believe their own press.

It is no accident, I believe, that companies that emphasize a perquisite-lean environment can often beat the pants off their competitors. Golden West Financial, an Oakland, California,-based company, is believed by many to be the best-managed S&L in the United States. And in case you don't think being the best-managed S&L is all that hard to achieve, it is considered to be one of the best-managed companies, period. According to the *Wall Street Journal,* Herbert and Marion Sandler, the husband-and-wife team who run the place, "do without corporate jets and corporate dining rooms and even corporate receptionists: Visitors to the company's 17-story headquarters are instructed by a placard to announce their own arrival on an old black telephone. Marion says she does allow herself the extravagance of a chauffeur: It is her husband, who handles that extra chore for free."

Capital Cities/ABC has been successful in recent years to the opposite degree that CBS has been unsuccessful. Its recently retired chairman, Thomas Murphy, is frugal with perquisites to the opposite degree that CBS's former chairman, William S. Paley, was lavish. Here again is what the *Wall Street Journal* has to say: "At ABC headquarters, the private dining room for top brass was shut down [shortly after Murphy merged his company, Capital Cities Broadcasting, with ABC]. So was the private executive elevator. On Mr. Murphy's first visit to the ABC Entertainment division in Los Angeles, he was greeted at the airport by a white stretch limousine. The next time? 'I took a cab.' On a recent afternoon, a hired sedan waits outside the headquarters building to drive him to a wedding. He pays the bill rather than charge the company. 'How do you think we got here?,' Mr. Murphy says, eyebrows arched. 'The business of business is a lot of little decisions every day, mixed up with a few big decisions. If the boss is chiseling, everyone else will feel they have a right to chisel.' "

Why do we have so many Bill Paleys in the world and so few Tom Murphys?

Thirteen

A Look Across the Waters

PERHAPS one could accept the high pay levels of U.S. senior executives if one could observe the same high pay levels in other major industrialized countries. But fans of high pay aren't going to find much comfort from their observations.

Before looking at pay levels in Japan, Germany, France, and the United Kingdom, let's construct a benchmark for the United States. A 1990 study showed that the average CEO among 202 major company CEOs studied was earning $1.4 million per year in total current compensation—a combination of salary and annual bonus—and $2.8 million per year in total direct compensation, a combination of salary, annual bonus, and the annualized present value of such long-term incentives as stock options, restricted stock, performance shares, and performance units. Excluded from this awesome $2.8 million total are the values for perquisites and for both regular and supplemental fringe benefits—such as pension and profit-sharing plans, and life and medical insurance coverages.

You should also keep in mind that in 1989, the year when the average major company CEO in the United States was earning $2.8 million, the average worker in the private, non-agricultural sector was earning $335.20 per week, or $17,430 per year. Hence, the average major company CEO was earning about 160 times the pay of the average U.S. worker. Even if you restrict the comparison to American's working-class bluebloods, those who work in manufacturing and whose average earnings in 1989 amounted to $429.27 per week, or $22,322 per year, the ratio is still 125 times. Either way, we're a long way from Plato's five times (which was applied to the lowest rate in the community and not the average) or J. P. Morgan and Peter Drucker's twenty times. And you should also keep in mind that the maximum tax rate on a U.S. senior executive's income is 31%, excluding any state and local income taxes. Now let's do some sightseeing.

According to Tatsuaki Kikuchi, who is manager of Human Resources-International for the giant NEC Corporation, the typical CEO of a major Japanese company earns a combination of salary and bonus of around 40 million Yen. At an exchange rate of 129 Yen to the dollar, which prevailed at the time this book was being written, that translates into total cash compensation of around $310,000 per year. The sum of $310,000 per year wouldn't even fund your typical American CEO's salary for half a year, much less his annual bonus.

Thinking that perhaps this wild pay difference would be made up by the use of lavish long-term incentives in Japan, I pressed Mr. Kikuchi in this area, only to find that there are, effectively, no long-term incentive plans in use in Japan. To be sure, many companies have broad-based stock purchase plans, in which almost any employee can purchase a few shares of stock at a modest discount from the prevailing market price. But stock options, as we know them, don't exist. And no one has even heard of restricted stock. So total direct compensation in Japan is essentially the same as total cash compensation—around $310,000 per year.

There is a considerable irony here. The Japanese regularly lecture Americans on their short-sighted behavior. How, they ask, are you ever going to be competitive unless you are willing to make long-term investments—investments that may produce only losses for years before they finally begin to pay off? Yet Japanese CEOs have no monetary incentives to engage in truly long-term behavior, while American CEOs, at least in theory, have huge monetary incentives. It is, of course, Japan that is cleaning our clock by looking to the long term.

Is it possible that money is not as strong a motivator of performance as all of us in the United States have all come to believe? In Japan, as I understand it, the game seems to be played for recognition or, if you will, standing in the community. The game is not being played for huge sums of money. Incredulous, I asked Mr. Kikuchi about the many Japanese billionaires that *Fortune* and *Forbes* talk about each year in their issues devoted to the rich and famous. He replied: "Those are the founding entrepreneurs and the real estate speculators; those are not, in most cases, the current CEOs."

Japanese senior executives do not, however, wear a hair shirt twenty-four hours out of each day. There are some pretty nice perquisites handed out, including a car and driver for senior executives and, in some cases, the use of company apartments in Tokyo (a perquisite that we've seen is not uncommon in the United States either, especially in New York City). And stories abound about the lavish entertaining that goes on nightly, with much of the talk centering on large quantities of sake consumed in the company of the fabled Geisha girls. But with total cash compensation of only $310,000, your liver would rot out or other of your vital organs would cease to work before your expenditures on entertainment rose to match the $2.8 million total direct compensation of an average American CEO.

Although Japanese executives earn far less money than their U.S. counterparts, they pay much more to the government in income taxes than in the United States. And these two facts are decidedly not counterbalancing! According to *The Economist*, the top marginal tax rate in Japan reaches 65% for taxable income above about $155,000 per year.

Because of its relatively low CEO pay rates and its relatively high income tax rates, Japan has forged a highly egalitarian society. The pay of the average industrial worker is around 2–3 million Yen. If we take the midpoint of that range, or 2.5 million Yen, and apply an exchange rate of 129 Yen to the dollar, we obtain annual pay of just over $19,000. Hence, the typical CEO earns pay that is a relatively low 16 times the pay of the average industrial worker. That is arguably more than Plato thought would be proper. But compared to the United States, Japan is egalitarian heaven.

The Germans are less egalitarian than the Japanese, but they still don't come close to the U.S. practice. According to Peter Domschke, a top executive compensation consultant in Frankfurt for Towers Perrin, a leading international compensation and employee benefits consulting firm, a typical major company CEO in Germany earns a base salary of around 800,000 Deutschemarks. At the current exchange level of 1.52 DM to the dollar, that translates into an annual base salary of around $525,000. To this is added an annual bonus opportunity of around 40% of salary, such that total current compensation is around 1.1 million DM, or about $735,000 per year. Hence, your typical German CEO earns total current compensation that is just about half the level being paid in the United States. Further, Domschke says that about half the bonus opportunity is effectively guaranteed and does not fluctuate with the company's profits. In contrast, at least half, and probably more like 75% of an American CEO's bonus, also is pretty set in concrete.

Long-term incentives are rare in Germany. Domschke notes that a tire company, Continental, adopted a long-term incentive plan, but that it didn't seem to work very well, since the company was subsequently raided by another tire company. I asked Domschke why German companies weren't jumping on the long-term incentive bandwagon, and he replied: "Germans are not very risk-oriented. They still remember the huge asset devaluations that occurred in the 1920s and right after World War II. Also, they have a certain skepticism about the equity markets, given some scandals that erupted in Germany in the 1950s."

Once again, we have a fiercely competitive country, which engages in long-term thinking, but whose senior executives have no economic incentive to do so. So, as in Japan, what you see is what you get. A German CEO's total current compensation of around $735,000 constitutes virtually all of his pay package.

Except for perquisites. German CEOs, like their counterparts all over, are given a car and driver. And the car is likely to be a very large Mercedes, one that can travel some 190 mph and frequently does—all quite legally, mind you—on the German Autobahn. They also have the usual complement of club memberships and get to fly first class. (Corporate jets are used less often, however, due to the small size of the country.) It is also not atypical to provide rent-free housing for the CEO. The company may purchase a house with a value of up to around $1 million and then either provide it rent-free to the CEO or else charge him rent at a rate that is substantially below the free-market rental value of the property, but high enough to satisfy the tax collectors that no economic benefit has been conferred. However, even if no rent at all is charged, the value of the free housing is not much more than $40,000 per year—a pittance when we are dealing with an average CEO pay package of $2.8 million per year in the United States.

German senior executives may also be given the services of a security guard and an armor-plated limousine. But in Germany there is a genuine threat of terrorism, as was recently demonstrated by the untimely murder of the CEO of Deutsche Bank while he was being driven to work in the company's limousine. In the United States, shareholders, even though angry, have not yet resorted to acts of terrorism, and the need for armor-plated limousines is comparably less.

Reflecting the same desire as in Japan for a more egalitarian society than is found in the United States, tax rates in Germany are comparatively high. The top marginal tax rate is 53%, and tax deductions are relatively limited. Once again, we find a country where senior executive pay is much lower than in the United States but where the tax rates are much higher. Curiously, churchgoing Germans who declare that they are churchgoing Germans are required to pay a church tax of around 8–9% of their income tax. Domschke jokes that few senior German executives seem to be devout believers, given a potential maximum tax of close to 60%, counting the church tax.

The $735,000 in total current compensation that the typical German CEO earns compares to wages of around $35,000 for the typical German industrial worker, according to Domschke. So the German CEO is earning about 21 times more than the typical worker—a ratio that J. P. Morgan would have found reasonably appealing and that Peter Drucker might possibly have accepted, too—although once again, the ratio is being applied to the pay of the average worker, not the lowest-paid worker.

Base salary levels for French CEOs are not too different from those in Germany. According to Vincent Regazzacci Stephanopoli, a partner with Progress, one of France's largest executive recruiting firms, a typical major company CEO will earn a base salary of around 3 million French francs. At the current exchange rate of 5.09 francs to the dollar, that translates into a base salary of around $590,000 per year. (As noted above, a German CEO earns a base salary of around $525,000 per year.)

Income tax rates in France are extremely high—at least theoretically. The top marginal tax rate is 57%, and with the added imposition of a tax on wealth, the combined tax can rise to as high as 80%. However, the French have been dodging their tax collectors since long before the United States was founded, and apparently they are still pretty nimble. It is often the case that a French CEO is paid, at least in part, by an overseas subsidiary. And that income, though taxable at whatever rates prevail in the other country, is not taxable by the French. (The United States is one of the few major industrialized countries that taxes the worldwide income of its citizenry.)

The British and the Americans speak the same language, although the former vigorously deny this fact. It is this linguistic bond, coupled with the rise of the Thatcherite self-made CEO who has little inherited wealth, that probably accounts for the fact that British CEOs are beginning to ape their U.S. counterparts in a major way.

John Carney, a vice president of Towers Perrin in London, says that the base pay of a major company CEO in the United Kingdom is around £350,000. At the current exchange rate of $1.97 to the pound, that translates into an annual salary of close to $700,000—easily the highest rate among the four major countries (other than the United States itself) that I studied. Add a typical annual bonus opportunity of another $180,000 per year, and you derive total current compensation of close to $900,000 per year.

As in the United States, the differences between CEO pay and average worker pay are growing more pronounced. According to James Matthews of the U.K.'s Incomes Data Services, the pay of the typical highest-paid director (usually the CEO) was 10.6 times the pay of an average worker in 1981, and 22.2 times in 1990. John Carney of Towers Perrin reckons the current differential for a truly major British firm to be even higher—about 33 times the pay of a typical worker. He notes that there has been a 119% increase in the total current compensation of a typical British senior executive over the past five years—but pay increases, he adds, show signs of slowing down. Still, though the pay ratio may be 22 or 33 times the pay of an average worker, neither figure comes close to the more than 50 times ratio of CEO total current compensation to worker pay in the United States, or to the substantially more than 100 times ratio for total direct compensation (including long-term incentives).

Whatever the true ratio, there is a growing controversy in the U.K. over the size of senior executive pay packages. Even the former prime minister, Margaret Thatcher, got into the act. James Matthews says she publicly chided British CEOs for neglecting to include themselves in their plans to meet her goal of restraining British pay packages and thereby enhancing the country's economic competitiveness.

U.S.-style stock options have found a home in the U.K. A bit of a tax break is afforded to government-approved stock option schemes, which limit the size of option grants that may be given to 4 times pay in any three-year period (that is, the product of the number of option shares and the strike price per share may not exceed 4 times the sum of the executive's base salary and annual bonus in a three-year period). By comparison, if we take the aggregate strike price of Steven Ross's most recent stock option grant, which was $270 million, and then divide it by the typical British CEO's total cash compensation of $900,000 per year, we find that the ratio, instead of being the approved U.K. level of 4, is 300.

U.K. companies can exceed the British government's limit of 4 times pay if they are willing to forego the modest tax advantage being offered. But to date few have done so. Indeed, many do not even grant the maximum 4-times-in-three-years permitted by the government, but rather stretch the 4 times over the ten-year life of an option grant. They do this in response to heavy pressure from British insurance companies and pension funds, which own large chunks of their stock.

But that may be changing. Because they speak English so fluently, the British are reading a lot of U.S. periodicals, and a lot of what is being written in the United States is finding its way into their own periodicals. As a result, British CEOs are quite in touch with how much more their U.S. counterparts are earning. Indeed, the news is being driven home in an even more dramatic way, as U.S. executives move to Britain to head local companies. In the recent merger of Beecham Products and Smithkline Beckman, the CEO continues to be an American, though he now works out of London. His U.S.-sized pay package is the subject of not-so-polite conversation in a lot of English club rooms. Matthews of Incomes Data Services says that while U.S. CEOs are trying to justify their pay packages by making comparisons to what U.S. movie stars and sports stars earn, British CEOs are trying to justify their need for greater income by making comparisons to what U.S. CEOs earn. And for good measure, he adds, they also take note of the earnings of people like Madonna.

In much the same way as has occurred in the United States, the British have taken a meat-ax to their tax structure. Not too many years ago, a British CEO could be subjected to a marginal tax rate as high as 88%. Now the maximum is 40%—a figure that is passably close to the U.S. level, if you include state and local income taxes in the U.S. figures.

When the British lowered their income tax structure, the government tightened up on the taxation of perquisites. (A similar tightening also occurred in the United States when top tax rates began to drop.) Nonetheless, perquisites are still something to behold in Britain, especially the heavy use of company cars. In addition, British employees enjoy much more holiday and vacation time than the employees in virtually every other developed country.

The tremendous imbalance in the pay levels of American senior executives, on the one hand, and their counterparts in such countries as Japan and Germany, on the other, opens significant public policy questions. As we have seen, if CEOs receive raises, the bucks don't stop there; they trigger many other, albeit smaller, raises and lead to a serious increase in company costs.

This cost increase can be handled in one of three ways. First, since the extra costs stem largely from the adoption of various long-term incentive plans, there is always the possibility that the plans might do what they are supposed to do, namely, stimulate smarter behavior. If that occurs, then there will be added revenues to offset, or maybe even more than offset, the added costs. However, the case for this happening is exceedingly weak, if not downright negative. The addition of more and more long-term incentive plans to the CEO's pay package, far from motivating him, seems merely to bloat his pay package even more and leads to a decrease in returns to shareholders.

If these added costs for executive compensation cannot be made to pay for themselves in the form of greater executive motivation, then someone has to foot the bill. And that leaves only two possibilities: shareholders or consumers. The company can stiff its own shareholders by giving them less net income and hence less total return. But that alternative is apt to lead to a lower rate of capital formation in America. And once shareholders figure out what is happening, it may even lead to some desertion of the American equity markets in favor of Japanese and German equities. Alternatively, the company can stiff its consumers. Under this scenario, the company produces the same net income to shareholders as it would have produced had it had a lower level of executive compensation costs. It accomplishes this seeming alchemy by raising prices to consumers. In this case, however, it is not the shareholders but the consumers who take a walk. They start buying Japanese and German products with considerable enthusiasm. After all, there's not much of a contest when the product is not only better but is cheaper to boot.

At the beginning of the 1980s, some of the most senior automotive executives in Detroit mounted the bully pulpit and lectured their workers on the need to cut their pay, or if not to cut their pay, at least to freeze it. The reason: the Japanese were killing our domestic automotive industry with lower factory-floor labor costs. The workers did agree to some pay actions which had the desired effect. Now, I believe that there is little difference between the pay of a Japanese automotive worker and his or her American counterpart.

It's high time for a Lee Iacocca to again mount the bully pulpit and to talk about the need to remain competitive. Only this time, the auditorium needs to be filled with the CEOs and other senior executives of virtually every major company in America.

In summary, CEOs and other senior executives in the United States earn far more than their counterparts in the other major industrialized countries. And they pay the least taxes. The country that comes closest to emulating the pay levels of the United States is the U.K. And that is also the country that, along with the United States, is the least competitive among the majors. By contrast, Japan, the country that gives the United States the greatest competitive fit, pays its CEOs the least, and has the most egalitarian approach to compensation. Moreover, it achieves great long-term performance without the use of any long-term incentive compensation at all.

Is there a lesson here?

Fourteen

The Culprits

Executive compensation in the United States did not go out of control simply through some random process; it went out of control because of the actions—or non-actions—of a number of parties.

The first culprits in what will be a litany of culprits are compensation consultants, company boards of directors, and, more specifically, board compensation committees. Almost all boards of directors of publicly owned companies of any size have formed a committee composed solely of outside directors and have charged that committee with riding herd on the company's compensation plans and compensation levels. A board compensation committee typically consists of about five outside directors—directors who are not employees of the company and who, at least theoretically, have no economic ties with the company. The committee meets several times a year, sometimes every time there is a board meeting.

Serving on a compensation committee is considered to be "the pits" by many outside directors. In most companies, there is a sort of hierarchy of committee service, and at the top is the executive committee, followed by the audit committee. At or close to the bottom is the compensation committee. Why the compensation committee should be so low-ranking is something I cannot pinpoint, but I suspect it has to do with the linkage of compensation to a company's personnel department. Since the personnel department typically fights it out with the public relations department for the bottom of the prestige heap, the linkage of compensation with personnel may be perceived in the same negative light by those outside directors who are asked to serve on the compensation committee.

From an economic standpoint, a CEO is the seller of his own services, the compensation committee is the buyer of his services, and whatever the executive receives in the way of pay is the price of his services. Under classic economic theory, a reasonable price is obtained through arm's-length negotiations between an informed seller and an informed buyer. There is nothing wrong with either the seller or the buyer, or both, asserting his own personal interests; indeed, Adam Smith's invisible hand is supposed to so operate as to bring those competing personal interests into a congruence that is beneficial to society.

Let's parse the above statement concerning an informed seller, an informer buyer, and arm's-length negotiations.

We'll start with the seller, who is the CEO. Since he has been a consumer of his company's compensation products for some years, even a fairly dim-witted CEO knows pretty well how various compensation plans operate, including their potential or non-potential for enriching him. So it is hard to view a CEO as being an uninformed seller of his services. In fact, it is impossible to so view the CEO when, as nowadays, he has working for him a professional compensation director and when, for added protection, he hires a compensation consultant to boot.

Executive compensation consulting, as an organized profession, did not get started in any meaningful way until the 1950s. An early superstar in the field was Arch Patton, a director of McKinsey & Co., one of America's premier management consulting firms. (A few years back, McKinsey abandoned its executive compensation practice.) Among other things, he helped the American Management Association design one of the first surveys of executive compensation, thereby permitting companies to obtain a better reading of how they stood vis-à-vis other companies.

The executive compensation consulting field grew at a steady but unspectacular rate until the beginning of the 1970s. From the end of World War II until the beginning of the 1970s, America enjoyed the greatest sustained Bull Market in its history. That in turn gave abundant life to stock options, basically the sole form of long-term incentive compensation then in use. (Stock options first came into vogue in 1950, when Congress passed legislation granting them favorable tax treatment.) So until the postwar Bull Market ended, few companies needed to spend much time on their executive compensation programs; they paid a decent base salary, offered a decent bonus, granted stock options, and watched their senior executives become painlessly rich through ever-rising stock prices.

The rationale underlying stock options was simple: Companies should tie executive pay to things that matter to shareholders. And, of course, what is of greater moment to a shareholder than the price of his company's shares? Hence, if the stock price rises, the executive should be rewarded. Left unspoken was a corollary part of the deal, namely, that if the stock price stays the same, or falls, the executive should not be rewarded. Stock options themselves also were simple. The measure of executive performance was not some complex calculation like discounted cash flow; it was the market price of the stock. And the measure could not be rigged by management. Rather, the measure could be looked up every day in the stock tables of any newspaper.

The unspoken corollary that, if the stock price fails to rise, or falls, then the executive should go unrewarded, was given its sea trials when the stock market fell apart in the early 1970s. And it promptly sank without a trace! A different outcome could have occurred, of course. Companies, harking back to the immortal words of J. P. Morgan to the effect that stock prices will rise and fall, could have elected to ride out the Bear Market and continue to make regular grants of stock options. To be sure, executives might not have received any rewards for a while, but stock options, after all, are exercisable for a ten-year period, and no Bear Market—even the Bear Market following the 1929 Crash—has lasted ten years. No one, it seems, thought of that alternative. Rather, an insidious process of rationalization ensued, namely, that the stock market had gone crazy and no longer knew how to value equity securities. This process of rationalization continued throughout the 1970s and into the early 1980s, finally reaching its apogee with a cover story by *BusinessWeek* entitled "The Death of Equities." Demonstrating that the ability to predict the future continues to elude humanity, the editors of *BusinessWeek* ran their story only a few months before the stock market turned around and the Dow headed toward 3,000.

It was at this time that compensation consultants came into their own. Capitalizing on the theme that the stock market was crazy, they tried to convince CEOs that the reason they were not receiving the same level of remuneration as in the past was not because the CEOs' performance was lagging, but rather because they were using the wrong measure of performance, namely, the market price of their companies' stock. It didn't take very much to convince your average CEO of the merit of this line of argument. And so the compensation consultant was commissioned to perform a study that would ultimately recommend new forms of compensation—forms of compensation that, by definition and by design, would sunder, or at the least attenuate, the linkage between a CEO's pay and the performance that shareholders desire the most, stock price appreciation and dividends.

If the market price of the stock was no longer going to be the centerpiece on the table, what would be the substitute? Various companies cast about for various alternatives, but the early favorite became growth in earnings per share. So plans were quickly designed to reward executives for increasing their firm's earnings per share over a period of three or four years. These new plans had, of course, to be integrated into the company's existing framework of compensation plans, and that chore necessarily required that someone attempt to measure their economic value. That in turn required that someone measure the economic value of existing forms of compensation, such as stock option grants. And all that work gave rise to a whole new generation of increasingly sophisticated compensation surveys—surveys that purported to tell the company how it stood competitively, not only in the aggregate, but in each of its many forms of executive compensation.

With lots of new compensation plan design work and with lots of new survey work, compensation consulting firms thrived. Towers Perrin quickly rose to the number one position, as measured by volume of business, followed by such companies as Hewitt Associates and Hay Associates, and by some of the Big Six accounting firms.

Ostensibly, compensation consultants were hired by the CEO to perform an objective analysis of the company's executive pay package and to make whatever recommendations the consultant felt were appropriate. In reality, if those recommendations did not cause the CEO to earn more money than he was earning before the compensation consultant appeared on the scene, the latter was rapidly shown the door. I learned this fact of life early on when I was hired by the CEO of a smallish conglomerate. (He is now the CEO of a very large company, and much admired by his peers.) His company paid base salaries to its executives, and it gave them stock options, but it did not have an annual bonus plan. He hired me to consider whether adopting such a plan was a good idea and, if so, to recommend its design, including such considerations as the size of the bonus opportunity. After interviewing a number of key executives to learn something about that particular company, and studying the compensation arrangements of the company's competitors, I duly determined that there was indeed a need for an annual incentive plan. However, I ran into a little snag. I had determined that a competitive level of base salary and annual bonus for my client's CEO was $160,000 per year, and that the breakdown, competitively, consisted of a base salary of around $100,000 per year and a bonus, in a year of normal performance, of about $60,000 per year. (As might be surmised from the tiny numbers just cited, this study was done many years ago.) But my client's CEO was already earning $160,000 per year, all of it in base salary. To add a 60%-of-salary normal bonus opportunity on top of his $160,000 salary would, of course, cause him to be paid at a super-competitive level. So, in my naivete, I recommended that he cut his salary to $100,000 to make room for a 60%-of-salary normal bonus opportunity. By so doing, I explained to him, he would, in a year of normal performance, earn what he was earning now; in a year of above-normal performance, he would earn more than he was earning now; and, fair is fair, in a year of below-normal performance, he would earn less than he was earning now.

The CEO did not take kindly to my suggestion. First, he tried to argue me out of the recommendation by challenging my survey data. But he wasn't successful. So he looked me in the eye and posed a question to me that I will never forget: "Just who do you think is paying your bills, anyway?" I replied to the effect that I hadn't been reviewing my accounts-receivable folder for a while, but that I suspected that the checks my firm was receiving were drawn on his corporation's bank account, and not on his personal bank account. I said to him: "Perhaps I am wrong about that, but if I am right, then I guess the answer to your question is that the shareholders are paying my bills, and not you!" There then ensued a scene reminiscent of *The Exorcist,* with the temperature in the room seemingly dropping some 40 degrees in a matter of seconds. After a desultory attempt to get the meeting restarted, we broke up, and I have never heard from him again. I'd bet, however, that he found another compensation consultant who was willing to recommend that the company adopt a new annual incentive plan without requiring executives to cut back on their base salaries.

Most executive compensation consultants are employed by firms that do more than executive compensation consulting. Towers Perrin, for example, has an immense employee benefits practice, which involves the design of pension and health plans, actuarial valuations, and the communication of such plans to employees. Indeed, in many cases, the revenues derived from a given client for such work as actuarial consulting dwarf by several orders of magnitude the revenues for executive compensation consulting. So, bucking a CEO and telling him that he ought to cut his bloated pay package can potentially cost a consulting firm not only the loss of executive compensation revenues but the loss of much larger revenues being generated from other services. This is not to suggest that a firm like Towers Perrin, or indeed any other consulting firm, will make recommendations in which it does not believe simply to keep some additional client business. But the pressure to do just that is always present.

The problem here is that the consultant is ostensibly being hired by a company's shareholders to give his/her best advice, but is actually being hired by the CEO. And the CEO's interests are not always those of the shareholders; if they were, there would never be a need to design incentives or even to hire a compensation consultant.

Compensation consultants come in two flavors; the great majority are ethical people, albeit with an institutional bias in favor of meeting the CEO's needs. But some are outright charlatans. One consultant wrote to the CEO of a giant investment banking firm and told him that, in her opinion, he was underpaid. Like Joan Rivers, she ended her letter: "Can we talk?" They talked, all right, and she was engaged to perform an extensive study. In due course, the CEO's pay package was increased significantly. In another instance, a lawyer who also functions as an executive compensation consultant wrote to the CEOs of a number of firms with the same siren song, namely, that they were being paid below the average and that they ought to do something about it. There is no evidence that this same lawyer wrote to an equal number of overpaid CEOs and suggested that they, too, do something about it.

Which brings up the whole subject of compensation surveys. Consulting firms such as Hewitt Associates, Towers Perrin, and Hay Associates generate significant amounts of revenues by conducting executive compensation surveys. Companies are solicited to complete often voluminous questionnaires on the types of compensation plans they use, how the plans work, and how much executives earn from them. These data are then analyzed statistically, and reports are sent back to participating companies. The reports generally hew to some standard of confidentiality. For example, a participating company will know the names of the other companies in the survey database, but will not know anything about each company's individual compensation data. Rather, the participating company will be given information on survey averages, medians, highs, lows, percentile ranks, and so forth.

A statistical average—whether it is average pay or average rainfall—is made up of a series of numbers, some of which must necessarily be lower than the resulting average and some of which must necessarily be higher. (The only exception is a series of numbers where every number is the same, and that is never encountered in the world of executive compensation.) That being the case, it does not follow, and it cannot follow mathematically, that every CEO is entitled to earn the survey average. But try convincing a CEO of the merits of this argument.

Companies have a sort of institutional pride, and consciously paying a CEO below the average constitutes a blow to that institutional pride. Talk to a member of the board about this issue, and he'll likely tell you that "our company is as good as anyone else's, and therefore we're not going to be cheap and pay below the average." This pernicious thinking leads to a phenomenon called "survey ratcheting." If a company shows to be below the average, the CEO is given a raise to the average; or, if not all the way to the average, at least an outsized raise. Unless CEOs who are being paid above the average are given pay cuts to the average, these raises cause the survey average to rise the next year and to contribute to another round of the same behavior. And, of course, it is virtually unheard of for a CEO to take a pay cut.

Rather, four sorts of rationalization emerge here. First, if the CEO is being paid above the average, the company and its consultants will immediately try to provide a justification. And the most obvious justification, of course, is above-average corporate performance. Studies will immediately be undertaken concerning earnings per share growth, return on equity, return on assets, cash flow growth, stock price appreciation, shareholder return, and any other conceivable corporate performance measure. And comparisons will be made to companies generally, to companies in the same industry, to companies of the same size, and even to companies with headquarters in the same city. Then the comparisons that "come out right"—i.e., show that the company is indeed an above-average performer—will be trotted in front of the compensation committee to justify the above-average pay. It never seems to bother anybody that the companies on which the performance comparisons are based may not be the same as the companies on which the pay comparisons are based. And it never seems to bother anybody that the measures of performance used to justify the premium pay positioning may change from year to year. Hence, stock price appreciation may be the justification this year, because it has been excellent. But if stock price appreciation isn't so good next year, then earnings per share growth will be the measure of choice, because it was decent in the past year. And so on.

Another form of rationalization involves restructuring the survey database itself by eliminating certain companies and adding others. Survey data tend to be believed to the extent that they confirm the preconceived prejudices of the reader. So, if you turn out to be overpaid, that's probably because you're being compared to the wrong companies. Choosing a new group of companies and rerunning all the survey analyses is a lucrative source of business for compensation consultants, especially since it may take several restructurings to produce the desired finding—namely, that the CEO is just your average-paid bloke, or better yet, just your below-average-paid bloke.

If neither of the above approaches—showing that the company is an above-average performer or picking a whole new group of companies against which to measure your CEO's pay—bears fruit, the company can still choose to travel down one of two further paths of rationalization. The first is to admit that the CEO is indeed being paid more than the average and that there seems to be no justification for the premium. However, rather than simply cut his pay back to the average, why not instead put him on a diet? Suppose other companies are granting pay increases of 10% this year, how about giving our CEO an increase of only 8%? Sooner or later, this sort of action will bring the CEO's pay into line with the average. Left unsaid, of course, is the fact that the CEO is apt to be in the ground long before the numbers finally work out. Also left unsaid is the fact that companies have notoriously short institutional memories. Thus, the CEO may well get only an 8% increase in the first year of his diet. But by the second year, everyone seems to have forgotten the commitment to keep the CEO on a diet for many years.

The last, and perhaps the most insidious, form of rationalization is to deny that the average is a proper place for the company to be and to adopt, as a matter of policy, a premium pay positioning. If a company goes this way, it is, for reasons that are shrouded in mystery, very likely going to opt for the 75th percentile. In other words, the CEO will induce the compensation committee to adopt a policy that says the company will henceforth pay a level of compensation that will be higher than the compensation levels of about three quarters of the companies that are considered to be valid comparators. When pressed to explain why the shareholders ought to pay more than the average as a matter of policy, the CEO will be heard to mumble that by adopting a premium pay positioning, the company will be able to attract a better grade of executive.

Interestingly, almost no company that adopts a premium pay positioning as a matter of corporate policy extends it below a handful of senior executives. When asked why he didn't aim for the 75th percentile for all his employees, and not just the top fifty executives, the CEO of one major company told me: "That would be too damn expensive." So maybe there's a need, after all, to pay a few people at the top a constant premium to the market; they have the daunting task of producing above-average performance from a bunch of average-performing blokes on the factory floor.

It wouldn't be so bad if some companies, as a matter of policy, paid above the average so long as other companies, also as a matter of policy, paid below the average. But that almost never happens. In one survey I conducted some years back of one hundred companies' pay policies, thirty-five stated that they were aiming for the 75th percentile of the distribution, sixty-five stated that they were aiming for the competitive average, and none stated that they were aiming for a position below the average. With that sort of pattern, is it any wonder that executive pay keeps spiraling ever upward?

Earlier, we were starting to parse the elements underlying reasonable compensation: an informed buyer of services, an informed seller of services, and arm's-length negotiations. So far, we can see clearly that the CEO is a more than adequately informed seller of his services. Aided by his knowledgeable and trusty compensation consultant, how can he be other than well informed?

But what about the buyers of the CEO's services, the shareholders and their agents, the compensation committee of the board of directors? Are they as well informed as the CEO? Absolutely not.

The first thing you need to know about compensation committees is that their members are not expected to spend much time analyzing the arcana of their company's compensation plans. And, obligingly, they don't. The second thing you need to know about compensation committees is that they are almost always reactive and almost never proactive. That is to say, they sit back and wait for the CEO to propose some course of action; they almost never propose the course of action themselves.

In the days when executive compensation plans were simple, the CEO himself used to present recommendations to the compensation committee. Nowadays, the job is more often than not left to the compensation consultant. Theoretically, the consultant gives the compensation committee members a balanced recitation of the pros and cons of any recommended approach; but you can be sure that the pros are given much greater play than the cons.

More important, there is the question of scenarios. Most executive compensation plans cannot really be understood until payouts are determined under various possible performance outcomes. It is only then that the weaknesses of a particular plan design, if there are weaknesses, can be exposed. Too often, the compensation consultant presents the outcome of a single scenario to the compensation committee and thereby fools it. To illustrate: I know of one consultant who sold a restricted stock plan to a compensation committee by focusing on one fact, namely, that if the company experienced compounded annual total shareholder return of 15% per year for the next five years, the CEO would receive shares having a total value of $5 million. The consultant was not, of course, conditioning the award of the stock on the achievement of 15% per year earnings per share growth over five years; rather, he was merely informing the compensation committee that the shares, which would be earned by the CEO in any event so long as he stayed with the company for the next five years, would be worth $5 million should the compounded total return to shareholders happen to be 15% per year during the same period.

Some members of the compensation committee immediately wondered whether that was enough of a reward for such an outstanding level of performance. With a little prodding from his admirers on the compensation committee, the CEO graciously accepted an increase in his contemplated restricted stock award so that, instead of earning $5 million of 15% compounded annual growth in shareholder return over five years, he would earn $10 million. No one, of course, bothered to tell the compensation committee members that if the company experienced no growth at all in total shareholder return, the CEO would still receive stock worth $5 million, and that if the company experienced a negative growth in total return of 5% per year, he would still receive stock worth $3.9 million. Perhaps if the compensation committee had learned what the payouts would be under these less-than-optimal performance outcomes, it would not have been so quick to double the size of the CEO's restricted stock grant. Indeed, perhaps it would have rejected the notion of restricted stock outright.

Or consider the compensation committee of H. J. Heinz when it approved a 4 million share option grant for Anthony O'Reilly. It probably focused on the money he would receive for, say, doubling the value of the stock. But did it focus on the fact that if Heinz's share price rises only a paltry $1 per share over the next ten years—a level of performance that ought to result in the CEO's being publicly humiliated in front of the shareholders—O'Reilly will nonetheless receive a reward of $4 million?

This failure to present the compensation committee with the results of scenarios is particularly onerous given that so many CEOs are engaged in trying to squeeze every bit of risk out of their pay packages. As we have already seen, companies are switching from stock options to restricted stock. And they are putting minimum floor prices under restricted stock plans. And they are assuming the burden of the executive's taxes. A lot of that risk-reducing behavior would be exposed for what it is if the compensation committee were presented scenarios showing the range of outcomes under the current compensation arrangements, as well as those for the contemplated new arrangements.

Another problem compensation committees have stems from

their poor institutional memories. If they give the CEO a grant of 100,000 restricted shares one year, they may well remember their action the next year. But don't bet on the year after that. Many CEOs have learned that you don't want to panhandle your compensation committee for big grants every year; just wait an extra year or so, and no one will think to ask what the company did for you in the past.

The poor institutional memory of compensation committees lies not so much in the fact that there is considerable director turnover but rather in that outside directors have no staff of their own to remind them of what actions they took in past years. They do not spend all that much time thinking about company executive compensation issues; and, most important, the CEO deliberately forgets to remind them of what actions they took in past years.

So, when you consider that compensation committees never spend enough time studying complex compensation schemes, and when you consider that they are at the mercy of whatever the CEO wants to tell them, can you honestly conclude that these buyers of the CEO's services are, in fact, well-informed buyers?

Thus far, we have a combination of an informed seller of services—the CEO—and an uninformed buyer of services—the compensation committee of the board. A lethal combination.

Finally, we come to the third element that must be present to produce reasonable compensation: arm's-length negotiations. Presumably that element is automatically taken care of due to the fact that the buyers of the CEO's services are outside directors. They do not work for the CEO, and they have no significant economic ties to the company. But consider here who hires the directors in the first place. That person is likely to be the CEO. To be sure, a growing number of boards have their own nominating committees, but the names produced by those committees are not going to go very far if the CEO doesn't approve of them. After all, the CEO, in most companies, also is the chairman of the board. Hence, in a subtle way (or maybe it isn't such a subtle way) he is the boss of all the outside directors.

Most board members are not willing to see that they must of necessity be in an adversarial position to the CEO—especially when it comes to his compensation. Rather, like members of the same parliamentary party in Great Britain, they see themselves as being part of a team, with the CEO acting as prime minister. In Britain, it is not considered good form to vote against your own party. And in U.S. boardrooms, it is considered well-nigh traitorous to buck the CEO. If things get bad enough, you can fire the CEO. But until you do, you'd better support him. Indeed, about the only time I have seen a board attack a CEO on his pay has been when it has already decided to get rid of him.

There is also another form of bias in compensation committees— bias that helps to defeat the presumption of an arm's-length negotiation. And that concerns the fact that most compensation committees contain one or more CEOs of other companies. Perhaps it will come as a surprise, although it shouldn't if you think about it, but the higher the pay of the CEOs who sit on the compensation committee, the higher will be the pay of the CEO whose pay the committee regulates. The correlation is not perfect, but it is statistically quite robust. Charles O'Reilly, the eminent organizational psychologist at Berkeley, says that a form of "social reference" is operating here. No one can think about pay in a vacuum. Before a person can decide on the reasonableness, or non-reasonableness, of a CEO's pay, he needs to know what other CEOs are paid. So that's one checkpoint. And his own pay—how much he earns when he's working at his regular job and not serving on the compensation committee—is, according to O'Reilly, another checkpoint. A CEO of another company who is earning $5 million per year may not blink at moving the pay of the CEO whose pay he regulates from $2 million to $3 million per year. So, one way for you as a CEO to assure you are paid at the maximum is to pack your compensation committees with other CEOs. But be careful here. First, you want CEOs who, right now, are actively working as CEOs; you don't want retired CEOs, whose perceptions of what a reasonable rate of pay is were formed when they were CEOs back in the 1960s. And second, you don't want just any active CEOs; rather, you want CEOs who make more than you do— indeed, a lot more than you do.

From the mid-1970s to the mid-1980s, I was a consultant to one of America's mightiest oil companies. My principal client was the company's senior vice president for human resources, but I met regularly with the CEO and, every so often, with the compensation committee of the board. At several meetings of the committee, an outside director, who had retired as the CEO of an even more prestigious company some five years earlier, fired broadsides at the pay package of the oil company's CEO. Before the run-up in oil prices, the oil company CEO had been earning around $800,000 per year; after the run-up, he was earning around $1.6 million per year. The outside director, when he was the active chairman of his company, had been earning only around $600,000 per year, and he was now languishing in Florida on his $300,000 per year pension. So, from his perspective, paying a CEO $1.6 million a year seemed obscene. No other member of the oil company's compensation committee agreed with his reasoning, and with the encouragement of the oil company's CEO, some of the other members of the compensation committee began to mount a rather personal attack on our retired CEO. In due course, he was removed from the compensation committee; not very much later, he was removed from the board of the oil company entirely.

There is another factor to consider here, and that is the almost incestuous relationship between the pay of outside directors and the pay of the CEO. Until just the last few years, an outside director was accustomed to receiving an annual retainer and then a fee for each meeting he attended. The sum of the annual retainer and the meeting fees was usually relatively modest—perhaps around $20,000 per year for an outside director of a major company. Then someone dreamed up the bright idea of giving the outside directors pensions. Now, in the majority of companies, an outside director can look forward to receiving a lifetime pension after serving as an outside director for perhaps only ten years. And the pension is apt to be 100% of his pay when he was actively working as an outside director, or at least 100% of his annual retainer.

Not too long after pensions began to be the vogue for outside directors, someone else dreamed up the bright idea of giving the outside directors restricted stock and also stock options. It is interesting to watch the rationalization that occurred here. Many academics and other critics of corporate behavior have noted that outside directors typically own hardly any shares of the companies they regulate. These critics have called for directors to own more stock, on the theory that they would take a more active interest in seeing that the company performed for its shareholders. Now, giving the directors more stock is not a bad idea per se. But I strongly suspect that the critics who were pushing for more stock had in mind cutting the cash compensation of the outside directors and then substituting shares of stock with an equivalent economic value. I strongly suspect that the critics didn't have in mind letting the outside directors continue to receive their usual amount of cash compensation and then giving them free shares of stock and stock options, too. But that, of course, is exactly what happened. It is now the case that the outside directors of some companies have begun to earn relatively huge amounts of compensation. For example, the outside directors of the Coca-Cola Company earn around $75,000 per year. Perhaps $75,000 per year, in the context of the millions the CEO is earning, seems a pittance. But that pittance is being earned for very little effort—possibly only around ten days per year.

The compensation committee of the board, as already noted, determines the pay of the CEO. But who determines the pay of the outside directors? Here, a sort of formal Japanese Kabuki has developed. If the CEO is on the ball, he will, without anyone asking him, commission the outside compensation consultant to study what other companies are paying their outside directors. Then, if the CEO's own outside directors are being paid below what the CEO considers to be an appropriate norm, he will, again without anyone asking him, suggest that the board approve an increase in its pay. At that point, the outside directors will ask searching questions of the CEO, questions like: "Are you really convinced, Sam, that we need an increase?" The CEO offers the necessary reassurance, and after a bit more handwringing on the part of the outside directors, the proposed pay increases are duly approved. The only glitch in this script occurs if the CEO is not on the ball and forgets to commission studies of outside director pay every other year or so. In that case, the outside directors themselves must get their hands dirty by suggesting to the CEO that they haven't had an increase for, say, five years, and isn't it time to look at their pay package?

So the board of directors determines the pay of the CEO, and for all practical purposes, the CEO determines the pay of the board of directors. Is it any accident, then, that there is a statistical relationship between how highly the CEO is paid and how highly his outside directors are paid? If the outside directors are paid, say, 10% above the market for outside directors, then the CEO is apt to be paid 5.2% above the market for CEOs. Perhaps it is a tribute to the integrity of boards that the CEO isn't paid a full 10% over the market when the outside directors are paid 10% above the market.

At the beginning of this chapter, I defined a reasonable pay level as one determined through an arm's-length negotiation involving an informed buyer and an informed seller. We can now see that only one of the three elements is present. There is an informed seller, to be sure. But the buyer is uniformed, and given the incestuous nature of boards of directors, the negotiation can hardly be considered to be at arm's length. Hence, it is hard not to conclude that the pay levels emerging from these flawed negotiations are, per se, unreasonable.

Executive compensation in the United States, however, didn't go out of control simply because of the efforts of compensation consultants and the non-efforts of board compensation committee members. It took more than that. Two other villains in the picture can be found in the guise of the regulators: the Financial Accounting Standards Board (FASB) and the Securities and Exchange Commission (SEC).

The Financial Accounting Standards Board is the industry-sponsored, rulemaking body for American accounting practices and procedures. Located in Norwalk, Connecticut, its board members are mostly drawn from among the partners of Big Six accounting firms, though an occasional academic or two wanders on to the scene.

Back in 1950, the predecessor organization to the Financial Accounting Standards Board, which was called the Accounting Principles Board, was first asked to rule on how companies should account for the grant of a new-fangled form of compensation, the stock option. To get the ball rolling, the Accounting Principles Board asked a number of experts to write papers on the accounting treatment they preferred. And to permit comparison from one paper to another, the Accounting Principles Board gave each expert a concrete example to use, e.g., what accounting treatment would you adopt for a stock option with a market price at date of grant of $50, a strike price of the same $50, and a term of ten years?

In due course, the experts submitted their papers, and one thing became immediately clear: there wasn't going to be any unanimity of opinion. For example, Expert number one outlined his way of thinking about stock options and concluded that a company ought to charge its earnings with $20 for a single stock option share having the above-described characteristics. Expert number two suggested an entirely different way of looking at the transaction, and concluded that a proper charge for the same option would be, not $20, but rather $25. And so forth, with perhaps some other expert recommending a charge as low as $15.

Confused by the variability of response it had received, the Accounting Principles Board, in one of history's more glaring non sequiturs, reasoned as follows: Inasmuch as none of the experts can agree on a single figure that a company ought to charge to its earnings with respect to a stock option grant, therefore the charge to earnings will be zero. Hold on a minute! Which expert came up with a recommendation to charge nothing to earnings? There wasn't one; the lowest came in at around $15. As Raymond Lauver, a former member of the Financial Accounting Standards Board, said of a more recent replay of the same exercise: "The difference between the lowest and highest estimates of value that we received was smaller than the difference between the lowest value received and the ultimate value adopted, namely zero."

Zero is a mathematical quantity that equates to nothing. Perhaps the Accounting Principles Board reasoned that if you can't decide what to do, you do nothing. In any event, that wonderful policy of not charging earnings with anything at all has persisted to this day.

Yet stock options do have value. Taking one away from an executive who has been given one is somewhat akin to snatching a piece of filet mignon out of the jaws of a Doberman who has missed several earlier meals; you'd better be very careful and very quick. Recently, I conducted a study of 500 companies with the largest market capitalizations (i.e., the value on the stock market of all the company's outstanding shares). Going back twenty years, I determined the economic trade-off between a stock option share and a common (or restricted) share, using the Black-Scholes option-pricing model. On the average, the model indicated that it would take 3.5 stock option shares to produce the same economic value as one free share. Then I moved forward ten years and determined two things. First, I determined the value of the one free share, including the value of all reinvested dividends during the ten-year period. Second, I determined the value of the stock option shares by multiplying (a) the amount, if any, by which the market price of a share of stock ten years later exceeded the value at grant; and (b) the number of option shares, e.g., 3.5 shares. I then moved ahead one year and repeated the exercise over again. And I kept moving ahead, until I had calculated values for each company for each of ten different ten-year option exercise periods.

My conclusion: As might be expected, stock options produced a lot more compensation than free shares at some companies and a lot less at others. But had an executive in the median company chosen to take consistently the greater number of stock option shares, he would have received 44% more compensation than he would have received had he chosen to take the fewer number of restricted shares. There is no question, therefore, that stock options can generate powerful economic benefits for executives.

Yet consider the decidedly non-level playing field that exists in the world of accounting. If a company gives an executive $100,000 in cash, it charges its pre-tax earnings with $100,000. And if it gives the executive $100,000 in free shares, it will at least charge its pre-tax earnings with the value of those shares at the time they were first handed to the executive. But if the executive exercises a stock option and then sells the shares for a profit of $10 million, not one cent of that $10 million is ever charged to earnings. To be sure, some dilution will occur since there will likely be a greater number of shares outstanding; but dilution, like periodontal disease, takes a long time to build up. And while periodontal disease, when it strikes, strikes your mouth, the cost of options, when it finally becomes manifest, is apt to strike, not *your* mouth, but the mouth of your successor's successor. By that time, everyone will have forgotten who gave away the farm.

Ray Lauver has a favorite slogan: "Never measured, never managed." For proof, he points to a parallel compensation problem, in this case the cost of providing health care for a company's retirees. Until the Financial Accounting Standards Board changed its thinking, companies were permitted to avoid charging their earnings for the costs of such promises until the doctors' bills started rolling into the claims center, i.e., until sometime after the employee retired. Then the costs were recognized and charged to earnings on a pay-as-you-go basis. Well, the CEO who first promised retirees lavish medical benefits didn't have to charge his company's earnings a nickel—at the time; he looked like a hero, and he didn't have to foot the bill. It is his successor who is stuck with the bill. And, ironically, the bill probably includes some stiff medical charges incurred by the very CEO who thought up the idea in the first place and who is now in retirement.

As Lauver's slogan suggests, if you don't charge earnings for the cost of providing an economic benefit—be that benefit retiree medical expense or a stock option grant—you are likely to start thinking that that benefit has no cost at all. And like any underpriced resource, you start to hand out too much of it.

Some companies are quite candid about the fact that they use options in preference to other forms of compensation because of the fire sale the accountants have been holding for some forty years now. Time Warner, for example, touts one advantage of giving its co-CEO, Steven Ross, an option on 1.8 million shares as being the fact that there will be no charges to earnings compared to an alternative way of compensating Ross that the company might have continued in place. Or consider the 4-million-share option grant recently given to Anthony O'Reilly of H. J. Heinz. Would Heinz's board seriously have considered making such a monster grant if its economic value at the time of grant (about $25 million, using the Black-Scholes option-pricing model) had to be charged to earnings;

or if the company had been required to charge to its earnings whatever benefits O'Reilly eventually received (in this case, $4 million for each 1-point rise in Heinz's stock price)?

A few years ago, the Financial Accounting Standards Board began to get serious about the subject of stock option accounting. The board came close to ruling that a company would have to take a substantial charge to its earnings based on the economic value of the option, measured at the time of its grant and spread over the number of years between the date of grant and the date the option first became exercisable. But its work was immediately subjected to a withering hail of criticism. At least a couple of major company CEOs started a movement to deny the Financial Accounting Standards Board a significant source of its funding, contributions from major companies. And a well-known compensation consultant opined to the board that its action could well end up destroying America's competitiveness, inasmuch as reported earnings would be substantially lower. So, succumbing to pressure or just plain sloth, the board has put its stock option accounting project on the back burner for the last couple of years. Perhaps it will yet do what it should do. But it also might not be a bad idea to consult an actuary to evaluate the odds of the members of the Financial Accounting Standards Board taking action before a higher power takes action on them.

The Financial Accounting Standards Board, because it has created a non-level playing field, has distorted the long-term incentives now in use. In a company like General Electric, which is engaged in multiple industries, introducing long-term incentives that pay out based on the long-term performance of each major business unit might well prove to be more motivational than giving business unit executives option shares on GE stock. After all, the correlation between the long-term performance of any single operating division of GE and the long-term performance of GE itself cannot be much better than the correlation between the long-term performance of any single operating division of GE and the U.S. gross national product. GE, in microcosm, *is* the U.S. GNP. So how would it sound to say to a GE executive: "If the U.S. GNP advances at the rate of 3% per year in real terms over the next five years, I'll pay you $2 million"? Obviously, no GE operating unit executive can hope to have any real influence over the nation's GNP. But, effectively, they are being given an incentive on the GNP whenever they are granted GE stock options. And perhaps they are being given GE stock options because someone has decided they are just too good a buy to pass up.

America's competitiveness won't be destroyed if the Financial Accounting Standards Board imposes a charge to earnings for stock options. Indeed, America's competitiveness will be destroyed if the board *doesn't* impose a charge to earnings for stock options. For by not measuring the cost, and not managing the cost, as Ray Lauver likes to say, true economic costs will continue to skyrocket, and America's competitiveness vis-à-vis its leaner, meaner, and lesser-paid competitors overseas will continue to diminish.

The organization that has ultimate accounting authority in the United States is not actually the Financial Accounting Standards Board, but rather a federal government agency, the U.S. Securities and Exchange Commission. If the Securities and Exchange Commission wishes to bestir itself, which it rarely does, it can overrule anything the Financial Accounting Standards Board does, or even order that board to adopt a certain accounting practice or procedure. But the Securities and Exchange Commission has a more direct impact on executive compensation, and that impact concerns the rules it promulgates on the subject of proxy reporting. It is here where all sorts of games can be played.

A major cigarette brand used to advertise: "It's what's up front that counts." Well, nothing could be truer with respect to proxy reporting. Each publicly held company is required to include in its proxy a table showing the "cash compensation" of each of its top five executives. Now, a novice might think that the phrase "cash compensation" means just what it says—the value of everything the executive received in cash during the past fiscal year. But that just goes to prove that the novice is indeed a novice.

Consider Paramount Communications, for example. Although

the Securities and Exchange Commission's proxy regulations require that a company report in its cash compensation table at least the sum of its base salary and annual bonus, Paramount, in its January 1990 proxy statement, reported only its base salaries. Hence, Martin Davis, the company's CEO, was shown to be earning a salary of $950,000. Someone accustomed to finding in other companies' cash compensation tables, not merely the base salary of the CEO, but the sum of the base salary and the annual bonus, could easily, and mistakenly, have concluded that what was only Davis's salary was actually his salary and bonus. On that basis, the reader would also have concluded that Davis was a terrific buy. However, if he persevered through several hundreds words of text following the cash compensation table, he would have found that Davis also received a bonus of $3,144,900 for his performance during the past fiscal year. Now that's more like it! And if he turned the page and waded through some more legal prose, he would have found that Davis also earned $855,100 through a long-term Performance Unit Plan that rewarded his performance for, effectively, the four preceding years. And if he read through three more pages without falling sleep, he would have found that Davis had also been granted 500,000 shares of restricted stock in the past year. Although the proxy did not offer the reader any help in determining the value of those 500,000 shares, he could have looked up stock prices during the preceding year and have determined that the grant was worth on the order of $25 million. So the figure of $950,000 reported in the cash compensation table—the table that probably 99.9% of shareholders rely on to inform them as to what the CEO makes—turns out to be merely a crumb that fell off of Davis's compensation plate.

And while you're reading Paramount's proxy, you might reflect on another improbable disclosure being made by the company, namely that the senior vice president–senior tax counsel was listed as the fifth-highest-paid executive for 1990. According to the proxy released in 1991, he earned $235,000 in base salary. Can he really be the fifth-highest-paid executive? Is Paramount one of those companies that will do anything, pay anybody what it takes, to cut its tax bill down to the lowest possible amount? But then, after you read the annual report, you develop the nagging feeling that something or, more accurately, someone is missing from the proxy statement. One of Paramount Communications' businesses is its motion picture and television operations, which in 1990 were headed by Frank Mancuso. Yet Mancuso's name doesn't appear in the cash compensation table, nor does the name of anyone working for Paramount Pictures. Then you recall that another of Paramount Communications' businesses is publishing, which is headed by Richard Snyder. Yet Snyder's name doesn't appear in the cash compensation table, nor does the name of anyone working for Paramount's publishing organization.

Here's what the SEC regulations say about who should be reported in a company's proxy statement: "[Companies] should be flexible in determining which individuals should be named in the Cash Compensation Table in order to ensure that disclosure is made with respect to *key policy making members of management.* Consideration should be given to the question of whether an individual's level of executive responsibilities, viewed in conjunction with such an individual's actual level of cash compensation, is such that the [company] reasonably may conclude that the person is among its five most highly compensated, key policy making executive officers. Under this standard, it may be appropriate, in certain circumstances, to include an *executive officer of a subsidiary* in the Cash Compensation Table" (emphasis is mine).

It's a pretty good bet that Frank Mancuso, chairman of Paramount Pictures in 1990 and at the time the 1991 proxy was released, and Richard Snyder, chairman of Simon & Schuster, earned more than Paramount's senior tax counsel, who occupied the number five position in the company's cash compensation table. And it's a certainty that Mancuso and Snyder were not corporate officers of Paramount Communications, the parent company.

Therefore, I have to conclude that Paramount Communications either failed to abide by the SEC regulations or, alternatively, decided that Mancuso and Snyder were not, in fact, "key policy making members of management" and therefore rightfully excluded them from the proxy statement. But could such a conclusion really have been valid? Throughout 1990 and at the time it released its 1991 proxy statement, Paramount Communications had no chief operating officer; Mancuso and Snyder reported directly to Martin Davis, the parent company's chairman. From that perspective, therefore, they could be considered chief operating officers themselves, each of his own operating unit. I know of no company that would stand up and say, with a straight face, that its chief operating officer is not a key policy-making member of management. Moreover, those two operating units constituted virtually all of Paramount Communications; in the 1990 annual report, Davis notes that "the company's fundamental strength is found in our truly outstanding core assets: Paramount Pictures and Simon & Schuster." Buttressing his statement is the first picture in the annual report. On page 2, we see a smiling, and standing, Martin Davis beaming down at Frank Mancuso and Richard Snyder, both of whom are also smiling, but sitting. So if Mancuso and Snyder are not key policy-making members of management, what are they doing running the company's "core assets" and yukking it up with the chairman? Consider also that if Mancuso and Snyder are not invited to sit around the table when key policy decisions are made concerning the company's core assets, how can the key policy decisions that are made be considered informed, much less wise? Unlike some companies, Paramount Communications has a truly tiny corporate staff. Therefore, it would seem difficult for Davis to do an effective job of managing the company without leaning fairly heavily on Mancuso and Snyder.

Granted that the SEC's regulations concerning the reporting or nonreporting of subsidiary heads in the proxy statement is a matter of interpretation. So it is possible that I am missing something here. But if I am not, then leaving Mancuso and Snyder off the proxy statement typifies the abuse and obfuscation to which the shareholders of not only Paramount Communications but many other companies as well are subjected.

And consider also RJR Nabisco, in the days before it underwent a leveraged buyout. Its flamboyant CEO, F. Ross Johnson, took clear title to formerly restricted stock worth approximately $20 million when his company was taken over. Yet the nondisclosure of all but a handful of the restricted shares made Paramount Communications' proxy look like a model of clarity; it was simply never mentioned in the RJR Nabisco proxy statement. Apparently, RJR Nabisco's board was relying on an unusual interpretation of the proxy regulations that held it was permissible to disclose the grant of restricted stock either when the grant was made or when the restrictions on the related shares lapsed. The board chose the latter course, perhaps thinking that its lavish grants to Johnson would never see the light of day. However, the restrictions on his shares lapsed as a consequence of the leveraged buyout, and so the board's largesse finally did become publicly known.

Once again, we are confronted with a matter of interpretation. The SEC regulations require that a company "describe briefly all plans, pursuant to which cash or non-cash compensation was paid or distributed during the last fiscal year, *or is proposed to be paid or distributed in the future*" (emphasis is mine). The issue here centers around when a "distribution" is made under a restricted stock plan. Is it made when the shares are first given to the executive, even though such shares cannot be sold at the time? Or is it made when the restrictions on the shares first lapse? Presumably, the board of directors of RJR Nabisco answered the first question with a resounding no and the second with a resounding yes. I am not an attorney and therefore not an expert in saying how the two questions should have been answered. But a senior attorney I talked to at the SEC expressed the opinion that grants of restricted stock should be disclosed at the time of the grant. And of 100 companies that grant restricted stock, at least 95% have interpreted the SEC regulations in the same way as the SEC attorney with whom I spoke.

Or consider the order in which the five-highest-paid executives of a company are reported in the proxy's cash compensation table. Some companies report the five executives in descending order of their pay, which means that the executive listed first is the CEO. Other companies, however, choose to report the five executives in alphabetical order of their surnames. As it turns out, if the CEO's surname starts with a letter late in the alphabet, there is an overwhelming probability that the company will choose to report the five executives in alphabetical order. That way, the high pay of the company's CEO is somewhat obscured. If the CEO's name happens to be Aaron Aardvark, however, the company doesn't have too many alternatives.

In fairness, the degree of executive compensation disclosure in the United States exceeds that of every other major country. But saying that isn't saying much. Perhaps a tight logical case can be made for having no disclosure at all—"You shareholders elected the board, and if you don't like what they are doing, elect another board. Otherwise, shut up." But there is no logic behind mandating disclosure of executive compensation and then permitting companies to make a mockery of your mandate.

Once again, a non-level playing field has been created—a playing field that favors those forms of executive compensation that have the least adverse disclosure or, to put it another way, that have the best "optics." In many of the board compensation committee meetings I attended over the years, I heard the chairman of the committee or some other member say: "Well, the suggested new plan looks okay to me. But how about dummying up a copy of the proxy statement so that we can see what it will look like when it is presented to the shareholders?"

The problem of proxy disclosure is partly the Securities and Exchange Commission's fault, but it is perhaps not wholly the Commission's fault. Proxy regulations urgently need to be redrafted so as to prevent the sort of reporting practiced by Paramount Communications and many other companies, too. But for many years now, the Securities and Exchange Commission has relied on an honor system; it does not review each and every company's proxy statement but merely assumes that the company is doing the right thing. That needs to be changed.

It's what's up front that counts. And until the Securities and Exchange Commission takes some vigorous action, what's not up front will not count for very much—except when the bill is ultimately presented to the company's shareholders.

Fifteen

Reforming the System

As you must by now be aware, there are problems aplenty in the world of U.S. executive compensation:

- U.S. senior executives are paid so far in excess of U.S. workers as to raise fundamental questions of equity, and even decency. And the gap is growing, not shrinking;
- U.S. senior executives are paid far in excess of their counterparts in the other major industrialized countries. And the gap is growing, not shrinking;
- U.S. senior executives are insulating themselves from pay risk to an alarming degree. In many companies, it seems as though there are almost no scenarios that could materialize to devastate the CEO's pay package, while there are an almost infinite number of scenarios that could materialize to enrich him.

So what are we going to do about these problems? One is tempted here to endorse the need for governmental regulation of senior executive pay packages. After all, we are no strangers in the United States to pay controls. They were in place in World War II, and President Nixon imposed them as recently as the early 1970s.

But since an executive's pay is the price of his labor, pay controls are merely price controls operating under a different name. And history is replete with horror story after horror story as to how price controls cause misallocation of resources and end up being abandoned. As Mikhail S. Gorbachev now ruefully attests, there is no substitute for a free market, with prices set by supply-and-demand conditions.

What we need to do, then, is to strengthen the ability of market forces to do their job, rather than abandon the free market altogether. And the first market force that needs to be strengthened is the compensation committee of a company's board of directors. They, after all, sit across the table from the CEO when it comes to negotiating the latter's pay package.

As you have read earlier, the CEO has ample resources on his side of the table, and principal among them is his outside compensation consultant. He also has his in-house director of compensation. Although many people who hold these positions are highly skilled, they tend to be perceived as having a conflict of interest, since they work for the company and can be summarily fired by the CEO. Which is sort of ironic, because what do you think is likely to happen to an outside compensation consultant who bucks the CEO? He, too, can be summarily fired. Perhaps his advice is a tad more objective, because he has a diversified portfolio of clients, and not the single client that the in-house director of compensation has. But we emphasize the word "tad."

If the CEO is going to have professional help on his side of the negotiating table, it seems obvious that the compensation committee should also have its own professional help. Hence, our first suggestion is to mandate that the compensation committee have its very own compensation consultant. To foster objectivity, however, the committee's consultant should not be permitted ties of any sort with the company's management. The consultant cannot work both sides of the street and also consult for the CEO. And if the consultant is employed by a multi-consultant firm, his colleagues cannot be allowed to offer pay advice to the CEO, or, for that matter, actuarial advice, or, for that matter, marketing advice, or, for that matter, advice on any subject whatsoever.

Once the committee's consultant is on board, he (or she) should attend all meetings of the committee, even including telephone meetings and definitely including so-called executive sessions. It does no good if the consultant is invited to some meetings and not to others, for it is probably the meetings to which he is not invited that carry the most danger for shareholders.

The consultant should also offer opinions in writing on all new or revised compensation plans and, at least annually, on the pay package of the CEO. Oral opinions are not unhelpful, but people have a tendency to remember what they want to remember, and not necessarily to remember what they should remember. An opinion in writing reminds committee members of the consultant's feelings on a subject. And because it becomes a part of the corporate record, it also is available to plaintiffs in subsequent lawsuits alleging the payment of excessive or unreasonable compensation.

The committee's own compensation consultant should present to the committee, at least annually, a written sensitivity analysis of the pay package of the CEO and the other senior executives, showing the degree to which each component of the pay package, as well as all components taken together, is sensitive to both short- and long-term accounting and stock performance. And the compensation consultant should prepare the same sort of presentation when a new or revised compensation plan comes up for approval. Sensitivity analyses are critical to educating the committee on the degree to which a compensation plan contains risk. If analyses of these types were routinely undertaken, few committees would adopt restricted stock plans, and almost no committees would give their approval to such items as tandem grants of restricted stock and stock options, which embody the "heads I win, tails you lose" behavior.

Finally, the committee's consultant should prepare an annual analysis comparing the pay of the company's CEO to the pay of ordinary workers in the company, as well as to the pay of CEOs of major companies in such key countries as Japan, Germany, France, and the United Kingdom. Perhaps the committee will not factor these comparisons in any formal way into its decisions, but that doesn't mean the committee should not be aware of trends in these key areas.

The name of the compensation consultant should be required to be divulged in the company's proxy statement each year. Among other things, this will permit gadflies like me to analyze the performance of compensation consultants who serve multiple compensation committees. If a consultant proves to be too open-handed, that fact will come out over time.

Since the consultant to the committee can be expected to give unpopular advice from time to time, he needs to have some protection himself. That could come in the form of requiring the company to make a disclosure in its proxy statement if it fires the committee's consultant, and to indicate the reasons therefor. Moreover, the discharged consultant also should be permitted to offer his own defense in the same proxy statement. That same sort of protection is afforded to a company's auditors, and it makes sense to extend it to the committee's compensation consultant as well.

Earlier, we noted the conditions for the determination of a truly fair price, namely, that the buyer and seller are informed and that they bargain at arm's length. By assigning the compensation committee its own consultant, the committee will clearly be more informed. And if it is more informed, perhaps its willingness to bargain with the CEO at arm's length will be enhanced.

The compensation committee should also be required to make certain decisions in a formalistic manner. First, the committee should approve a list of companies against which it intends to measure the competitiveness of the company's compensation arrangements. Deciding on the so-called comparators forces the committee members to think about just who the company competes with for management talent. Next, the committee should adopt a series of guideline competitive positionings for various levels of long-term performance. For example, the committee might mandate that the company pay its CEO around the median of the comparator group if its long-term performance is normal, around the 75th percentile of the comparator group if its performance is also at the 75th percentile, and around the 25th percentile of the comparator group if its performance is also at the 25th percentile of the comparator group. Or, if the company wishes to adopt a more risk-taking posture, the committee might mandate that the company pay its CEO around the median of the comparator group for median performance, around the 90th percentile for performance at the 75th percentile, and at around the 10th percentile for performance at around the 25th percentile. Establishing these guidelines positionings is critically important because, without them, there is an overwhelming temptation to pay the CEO around the competitive median no matter what the performance of the company. And if that happens, pay-for-performance is a dead duck.

To dampen the incestuous relationship between the pay of the CEO and the pay of the outside directors, boards should adopt policies that peg their own pay to the median of a group of like companies. If their pay is below the median, they should raise it forthwith. If their pay is above the median, they should cut it forthwith. In short, they should insulate themselves from being bribed by a CEO who is bent on improving his own pay package.

There's one further suggestion that deals with boards and CEOs. Jay Lorsch, a professor at the Harvard Business School, has recommended that the chairman of the board not be the CEO of the company, but rather an outside director. Indeed, he goes a step further and urges that the CEO not even be a member of the board. In his view, the CEO should only be invited to meet with the board at the board's pleasure. Perhaps removing the CEO from the board would help to dampen the perception that he is the natural boss of the outside directors. If it does, then the outside directors will be in a better position to represent the shareholders when it comes time to bargain over the CEO's pay package. Arrangements like those proposed by Professor Lorsch have been common in Germany for many years. Perhaps it is no coincidence that the pay of German CEOs is much more reasonable than that of their American counterparts.

The Financial Accounting Standards Board, the Securities and Exchange Commission, and the IRS can also play pivotal roles in reforming the system. The accountants need to mandate charges to earnings for every form of executive compensation, most notably for stock options. As you have read, there has been a sale on stock options going on for forty years now, and that in turn has caused companies to grant them with abandon. A reasonable charge to earnings based on the true economic value of the grant will be a clear shot across the bow of open-handed compensation committees. To ensure that this desired action is actually taken, the Securities and Exchange Commission can signal the Financial Accounting Standards Board that if it doesn't act, the Securities and Exchange Commission will—by using the authority it has to impose its own accounting rules.

The Securities and Exchange Commission also needs to clean its own house in the proxy-reporting area. As it now stands, companies are permitted tremendous latitude to engage in obfuscatory behavior. What is needed here is a clear set of guidelines that every company must follow in providing its shareholders with a concise but accurate depiction of how much its senior executives are earning. At the least, the Securities and Exchange Commission ought to incorporate the following in its guidelines. First, the company should be required to report the pay of its five-highest-paid executives, whether those executives are employed by the parent corporation or any of its subsidiaries. The practice of letting a Paramount Communications avoid reporting the pay of the head of Paramount Pictures and the head of its publishing operations should be stopped.

The company should also be required to report separately the base salary of its top executives. The practice of permitting the company to lump together the base salary and the annual bonus should also be stopped. In this way, shareholders can obtain a more accurate picture of the responsiveness of the annual bonus to annual performance.

In the stock option area, the company should be required to provide the following information for each stock option grant made during the past year to each of the five executives being reported: the date(s) of the grant, the market price per share of the company's stock on the date of the grant, the strike price, the length of the option term, and the restrictions governing its exercise. By requiring the company to report on each option transaction during the year for each executive, rather than lumping them all together, there will be less temptation to try to capitalize on inside information. The company should also be required to report the following information for each option exercise that has occurred during the preceding year: the date(s) of the exercise, the number of shares exercised, the market price per share of the company's stock prevailing on the date of exercise, and the strike price per share.

In the restricted stock area, the company should be required to provide the following information for each grant of restricted stock made during the past year to each of the five executives being reported: the date(s) of the grant, the number of shares granted, the market price per share prevailing on the date of grant, and the restrictions imposed on the grant (e.g., restrictions on 20% of the shares granted lapse each year, commencing on the first anniversary of the date of the grant).

In the performance share and performance unit area, the company should be required to disclose the following information: the date(s) of each grant of performance shares, the number of shares granted or, in the case of performance units, the maximum amount of cash that may be earned, the market price per share prevailing on the date of grant, and the number of years in the performance measurement period. Moreover, the company should be required to show the number of shares or the sum of cash that will be earned for at least five representative points in the future performance spectrum, as well as the exact level of company performance that has to be achieved for the particular level of payout. This way, an analyst will be able to understand just what the company is "incenting" and the degree of pay risk being incorporated in the compensation plan.

In the perquisite area, the company should be required to disclose the estimated value of all perquisites being offered to the executive, as well as a description of each perquisite having other than some minimum value.

With such detailed disclosure, shareholders, the media, academics, and other interested parties will, for the first time, be able to place a price tag on the entire executive compensation package. And they will also be able to simulate the package to understand how it responds to various types of corporate performance. When those results are then published in the major media, the feedback effect should go a long way to persuading somnolent compensation committees to mend their ways.

As mentioned earlier, there is a case to be made for no disclosure of executive compensation at all, although I, for one, feel that to abandon disclosure would only make matters worse in the long run. But there is no case to be made for the halfhearted disclosure regulations that the Securities and Exchange Commission currently imposes. If you're going to do the job at all, do it right.

Our last recommendation for reforming the system involves the IRS. From probably about two days after the income tax law was first enacted in 1916, the government was thrust into the incentive compensation business. When the government permits taxpayers to deduct the interest on home mortgages, it implicitly "incents" home ownership and "disincents" rentals. Or when the government permits taxpayers to deduct contributions to charity, it implicitly "incents" giving and "disincents" stinginess.

In the world of executive compensation, the government has been in the incentive business ever since the first stock option plan was inaugurated in 1950. At that time, the government offered long-term, capital-gains tax treatment to stock options that met certain requirements. Among them was the condition that the strike price of the option could not be less than 85% of the market price of the stock on the date of grant. (By 1964, the requirement was stiffened to provide that the strike price be not less than 100% of the market price of the stock on the date of grant.)

Unfortunately, the conditions the government imposed on stock options did little to ensure that they would "incent" the desired long-term behavior. As already noted, we have executives like Stephen Wolf of UAL receiving millions for short-term run-ups in his company's stock price, and we have executives like Frank Lorenzo of

Continental Airlines Holdings receiving millions for producing horrendously negative shareholder results.

But the government could do the job right if it wanted to. It could offer a tax deal to a company that adopted a long-term incentive incorporating a number of key principles. First, the initial strike price should not be the market price per share on the date of grant. Rather, the strike price would be established by averaging the market prices of company stock during the preceding two years. In that way, it would be almost impossible for the CEO to capitalize on inside information by arranging a date of grant that gave him an ultra-low strike price.

The initial strike price, once set, would then be increased to include a minimum acceptable shareholder return. That return would be equal to what a shareholder could receive by investing in government bonds carrying a ten-year maturity. Assume here that the initial strike price is $50 per share and that the risk-free rate on a ten-year government bond is 9%. In that case, the final strike price would be determined by compounding $50 at 9% for ten years, thereby producing a figure of $118.37. Hence, the executive would receive no payout from his long-term incentive grant unless the market price at the time of exercise was greater than $118.37, thereby assuring shareholders of a minimum return equal to the risk-free rate before the executive began to be rewarded.

A company would be permitted to adopt a final strike price that was higher than the one just described, but not lower. So, if the minimum final strike price was the aforementioned $118.37, the company could adopt a strike price of $130 per share, if it wished.

The final strike price, once established, would be lowered whenever dividends were declared during the ten-year period following grant. Hence, if the final strike price were $118.37, and if a quarterly dividend of $1.00 were declared three months after grant, the strike price would be lowered to $117.37. (Actually, the reduction in the strike price would be greater than $1 to credit the executive with an assumed rate of return on the $1 dividend for the next 9.75 years.) In this manner, the executive would be "incented" to maximize long-term total shareholder return, and not just long-term price appreciation. Thus, a level playing field would be set up—one that would discourage the CEO from retaining earnings in the business and avoiding the payment of dividends, even though the company is incapable of earning a satisfactory rate of return on the incremental earnings being retained.

Exercise would not be permitted until the end of ten years following grant. Indeed, there would be no exercise at all; the executive would simply be given a payment—or no payment—shortly after the end of the tenth year following grant. This requirement would ensure that the long-term incentive plan would be just that: a long-term incentive plan, and not an opportunity for the executive to cash in early simply because the stock price was at some high point.

At the end of the tenth year following grant, the executive would finally be eligible to receive a payment, but only if the company's performance warranted it. First, the company would determine an "adjusted final market price per share" by using the same sort of two-year averaging procedure employed in determining the initial strike price per share. In this case, however, stock prices would be averaged for the two years preceding the *end* of the ten-year life of the grant, rather than the two years preceding the *beginning* of the grant. This adjusted final market price per share would then be compared to the final strike price per share, the strike price that had been increased to reflect a minimum shareholder return rate. If the adjusted final market price per share was less than the final strike price per share, the executive would receive no payment at all, even though the company's stock price had advanced to some modest extent during the ten-year period. But if the adjusted final market price per share was greater than the final strike price per share, the executive would receive a payment on each of the shares in his grant equal to that positive spread. To illustrate: suppose that the average market price per share during the two years preceding the end of the ten-year life of the grant is $150. Using the earlier example of an initial strike price of $50.00 per share and a final strike price of $118.37 per share (the result of increasing the $50.00 initial strike price to reflect a 9% compounded return to shareholders during each of ten years), the executive would be entitled to a payment on each of the shares in his grant equal to the amount by which $150.00 exceeded $118.37, or $31.63. Thus, if the executive had been granted 10,000 shares, his or her payment would be $316,300. On the other hand, suppose that the average market price per share during the two years preceding the end of the grant was not $150 but $100. In this case, the executive would receive no payment at all, even though the stock price had doubled—from $50 to $100— during the ten-year year life of the grant. The reason: though the stock price doubled, the compounded return to shareholders was less than the mandated 9% per year.

No "swaps" would be permitted. The executive is either going to be paid for good long-term performance, or he is going to earn nothing at all. And charges to earnings would be required for all such grants.

If a long-term incentive plan met all these characteristics, Congress might presumably be induced to grant it a favorable tax rate. For example, the tax rate might be 50% of the marginal rate then in effect. So, if the executive's marginal tax rate were 31%, the tax rate applicable to a long-term incentive payout meeting the above conditions would be 15.5%.

How, you might ask, can the government give a highly paid executive a tax break when we are running such a large budget deficit as it is? The answer is disarmingly simple: By increasing the taxes the executive pays on his base salary, on his annual bonus, on his restricted stock grants, and, indeed, on any compensation other than compensation received under the tax-approved, long-term incentive plan. Based on one analysis I ran for an article in the *New York Times,* the tax rate on those other forms of compensation might have to be raised as high as 60% on all salary and annual bonus to achieve what the economists call "revenue neutrality"—i.e., that point where the lost tax revenues from the approved long-term incentive plan are counterbalanced by the increased tax revenues from the higher taxes imposed on base salaries, annual bonuses, and so forth.

Think of the wonderful world that would be created by this proposal. Companies would be persuaded to go easy on unproductive forms of executive compensation. Paying an executive a base salary of

$1 million never did anybody any good—except the executive himself. Companies would be persuaded to make up the difference with a true long-term incentive plan. Over time, the difference in pay between a CEO who hit the ball out of the park for his shareholders and another CEO who grounded out to third would be awesome. And the CEO who grounded out to third might even be persuaded by his lack of pay to try some other field. Or if he doesn't take the hint, maybe his board, by having to confront how little he is earning, will push him out and get someone better to do the job.

The major problems besetting U.S. executive compensation aren't going to be solved by doing nothing. We need to buttress compensation committees and thereby help them to negotiate in an informed manner and at arm's length. We need to make sure that the true cost of every economic benefit a company gives its executives is charged to earnings. We need to assure that every economic benefit a company gives its most senior executives is duly reported in the company's proxy statement and in a way that outside analysts can understand fully. And finally, we need to harness the tax system to encourage the right forms of compensation and to discourage the wrong ones, all without making the federal budget deficit any worse than it is.

If we take these actions, we have a decent chance to put greed to work in the service of the U.S. economy and to begin to regain the economic glory that once was ours. If we do nothing, our dwindling competitiveness will dwindle even more. And, irony of ironies, the widening gap between CEO pay and worker pay may even inspire a new Marx and a new Lenin, but with American names, and all at a time when the original Marx and the original Lenin have been so discredited. All it takes is an understanding of the need for change. And an effort of will.

Sixteen

Counterattack 1992: The CEOs Respond

AT THE BEGINNING of this book, describing my transition from being a compensation consultant to a critic of excessive CEO pay, I said that I felt like the reformed sinner, Mary Magdalene. Well, in the year since the hardcover publication of this book, the proponents of high CEO pay have been trying to turn me into Saint Sebastian. They've shot so many barbed arrows at me, in fact, that I can hardly believe I'm still in one piece.

CEOs and consultants alike have sniped at me in the press, and lambasted me at business roundtables and seminars. Two regular writing assignments, at *Fortune* and *Financial World* magazines, soured because of corporate pressure. In the first instance, repeated urgings to change the content of my articles, in order to place the pay of Time Warner executives in a more favorable light, made it impossible for me to continue writing for *Fortune*. In the second, so many CEOs and their henchpersons voiced their displeasure with my articles that I was soon out of a job at *Financial World* too. Somebody there should have remembered the adage, "If you can't stand the heat, get out of the kitchen," before they hired me to roast overpaid CEOs. Fortunately, editors elsewhere don't seem to mind my culinary technique, and I am now contributing articles to the *New York Observer* and *Pensions & Investment*, as well as continuing to publish my newsletter, "The Crystal Report."

The attacks on me have been a side issue in the national debate which *In Search of Excess* has triggered. From the headlines to the editorial pages of the country's newspapers and magazines, on "60 Minutes," "ABC News Nightline," "Today," "Good Morning, America," and National Public Radio, and on the floor of the Congress and in the presidential election, the country has been wrestling with how closely CEO pay should be linked to company performance. At stake is nothing less than our national sense of fairness and our competitiveness in the global economy.

Along the way my position on CEO pay has found more than a few allies and supporters, from *Business Week* and the *Economist* to Bill Clinton and the Archbishop of Canterbury, who spoke out against American pay practices being imported into Britain. But the interesting thing, getting back to those barbed arrows, is how often my attackers have wound up shooting themselves in the whatsis and bringing even more public scrutiny to bear on executive pay. In my wildest imaginings, and they are pretty wild, I couldn't have dreamed up President Bush's traveling to Japan with a posse of overpaid American CEOs to whine about the Japanese playing hardball in the automobile business. Nothing could top that, unless it was the day a CEO acquaintance sent me a copy of a letter from Peat Marwick's Houston office—it went to two hundred CEOs around the country, along with a copy of this book—announcing the start-up of Peat Marwick's CEO COMPLINE, to help CEOs outfox my criticisms of their pay. The way I figure it, the only effective response to the criticisms in this book is for CEOs to clean up their act. So how about tripling that order, Peat Marwick? A lot of CEOs still haven't got the message.

Some have. In the past year a number of CEOs, including a few taken to task in the preceding chapters, have seen at least a part of their compensation packages reformulated. Among other companies, American Express Company has made large, no-fooling cuts in the pay package given to its CEO, James D. Robinson III, and in the process brought his pay closer to where it should be, given the company's size and performance. The company has done so without using the backdoor to rescind the cuts it made.

From 1990 to 1991, Robinson's total compensation package declined from $4.1 million to $2.3 million, a reduction of 44%. That's more like it, especially when you consider that in his 15 years on the job as American Express's CEO, Robinson has produced a compounded total shareholder return of 9.9% per year, a level of performance that ranks at only the 13th percentile among the 300 companies with the largest current equity capitalization.

If anyone was the poster child for compensation excess in 1990, it was Rand V. Araskog, the CEO of ITT Corporation. His company's performance had been lackluster, his pay package was spectacular, and he was the subject of considerable attention, not only from the media, but also from one of his largest institutional investors, the giant California Public Employees Retirement System, known as CalPERS. Indeed, CalPERS became so incensed about Araskog's pay that last year it voted its shares against the reelection of ITT's board of directors.

All that furor was not without effect. ITT has made extensive changes to both the size and design of Araskog's pay package. For 1991, Araskog received total compensation of $7.4 million. A year earlier, he received $11.5 million. Hence, he saw his pay reduced by 36% in the last year.

As pay reductions go, Araskog's cut was large. But it was not as large as it should have been. Although ITT is a huge company, it is not a high-performing company. Araskog has been CEO since July 1979, and between that date and the beginning of 1992, he has generated compounded total shareholder returns of 11% per year, a level of performance that ranks him at the 15th percentile of total returns achieved during the same period by the 300 companies with the largest equity capitalization. A fair level of total compensation for

Araskog would be $2 million per year. So he still is receiving more than triple what he should be.

Moving from the size of Mr. Araskog's pay package to its design, a number of praiseworthy qualitative changes have been made. First, ITT is no longer making grants of restricted stock to Araskog. Rather, it has switched to stock option grants. With the 80,508 restricted shares he was granted in 1990, Araskog can reap a huge reward of $2.1 million even if ITT's stock price drops in half. With the 170,000 option shares he was granted in 1991, he will receive nothing if ITT's stock does not rise above the strike price. Of course, if the stock does rise, Araskog will benefit hugely because the option grants him more than twice as many shares as the restricted grant.

But ITT has done more than switch from restricted stock grants to stock option grants. It has incorporated a provision that makes the option grants far riskier than the normal stock option grant. During the first nine years of the ten-year option term, Araskog may not exercise any of his option shares until the market price of a share of ITT stock increases 40%. Hence, during the first nine years of the term of the grant, the strike price is effectively $71.40, not $51.00. In the tenth year, he may exercise the option no matter how little the stock price has appreciated.

ITT has also changed its performance unit plan design. First, it has lengthened the performance measurement period from three years to four, thereby giving the plan that much more of a long-term performance focus. Second, it has changed the definition of performance from growth in earnings per share to return on equity, which is a much more solid measure of performance. Third, for managers of ITT divisions, it has predicated payouts on long-term divisional performance, instead of long-term corporate performance. That change ought to make the plan more motivational for executives who run profit centers.

Finally, ITT has improved its proxy disclosure tremendously. Like Citicorp, the company has provided a sort of roadmap of the various types of compensation it offers. Its proxy statement goes on to provide just about everything you need to know in easy-to-read tables that are grouped closely together.

All in all, ITT has made highly significant improvements. Araskog's pay needs to be cut further, unless he can effect a rapid turnaround in his company's stock price performance. But one theory holds that there's only so much that can be done in a single year. If that theory is correct, then ITT, to its immense credit, has done it.

Among the other good-guy CEOs is William Ruckelshaus of Browning-Ferris Industries, the Houston-based refuse systems firm, who has voluntarily given up an annual bonus equal to at least 25% of his salary. Edward Brennan of Sears, Roebuck also relinquished a bonus that was otherwise due him. His reasons, according to Sears' 1992 proxy, bear quoting: "Mr. Brennan . . . withdrew from [bonus] consideration to reflect the spirit of the salary freeze that was in effect for salaried employees in the Merchandise Group and Corporate staff during 1991." In a year when millions of hardworking Americans have suffered plenty of recessionary pain, Mr. Brennan's demonstration of team spirit deserves three hearty cheers.

James Preston, the CEO of Avon, made an even bolder move last December. He froze his salary for five years and also reduced his target short-term incentive award from 65% of salary to 50% of salary. In return, he was granted a one-time option on 50,000 shares of Avon stock. The option carries a strike price of $40.19 per share, the stock's market price on the date of the grant.

Preston's move may have been too bold. His stock option should actually have been twice as large as it was to compensate him for the loss of future salary increases and the reduction in his bonus opportunities. Though it is entirely possible that he will earn enough from his one-time stock option to repay himself for his foregone base salary increases and higher annual bonus payments, it is much less likely that he will come out whole when the substantially greater risk associated with a stock option is taken into account.

Two airline executives who took a lot of heat in the foregoing chapters have now shown a new, and welcome, appetite for pay risk. At AMR, the parent company of American Airlines, Robert Crandall has had his bonus cut to zero. This is quite a contrast to prior years, when Crandall's bonus seemed to float free of such mundane considerations as the company's profits. AMR's new bonus plan has two features that respect the interests of shareholders and rank-and-file employees, a vigorous minimum-performance threshold and a stipulation that no executive may receive a bonus as long as ordinary employees do not receive profit-sharing. (Lee Iacocca, please take note.) Robert Crandall has now shown himself to be the business world's answer to George Patton, an executive who doesn't just order the troops to attack but rides in the lead tank himself.

Stephen Wolf of UAL, the parent company of United Airlines, was the target of a lot of criticism, not just mine, when he earned millions in stock option profits just before the stock price slid toward the basement. Not only has the company's performance improved considerably since then, Wolf has relinquished his bonus for 1990 and 1991. In the latter year, the other senior executives of United have followed suit.

At the same time, Wolf has been granted stock options with what is called a tranche provision. Here's how it works. In 1991 Wolf was granted an option on 225,000 shares of UAL stock. The stock price at the time of grant was $147.88 per share. But only the first tranche of shares, 75,000 of the 225,000 shares granted, carries a strike price of $147.88; these shares can be exercised after May 1993. The next 50,000 shares carry a higher strike price of $170.06, 15% higher than the market price at grant, and they cannot be exercised before May 1994. The next 50,000 shares have a strike price of $195.56, 32% higher than the market price at grant, and can be exercised after May 1995. The final 50,000 shares carry a strike price of $224.90, a price that is 52% higher than the market price at grant, and can be exercised after May 1996.

In all, the four option tranches have a combined present value of $19 million. That's a stupendous amount of present value for one year's worth of options. But UAL, unlike most other companies, does not make option grants every year, and Wolf has not had a salary increase since he joined UAL in 1987. Most important, the option grant incorporates an appropriate measure of risk. Wolf will really have to perform for the shareholders in order to reap all the profit potential in the option.

UAL doesn't deserve sole credit for tranche options. The provision was also adopted by AT&T, which has recently made a number of mega-option grants to its top executives. CEO Robert Allen was awarded a 250,000 share grant in 1991. Sixty-two thousand five hundred shares carry a strike price of $38.625, the market price of a share of AT&T stock on the date of the grant. The next 62,500 shares carry a strike price 20% higher, $46.35 per share. The next 62,500 carry a strike price 30% higher, $50.21 pr share. And the last 62,500 shares carry a strike price that is 50% higher than the price prevailing at the date of grant, $57.94 per share. The four tranches are exercisable at two-year intervals after the grant.

The use of tranches, rather than a 250,000 share grant at the market price at the date of grant, has two advantages for AT&T's shareholders. The first is that tranches reduce the cost of the transaction. Obviously, 62,500 shares at a strike price of $57.94 are worth a good deal less than the same number of shares carrying a strike price of $38.625 per share. Even more important, the tranches offer an accelerating incentive. CEO Allen can't collect all his marbles and go home unless he meets increasingly stiff performance thresholds.

Sad to report, there is a lead lining in AT&T's cloud: its tranche grants come on top of normal option grants. Piling up incentives hasn't worked for most companies. Let's hope it does for AT&T.

AT&T's tranche grants are the brainchild of retired Warner-Lambert CEO Joseph Williams, who sits on AT&T's board of directors and its compensation committee. Joe Williams believes mega-option grants played a significant role in the huge success achieved by Warner-Lambert during his tenure as CEO. All we need to do now is sit back and see if AT&T's shareholder returns go through the roof like Warner-Lambert's did. Or, if you don't want merely to settle back, you can buy some AT&T shares and help make it two for two.

There have also been some encouraging moves outside the executive boardroom. As of this writing, the SEC is in the final stages of proposing new proxy reporting regulations for executive compensation levels and practices. These proposed regulations will make it far more difficult for a company to fudge the amount it is paying its CEO, and will allow shareholders to see much more quickly just how far a CEO's rewards depart from the company's performance.

Unfortunately, it will take many more such steps to bring rationality and a truly free market to executive pay. The backlash against pay reform is in full swing. And although the CEO/consultant counterattack hasn't amounted to much in terms of substantive argument, the 1992 proxy statements show that the unearned millions are still pouring into executive pockets.

In responding to this book and arguing that the ordinary CEO really isn't overpaid for his performance, CEOs and their consultants have flourished four red herrings. They have claimed, first of all, that my findings have been skewed by a few bad apples in the CEO compensation barrel, folks like Steve Ross whose pay is far greater than the average CEO's. Remove those bad apples, the experts say, and you will discover a robust relationship between pay and performance. They have pointed a finger at my use of average (mean) pay figures, which tend to be higher than median figures. They have opined that my habit of comparing CEOs across industries lumps apples (bad and good, I suppose) together with oranges. And they have reserved their bitterest criticism for the way I calculate the present value of a CEO's stock options: the consultants' position is that my methods produce a compensation figure for one year that ought to be spread out over the many years of the stock option grant.

These arguments aren't new, but they've been delivered with extra force in newsletters and opinion columns, and on talk shows, since this book was published. Having their say no doubt makes the consultants, and the CEOs who employ them, feel better. And I'm willing to admit there is even a grain of truth in what they say. Unfortunately for them, it's far too tiny to justify runaway CEO pay.

Let's see what happens when we throw those few bad apples out of the CEO pay barrel. In recent studies of 459 companies for *Financial World* magazine and 919 companies for the United Shareholders Assocation, I found an exceedingly weak link between pay and performance. In both studies, only about 5% of the variance in pay could be accounted for by difference in total shareholder return.

Taking the 459 company database for the purposes of this experiment, let's immediately throw out three extremely high and three extremely low pay outliers. Then let's regress CEO pay on company size. This gives a predicted appropriate pay level for each company, based on that company's size. We can then calculate the amount by which that predicted pay level exceeds the average pay level for the remaining 453 companies, and deduct that difference from the amount the company actually pays its CEO. The net effect of this process will be to produce a series of adjusted pay figures, giving larger-than-average companies pay credit for their greater size and giving smaller-than-average companies a pay penalty.

Now that we have adjusted actual pay for company size, we can regress each CEO's pay against his company's performance. The result, for the 453 CEOs left in the database, is that 9% of CEO pay can be pegged to company performance. Not much of a case for the bad apples argument, is it?

Wait a minute! I can hear those consultants shouting, you didn't throw out enough bad apples. Okay, suppose we rank the 453 companies in ascending order of the amount by which the CEO's adjusted pay exceeds what would be appropriate, given his company's performance. At the top of the list will be companies with the relatively lowest pay in relation to their performance, and at the bottom of the list will be the companies with the relatively highest pay in relation to their performance. The companies at either end of the list must be the bad apples. After all, what will better destroy the relationship between pay and performance than a CEO whose pay is wildly high in relation to his performance or, for that matter, wildly low in relation to his performance?

Following that reasoning, let's remove the top ten and the bottom ten companies from the list. Rerunning our regression analyses produces an 11% link between pay and performance. Must be a lot of bad apples left in that barrel of CEOs, eh? Let's hack another ten off the top and another ten off the bottom. This time the regression analyses show a 13% link between pay and performance. Could it be that all the CEOs in the barrel are bad apples?

Remember that Kenneth Lehn found that he could account for 74% of a professional baseball player's salary on the basis of the player's performance. Ironically, to show the same kind of correlation between CEO pay and performance, you'd have to throw 330 bad apples, 73% of the total, out of our CEO barrel. So there are a few good apples in there after all.

Some critics have moved on from the bad-apples argument to say that I've distorted the pay picture by using pay averages rather than pay medians. One such critic took issue with the assertion that the ratio of American CEO pay to that of the American worker is 160 times. The 160-times figure is indeed based on an average, the average CEO compensation of the 200 companies in a 1991 study I conducted for *Fortune*. A ratio based on median pay would be a much lower 108 times.

Now which is right? The best answer is probably another question. When was the last time an executive compensation consultant used a median in a report to his or her client, rather than the much higher arithmetic average, or mean, that will in turn support a much higher pay increase for the CEO?

To my way of thinking, insisting on the use of a median, rather than an average, is sheer hypocrisy. Pay rates, after all, are abnormally (or if you like the technical term, logonormally) distributed. That is to say, the old bell-shaped curve has a long right-hand tail. To ignore this maldistribution by choosing a median rather than an average figure is to underestimate true executive pay.

On the other hand, including extremely high and extremely low paid outliers does distort an average figure somewhat. Excluding two exceedingly high and two exceedingly low pay outliers from the *Fortune* study group lowers the ratio by which a typical CEO outearns a typical worker from 160 times to 144 times. So I will continue to use averages, after first excluding high and low statistical outliers. I hope this procedure will satisfy my average critic, though I suppose the median critic will continue to grumble.

Clifton Wharton, the CEO of the giant investment fund, TIAA/ CREF, recently argued that I would find a greater correlation between CEO pay and performance if I looked at pay statistics within industries rather than comparing the pay of CEOs across industries. Taking up Dr. Wharton's suggestion, I divided the 459 companies in my *Financial World* study into 20 different industry groups, ranging from pharmaceuticals to entertainment and from aerospace to railroads. I next removed from each group all the significant outliers, CEOs with either very high or very low pay, and performed three series of regression analyses on each industry, one for company size, a second for company performance, and a third for size and performance combined.

In the CEO pay versus company size regression, there was a statistically significant relationship in only five of the 20 industries. The five industries were food and consumer products, paper, pharmaceuticals, telecommunications, and power utilities. Two other industries, aerospace and petroleum refining, got close. In all other industries, there was no significant relationship between CEO pay and company size.

In the pay versus performance study, the results were even more disappointing. Of the 20 industries, only two proved to be relating pay to performance. They were food and consumer products and petroleum refining. Three industries came close to the mark: metals, publishing, and aerospace.

In the combined study of pay versus size and performance, only three industries had a statistically significant correlation. In petroleum refining, the figures show that a very high 69% of CEO pay can be accounted for on the basis of company size and performance. The comparable figure for food and consumer products is 67%, and that for aerospace is 54%. None of these correlations quite matches Kenneth Lehn's for baseball players, but they are, you might say, at least in the same ballpark.

For 17 out of 20 industries, however, an industry-by-industry analysis does not really help to explain why there is so little relationship between pay and performance. But I think Dr. Wharton has raised a useful point, and I will continue to run industry-by-industry regressions. The notion that there is not a monolithic market for CEOs' services, but rather a number of fragmented markets, each covering a different industry, certainly deserves continuing examination.

That brings us to the vexed question of arriving at a present value for stock option grants. Many defenders of high CEO pay maintain that it is not fair even to try to calculate a present value for stock options, which have a grant term of many years, and add that figure into an executive's current compensation.

Well, it is a judgment call to assign a present value to stock option gains. I've never said that it wasn't. But it is a judgment call that two major business magazines, *Fortune* and *Financial World*, continue to make regularly in their surveys of executive compensation. More important, it is a judgment call that CEOs themselves make all the time. So far as I know, every major consulting firm in the United States employs an option valuation methodology that is not unlike mine. Every month, perhaps 100 CEOs and board compensation committees are subjected to the torture of trying to understand the rationale underlying their consultant's statement that an option granted today has a present value of, say, $17.51 per share.

I read recently that H. Brewster Atwater, Jr., the chairman of General Mills and a key member of the Business Roundtable, claims that it is pretty much impossible to value an option at its grant date. Yet Mr. Atwater has introduced a pioneering compensation plan at General Mills, under which an executive can give up bonus dollars or salary dollars and obtain a greater number of stock option shares in return. Mr. Atwater has himself made such exchanges. Either Mr. Atwater and his fellow General Mills executives are playing blind hunches when they trade current dollars for option shares, or they have a pretty fair idea how many current dollars an option share is worth. My call is that it's the latter.

The plain fact is that however flawed a process present valuing stock options may be—and if it's good enough for Mr. Atwater it's good enough for me—the alternative would be worse. Because of the way stock options are reported, as well as because of the way they are cashed in, calculating a present value is often the only way to catch these payouts and assess their costs to shareholders.

Although the reports that my analysis of CEO pay was fatally flawed have been greatly exaggerated, America's CEOs have by and large acted as if the dirt were already piled on my grave. Over the last year they've paid lip service to the notion of linking their pay to their performance, and then gone on raking in money from the shareholders' asset fund. Two CEOs who have presented them-selves as reformed characters, yet kept on taking excessive pay, are John Akers of IBM and Paul E. Lego of Westinghouse.

IBM's 1992 proxy statement at first seems to give shareholders some long-overdue news. IBM's board has cut CEO Akers' pay significantly. For 1990, Akers received total pay of $7.4 million. In 1991 the figure was $4.9 million, a reduction of 34%.

Now a reduction of more than $2 million in pay is nothing to sneeze at. Rather, Akers and his board of directors should be con-gratulated for taking a step in the right direction. But the operative word here is "step," for they have a long journey ahead. Judged on company size and performance, IBM ought to have paid Akers $1.3 million in 1991. On that basis his current pay of $4.9 million needs to be cut more than $3 million more.

The primary reason underlying the need to make more drastic cuts in Akers's pay package lies in IBM's simply awful performance. Akers's pay and performance can be put in perspective by revisiting Michael Eisner of Walt Disney. During his time at Disney, Eisner has been hugely compensated. But what bears repeating is that the rewards have been earned fairly. Eisner's salary remains frozen at $750,000 per year until 1998. And remember that his bonus, 2% of Disney's after-tax net income, has a stiff performance threshold, 11% return on the company's average shareholders' equity during the year. As a result, Eisner has seen his pay drop dramatically, from $11.2 million in 1990 to $5.4 million in 1991, a reduction of 52%.

Michael Eisner's pay now nearly equals that of John Akers at IBM. But what is different is the two men's performance. Akers took the CEO's job at IBM in February 1985, while Eisner first sat in the CEO's chair at Disney in September 1984. Since his start, Akers has managed to produce a compounded shareholder return of minus 2.4% per year, putting him in the 1st percentile of CEOs at Amer-ica's 300 largest companies. During his tenure, Eisner has produced a compounded shareholder return of 37.7% per year, which ranks him at the 97th percentile. Obviously, something is wrong here. If

Akers is paid correctly, then Eisner is underpaid. Or, if Eisner's pay fits his performance, then Akers is overpaid.

John Akers probably feels pretty bad about his performance. He's had to take some tough personnel decisions lately, laying off several thousand employees. It'd be interesting to know if IBM's board ever considered trading off any more of Akers' pay to keep some of that valuable human capital working for the company.

At Westinghouse, CEO Paul Lego seems to have cut his pay, but really hasn't. In the process, he has managed to take in such observers as the *Wall Street Journal* and *Time*. Lego's maneuver was simple enough: he traded cash for mammoth stock options.

In 1990, Lego's cash compensation was a hefty $2,194,252. In 1991, it was a scant $677,083, a drop of 69%. But at the same time, Westinghouse's board dropped two option grants of 350,000 shares each in his lap. The present value of these two grants is $2,574,379. Lego also received a stock option grant in 1990, but the grant was considerably smaller, 124,000 shares with a present value of $1,173,650. As a result Lego's total compensation went from $3.4 million in 1990 to $3.3 million in 1991, not really a drop at all.

Lego's pay has held steady even as company performance slumped. On the day before he took over at Westinghouse, the stock priced closed at $36.75 per share. Then it proceeded to drop. When it got to $28.56 per share, Westinghouse's board rewarded Lego with the first of his two monster option grants, 350,000 shares with a strike price of $28.56 per share. When the stock dropped still further, to $16 per share, Lego received the second 350,000 share grant, with a strike price per share of $16.

As things now stand, if Lego succeeds in moving Westinghouse's stock price back to the $36.75 at which it was trading on the day he got the CEO's job, his two monster option grants will contain a combined paper profit of $10.1 million.

Consider for a moment how the game of football would look if it were played like the game of executive compensation. The ball is snapped, and the quarterback is nailed 20 yards behind the line of scrimmage. Nonetheless, if he and his team can gain 10 yards by 4th down, they are awarded a first down. The fact that they are still 10 yards behind the original line of scrimmage is overlooked. And if they gain a further 10 yards, thereby returning to where they started, the fans (that is, the board of directors) go wild. On that basis, you can win the game without ever getting beyond the 50-yard line.

Then there's the always fascinating case of Time Warner, where a merger that has already cost shareholders millions in lost profits will bleed them even more in the future. It's the only company around where shareholders get two CEOs for the price of four.

When Time and Warner Communications were being combined into Time Warner, the prospective co-CEOs, Steve Ross from Warner and Nicholas J. Nicholas from Time, were signed to 15-year contracts. When you examine these contracts you grasp immediately that Ross and Nicholas did not engage in a form of job sharing under which each took half the normal pay of a CEO. On the contrary, each took twice the normal pay of a CEO.

Three years down the road, Time Warner's board has decided that this kind of sharing doesn't buy good performance and it has sacked Nicholas from the co-CEO job. But it didn't want to leave him feeling completely jilted: in severance Nicholas has received a lump-sum payment of approximately $15,750,000, representing the present value of many of the 15-year obligations the board had undertaken in his employment contract. But that is not all the board has done. It has also kept Nicholas on at $250,000 per year until mid-1999. According to Time Warner's proxy, "Mr. Nicholas's services to the Company will not require a material portion of his time. . . . Mr. Nicholas is free to accept other employment, subject only to certain restrictions on competition with the Company and its subsidiaries, and to retain all proceeds therefrom." As a result Nicholas will continue to participate in Time Warner's various employee benefit plans, including health insurance, life insurance, and pension. And that's not all. The board has ensured that Nicholas's hundreds of thousands of stock option shares will remain alive for up to five years past his official termination of employment in 1999, and will allow him to earn out the thousands of restricted shares he was awarded previously.

As for Steve Ross, he has lost the title of highest paid CEO to Roberto Goizueta of Coca-Cola (of which more in a minute), but he's not doing too badly. Indeed, he's doing a great deal better than Time Warner's shareholders. Because Time Warner defines profits differently for Ross than for shareholders, Ross's bonus went up from $2,075,000 in 1990 to $2,864,000 in 1991, even though shareholders saw the company lose $99 million. Ross also received an additional 1991 bonus of $4 million, via a holdover from his days as CEO of Warner Communications whereby he pockets the tax savings the company receives from deductions for his deferred income. Thus Ross managed to earn $8.1 million for himself in a year when his shareholders continued to lose money as well as smart over what might have been.

Back in June 1989, Paramount Communications offered Time's shareholders $200 per share for their stock. Since then, Time Warner's shareholders have enjoyed (!) a return on their investment of minus 16.2% per year. Had someone invested $182.75 in Time stock (its high for June 1989) and reinvested dividends in more stock, that shareholder would have seen the value of his investment shrink to $109 by April 30, 1992. That performance level was lower than 95% of the 300 largest companies during the same period.

If the hypothetical shareholder had been permitted to accept Paramount Communications' offer of $200 per share and if that investment had increased at the 14.1 percent compounded annual rate of return enjoyed by the average company among the 300 largest companies, the shareholder would have seen his investment increase from $200 to $293. Interestingly, a value of $293 is within the range of stock prices that famed investment banker Bruce Wasserstein, who advised Time to turn its back on Paramount, estimated that the Time Warner combination might achieve by 1993. Mr. Wasserstein opined that Time Warner's stock ought to be trading somewhere in the $280 to $402 range by next year.

The difference between the $109 value per share of the investment that is and the $293 value per share of the investment that might have been, when multiplied by the 64.4 million shares of Time Warner stock outstanding when Time acquired Warner Communications, suggests that the value for shareholders that Ross and Nicholas have produced over the last three years has been minus $12 billion dollars.

That is a huge figure. Now if we could just get rid of the minus sign.

The shareholders may be taking a beating, but one group at Time Warner has done astonishingly well in the Ross-Nicholas regime, the board of directors. Before Time bought Warner Communications, it had 15 directors, and each outside director received basic pay of $38,000 per year, excluding extra pay for special board meetings and attendance at committee meetings not held in conjunction with board meetings. The combined companies needed a bigger, better-paid board. A Time Warner document issued in December 1989 revealed that the number of directors had risen from 15 to 24, that each outside director would now receive basic pay of $60,000 per year, and that a new pension plan had been created for directors. All of which goes to show that a happy board of directors makes for a happy CEO, or two.

On the evidence, Coca-Cola's board and its CEO must have quite a mutual admiration society going. Determined to show that Steve Ross's pay at Warner Communications and Time Warner was not the highest in the land, Coca-Cola's board has made strenuous efforts to establish CEO Robert Goizueta as the true Prince of Pay. The result is staggering. Including such items as a 1991 restricted stock grant of 2,000,000 free shares, Goizueta's pay over the past eight years has exceeded $400 million.

Given that Goizueta has performed brilliantly as CEO, is there anything wrong with this level of pay? Coke's shareholders have received total returns of a compounded 31.7% per year since Goizueta became CEO in 1981. So the sky may well be the limit for his pay. But I can't help noticing that shareholders of Gillette, Philip Morris, Gerber Products, Merck, General Mills, Food Lion, and Sara Lee have reaped similar rewards without paying nearly so much for CEO talent. I also can't help noticing that no one else in Coke's executive suite receives the kind of treatment Goizueta does. His second-in-command, Donald R. Keough, receives no restricted stock at all, and his stock options carry a stiff strike price. Looking farther down the company roster, I can't help wondering how Coke's rank-and-file have been rewarded for their company's stellar record.

Business Week recently quoted Ralston Purina CEO William P. Stiritz as saying that all the media hype concerning CEO pay is ". . . the lowest form of yellow journalism." And a member of Mr. Stiritz's board, Fletcher L. Byrom, ex-CEO of Koppers Company, blasted this book in particular for its "strong adverbs and adjectives, pejoratives, and neatly manipulated phrases." I've checked with my publishers, and they have assured me that these are hallmarks of good writing, but I can't help feeling that Mr. Byrom wants to take me to task as the sort of "yellow journalist" detested by Mr. Stiritz. What follows won't give him much comfort.

Apparently, there was a motivational crisis at Ralston back in early 1986. The company's board compensation committee, of which Byrom was a member, seems to have been dismayed at the startling lack of motivation being exhibited by Mr. Stiritz. Oh sure, he was earning a good salary, a good bonus, and he participated in some stock plans. But all that money was simply not doing the trick of turning him into a fierce carnivore. What else could the compensation committee do? It decided on a restricted stock grant of 160,000 shares.

At the time of the grant, the price of Ralston Purina stock was $63.38 per share (before adjusting for a subsequent 2:1 split). So the shares were then worth $10.1 million. But the grant came with a catch: Stiritz had to get Ralston's stock price up to $100 per share and keep it there for ten consecutive trading days, sometime within the next ten years, or else he stood to forfeit all the shares. To put it another way, he stood to earn either $16 million (160,000 shares at $100 per share) or nothing.

Now that's a powerful incentive, and apparently it had the desired effect of jumpstarting Stiritz. He doubtless continued to take an interest in Chex cereals and Ralston Purina pet foods. But he also continued to rely on a strategy he had been already been following: buying in the company's shares in the open market.

Using cash to buy in shares is not supposed to change the overall value the stock market puts on a company. If your business is worth $10 billion, including $1 billion in cash, and if you then take the cash and buy in shares, some shareholders end up receiving $1 billion in cash and the rest of the shareholders end up owning a company that has to be worth only $9 billion. But try selling that notion to the

average speculator. He will likely reply, "Sure, the company probably won't be worth more in the long run, but if everybody is buying
the stock in anticipation of an imminent buyback, the stock price, at
least in the short run, is going to go up fast."

And buy Stiritz did. From the second quarter of fiscal 1986
through the second quarter of fiscal 1991, Ralston's outstanding
shares shrank by 26%. There were a few near misses along the way,
but by February 22, 1991, Ralston Purina's stock crossed the magic
$100 line for the tenth consecutive day, and Stiritz took clear title to
$16 million of stock. He also stopped buying in large quantities of
shares. From the second quarter of fiscal 1991 through the first quarter of fiscal 1992, the number of shares outstanding decreased by only
1.3%, presumably reflecting the fact that increasing the stock price to
some arbitrary point was no longer of great importance.

Had Stiritz taken the full ten-year term to clear this hurdle, the
boost in stock price, together with the dividend yield, would have
amounted to total return for shareholders of 6.7% per year. Is that
the sort of performance that is worthy of a $16 million reward?
Ralston Purina's board could easily have bought a long-term Treasury bond and locked in a ten-year total return of close to 10% per
year, instead of dangling $16 million in front of the CEO.

Given the heavy random influences in the stock market, and the
resulting volatility in stock prices, you have to wonder whether
judging a stock's price over a period of time as short as 10 or even 20
days really offers a good measure of company performance. When a
board of directors also stipulates a go/no go provision, so that a
CEO gains hugely or not at all, it has created an incentive for sharp
price swings rather than steady accumulation of value.

Stock volatility is also the key to a recent maneuver by Georgia-
Pacific's CEO, T. Marshall Hahn. Remember that he co-pioneered
the tax-reimbursement feature for CEO pay with Roberto Goizueta.
He has just pulled off an even niftier feat. He has been paid three
times for the same performance.

In January 1988, Georgia-Pacific's stock price was $33.47 per
share. At that point, the company instituted a Long-Term Incentive Plan which provisionally allocated Hahn 140,000 shares. Hahn

could take title to all the shares if the price of Georgia-Pacific's stock doubled within five years. But if the stock didn't get that far, he was not to be left with nothing in the bag. For every 20% increase in the share price over $33.47, so long as it was sustained for ten consecutive trading days, Hahn would earn 20% of his 140,000 share allocation.

By the fall of 1989, Georgia-Pacific's stock price had risen to more than $60.25 per share, and Hahn had earned 80% of his shares. Then a funny thing happened. The share price dropped to $44.20, and Georgia-Pacific cancelled the Long Term Incentive Plan and replaced it with a new one that provisionally allocated Hahn 100,000 shares. The same provisions applied: Hahn would get all the shares if the share price doubled, and 20% of his allocation for every 20% increase in share price. And Georgia-Pacific set the base price from which the increases would be measured not at $44.20 per share, but at $50 per share.

That sounds like a tough performance hurdle, and *Fortune* magazine took pains to praise it. Looked at a little more closely, the new Long Term Incentive Plan gives Hahn 20,000 shares, worth $1.2 million, for moving the share price back to where it was in 1989, effectively paying him twice for the same performance. Georgia-Pacific's board felt so good about this double dip that it gave Hahn a third scoop of ice cream. In 1991, Hahn received a provisional allocation of 50,000 shares, this time carrying a base price of $54.10 per share. He will take title to 20% of these shares, worth $1 million, when Georgia-Pacific's stock price rises to $64.92 per share. Georgia-Pacific thus arranged to pay Hahn three hefty sums for yo-yoing the price of a share from $50 to $60.

My account of the CEO/consultant counterattack wouldn't be complete without mention of two more episodes, involving Champion International CEO Andrew C. Sigler and the *Harvard Business Review.*

In December 1991 and February 1992, Ira M. Millstein, a partner in the New York law firm of Weil, Gotshal & Manges, and one of the top corporate lawyers in the United States, wrote to me in care of *Financial World* magazine. In these letters, he complained, rather stridently, that I had unfairly criticized Andrew Sigler's pay at paper products giant Champion International, and he suggested that I had done so out of personal animus. When I offered to print Mr. Millstein's letters, and my rebuttal, in my newsletter, "The Crystal Report," he asserted his copyrights in the two letters and warned me not to publish them. I in turn asserted my first amendment rights as a working journalist and released copies of his letters and my reply to the press. I also explored the matter of Sigler's compensation at some length in my newsletter. The ensuing controversy gave the *Wall Street Journal*, the *New York Times*, and others in the media plenty to talk about.

The heart of Mr. Millstein's complaint was twofold, as I saw it: that Mr. Sigler was not such a bad performing CEO as to merit attention from me, and that I had distorted his pay in calculating the present value of the stock options Champion had granted him. Mr. Millstein had other bones to pick, but they were pinky-finger bones compared to these two issues.

Let me emphasize that I have no personal animus against Andrew Sigler, whom I've never met or spoken to. But as a student of executive compensation in relation to company performance, just what am I to make of Andrew Sigler's more than 17-year tenure as CEO of Champion International? Sadly for Champion's shareholders, his pay has been big and his performance has been nothing short of woeful, whether compared against large companies in many industries or only against those in the paper industry.

Over the 17 years ending in January 1992, Champion International has delivered a compounded annual total return to its shareholders of 7.6%. In contrast, a shareholder who invested in the average company, among the 403 large companies in my *Financial World* study whose stock had been publically traded for the same 17 year period, would have earned a compounded annual return of 16.6% per year. When weighed against this group of 403 companies, Champion ranks at the 8th percentile. When compared to the 15 companies in the 403 company group active in the paper industry, Champion ranks at the 7th percentile. In fact, throughout the 17 years studied, Champion has not once managed to give investors a return on investment that beats the safest of all securities, 90-day

United States Treasury Bills. To perform badly is bad enough. To perform consistently badly, and over a 17-year run as CEO, must be little short of intolerable to Champion's long-suffering investors.

Along with this low-level performance has gone some pretty high-level compensation. Sigler has never failed to collect a hefty bonus, even during periods of low or negative profits. He has also regularly collected large stock option grants. Interestingly, the lower the stock price has dropped, the larger his option grants seem to have been. If he can recover even part of the ground the company has lost under his leadership, he will be rewarded munificently.

Which brings up Mr. Millstein's second criticism, that the present value I calculated for Sigler's options distorted the true extent of his pay. As we've seen, there is no sensible alternative to present valuing stock option grants. And there is no getting around the fact that Sigler has amassed a mountain of stock option shares. In 1990, Sigler received an option on 47,000 shares carrying a strike price of $27.09 per share, and in 1991 he received an option on 200,000 shares with a strike price of $26.875 per share. The present value of these grants is $2.2 million.

In its May–June 1992 issue, the *Harvard Business Review* published an article entitled "Executive Compensation" by Andrew R. Brownstein and Morris J. Panner, two lawyers in the New York firm of Wachtell, Lipton, Rosen & Katz. Casting a beady eye on my research finding that only about 5% of the variation in CEO pay can be accounted for on the basis of company performance, Brownstein and Panner argue that there is in fact a strong correlation between CEO pay and company performance.

The basis for this contention, which would demolish my work in an instant if it were true, lay in a study of 129 unnamed companies by Michael S. Kesner, a partner of the consulting firm Arthur S. Andersen & Company. As you can imagine, I was pretty curious to see what Mr. Kesner had up his sleeve.

To begin with, Kesner published statistical results showing high correlations, "r-squareds," between pay and performance. But looked at closely, the r-squareds turn out be r's. And even these numbers rest in many cases on the influence of a single statistical outlier. Moreover, he obtained these numbers by working with as few as seven data points, each of them a median or average of grouped data. Calculating statistics with a few averages is a very handy way to hype your results, but it doesn't produce reliable numbers.

Like Dr. Wharton, Kesner also made a fuss about inter-industry pay differences. To account for such differences, Kesner devised his own subjective scoring system, involving his assessment of what he labeled Management Control, Complexity, and Business Risk in seven industries. The way he went about his task smells strongly of manipulating his factors and his factor weights to produce the results he desires. He also erred by defining Business Risk as the ratio of a company's equity to its assets and then declaring that "higher-risk businesses will have the greatest ratio of equity to assets." Even the beginning student of finance should know that it is the other way round.

In trying to prove that there is a high correlation between CEO pay and company performance, Kesner has defined company performance to be one-year growth in sales and one-year return on equity. His choice of an exceedingly narrow time window aside, what happened to that most critical performance measure of all, total shareholder return?

In addition, some of Kesner's mathematical transformations do not appear to be accurate. When I called him to ask about the apparent errors, he replied that, it being the end of the business day, he could not enter his "data room" to re-check his results. Although he said he would do so promptly and get back to me, some months have passed with no sign of his doing as promised.

Ironically, even if you accept Kesner's flawed data, they do not in fact show a high correlation between CEO pay and company performance. Rather the data, analyzed in a straightforward manner, prove my conclusion that there is hardly any relationship between CEO pay and company performance.

Brownstein and Panner also relied heavily on the work of Professors Michael C. Jensen and Kevin J. Murphy of the Harvard

Business School. Professors Jensen and Murphy are serious scholars. In 1990, they published in the *Harvard Business Review* the results of an immense study of 430 companies, arguing that increasing the sensitivity of CEOs' pay packages to total shareholder return would benefit the American economy. The only problem with their research is that there is no significant relationship between pay-package sensitivity, using their 430 companies and their sensitivity numbers, and total shareholder return, whether the time window is one year, ten years, or any intervening period. Their research raises the troubling question of whether all the money being spent on designing motivational pay plans will, at the end of the day, do anything for America's shareholders except increase their costs of doing business. I published my research in my newsletter and sent a copy to Professor Jensen. He took the time to meet me and a colleague from the University of California (Berkeley) Business School. But he did not at that meeting offer any cogent explanation for my findings. Nor has he offered one since.

As you can see, the war over CEO pay is by no means at an end. CEOs and their consultants will naturally follow their self-interest and attempt to justify the huge payouts CEOs draw from shareholders' assets. What has changed is that CEOs now must make a real effort to justify their pay to their shareholders, the press, and the public at large. That is the best sign we could have of the greater scrutiny that is at last being applied to executive pay. At a time when the American economy has shown itself to be all too fragile, every step to bring CEO pay into line with company performance is a step toward renewing American competitiveness.

Appendix

CEO Pay and the Investor—
Cautionary Tales for Stock Pickers

Aᴄᴄᴏʀᴅɪɴɢ ᴛᴏ the efficient markets hypothesis—one of the sacred beliefs of modern financial economists—rational investors project a company's earnings (or, alternatively, its cash flow) far into the future and then discount it back to the present, using a discount rate that is reflective of the risk they are taking. The present value of the discounted future earnings then becomes the price they are willing to pay today for a share of stock. To take a very simple example, assume that someone offered you a single cash payment of $100, ten years from now. How much would you pay now to secure that future cash payment? If you desired to earn, say, 15% per year on any investments you made, you would discount the $100 future payment at the rate of 15% per year for ten years, and you would therefore offer the seller a cash payment of $24.72. Or think of it another way. If you placed $24.72 in a bank account, and it earned interest at the compounded annual rate of 15% per year, you would have $100 in your bank account ten years from now. In determining the price of a stock, of course, you will be discounting not a single cash payment ten years from now, but rather a stream of cash payments, and possibly some losses as well. The sum of all those discounted cash payments becomes the price you are willing to pay for the stock. That price will vary from day to day, depending on what you learned the day before about the company or about any other salient factor that might impact stock prices. At least that's what the efficient markets hypothesis contends.

If all that is true, what does the pricing of a stock have to do with how much, or how, a CEO is paid? In truth, the CEO's pay package probably doesn't have much to do with stock values. But it should.

The reason it probably doesn't at the moment lies in a mistaken belief on the part of sophisticated investors (Wall Street types, institutional investors, etc.) that the cost of the CEO's pay package is a drop in the bucket of company costs and hence is likely to be lost in the rounding of earnings. But consider for openers that the CEO's pay package, as has been detailed time and again in this book, has grown to gargantuan proportions. The $7.6 million value of the 1990 pay package given to John Akers, the CEO of IBM, is not going to get lost even in the rounding of IBM's earnings, and IBM has more earnings than any other American company. Moreover, investors may be overlooking the multiplier effect that the CEO's pay has on the pay of others in the organization. Before considering this, however, let's look at a controversial theory now running through academe—the so-called Tournament Theory.

The creators of this theory started by posing a hypothetical situation that went something like this: Five executive vice presidents report to the CEO, and all are vying to succeed him when he retires. Each executive vice president earns $500,000 per year. The CEO retires, and one of the five executive vice presidents gets the nod. He is paid $1 million per year. Question: Why doesn't one of the four losers step forward, raise his hand, and offer to take the CEO's job for $500,001? Why, in other words, is there such a big difference in the pay of the four executive vice presidents on the one hand and the CEO on the other?

The creators of the Tournament Theory explain the large compensation gap by asserting, ironically, that the executive vice presidents are underpaid. The theory holds that a tournament is in progress and that the winner of the tournament becomes CEO. The entry fee for competing in the tournament is for the executive vice president to give up some of what he is truly worth and to contribute that foregone sum into a pot, which then becomes prize money for the CEO. Or, to state the reverse, in a world in which none of the executive vice presidents were permitted to compete for the CEO's job, they would demand more money and might earn, say, $600,000 per year. Then, since they were not each contributing some of their worth to a prize pool, the CEO might earn only, say, $800,000 per year.

There is some intuitive support for the Tournament Theory. For example, think about how law firms run—or at least, how they used to run. A graduate fresh out of law school agreed to work for a law firm for close to slave wages in order to compete in a tournament that might end in a coveted partnership some seven years later. These young law graduates might be argued to have contributed some of their true worth to a pool to be used to reward the winners of the tournament, the partners of the firm.

The creators of the Tournament Theory argue—seemingly logically—that if the prize for winning a tournament is small, then the competing players will not be willing to contribute much of their true worth to the prize pool. Hence, there is a huge pay differential between the pay of the CEO and the pay of the executive vice presidents because the prize of becoming CEO is so great. But when the prize is to be a first-level foreman, who earns perhaps only 15–20% more than his workers, the workers will not be willing to contribute very much, if any, of their true worth to the prize pool.

If the Tournament Theory is really true, it might make sense to wildly overpay the CEO of a major company. The prize being so great, the players who are competing in the tournament to become CEOs might be willing to give up even more of their true worth. The result: Overall executive compensation costs in the organization might be lower than they would have been had the CEO been paid more moderately.

Nice theory, but it doesn't work. As already mentioned, research I have conducted shows that if the CEO is being paid above the market, so will his number two executive be paid above the market (though not perhaps by as much). And so will his number three executive. And on and on. Hence, when the CEO is paid $1 extra of compensation, the cost to the organization is not simply $1. Rather, the number two executive's pay is likely to rise around 50 cents. And so forth with other executives. Perhaps, then, the overall cost to a company to give the CEO $1 extra of compensation is on the order of $40 to $50. And if that is so, the added costs are certainly not going to get lost in the rounding.

Compounding the problem is the fact that CEO pay abusers rarely are content to stop with being just a bit overpaid. Rather, they continue to savage their shareholders year after year, and their pay package grows disproportionately to the size and/or profitability of the company. That in turn means that earnings forecasts made by the rational investor may turn out to be too high, thereby producing a current stock price that is also too high, thereby cutting the investor's future returns on his investment.

There is a further overlooked cost here, and that concerns the reactions of the company's workers to overly high CEO and other senior executive pay. A few years back, I asked a senior executive of Walt Disney what the workers thought about Michael Eisner making so much. He said: "The workers are not socialists, and therefore the reaction is not what you might have anticipated. Rather, the workers are all for Eisner making huge amounts of money. They just want a little more for themselves—like a dollar or two more per hour." So the presence of huge CEO pay most likely creates greater pressure on the part of the workers for more pay. And though the results of this pressure cannot be quantified, any extra pay that is won can have an awesome effect on future earnings, given the huge number of workers involved.

One has to wonder here what the reaction of the employees of Chrysler will be to the restricted stock that was given to Lee Iacocca and some 1,800 other Chrysler managers in lieu of a cash bonus for their 1989 performance—or should I say, non-performance. Will the workers, through their union, the United Auto Workers, reason that things can't be that tight at Chrysler, and therefore, the company can afford to do something extra for the workers the next time the union contract comes up for renegotiation?

Thus far, we have talked about the size of the CEO's pay package. But sophisticated investors also need to think about the composition of the pay package. If the CEO is earning an inordinately high base salary, that is a sign that the company's ratio of fixed costs to variable costs is too high. In turn, that will likely mean that the company will respond less well in an economic downturn.

The same holds true if the CEO's annual bonus is relatively unresponsive to changes in company profitability. A number of Time Warner's most senior executives were guaranteed bonuses of not less than 125% of base salary. At the end of the day, there is no difference between a base salary of $800,000 per year and a guaranteed bonus of 125% of salary, and a base salary of $1.8 million per year. But the bonus doesn't have to be formally guaranteed to prevent it from being unresponsive to changes in company profitability. A willing compensation committee can simply make sure that the bonus varies little with company results.

Companies that rely heavily on restricted stock grants in structuring the pay packages of their CEOs and other senior executives are generally, though not always, dogs. The alternative to a grant of free shares is to accept a stock option on perhaps three to four times as many shares. Hence, if a CEO is relatively bullish on the company's future, he will always prefer a stock option, because that leverage of three-to-four times as many shares will produce greater compensation than he might have received from the much smaller number of free shares. That being the case, it can be argued that a CEO who accepts free shares is either highly risk-averse, or not very bullish on his company's future, or, worse, both. In several studies I have conducted, I have found that investors could earn superior long-term returns simply by dumping from their portfolios any companies that make restricted stock grants to their CEOs and retaining the stock of any other companies that, whatever else they do, don't make restricted stock grants to their CEOs.

Companies that rely on performance shares and performance units as long-term-incentive-reward vehicles are not in the same dismal camp as the restricted stock granters. But a sophisticated investor still ought to consider how much performance is being demanded for the reward being offered. Has the company kept the tennis court net at regulation height? Or has it lowered it to two inches from the ground, thereby making the game a lot more satisfying to the players, if not perhaps to the gallery? Moreover, investors need to see what happens when a company's performance share plan or Performance Unit Plan fails to pay out. Does the management accept its lumps graciously? Or does it immediately find another way to reward itself? W. R. Grace adopted a restricted stock plan shortly after its performance unit plan failed to pay out. Perhaps the timing was merely coincidental, perhaps not.

Investors also need to pay more attention to how many stock option shares are being granted. The total number of shares the company grants each year to all employees is shown in the footnotes to its annual report. Remember here that a company granting a huge number of option shares incurs no charges to earnings; rather, it dilutes its future earnings per share, inasmuch as future earnings are going to have to be divided by a larger number of shares outstanding. So the investor who fails to make some windage adjustments for stock option grants when he estimates the company's future earnings is looking for trouble. Note here also that the trend of option share grants may be as important as the sheer volume of shares granted. Is the company granting 1 million shares each year? Or did it grant 500,000 shares a few years back, 750,000 shares the year before last, and 1 million shares last year? Attention should also be paid to mega-stock grants given to the CEO and other senior executives. These are not only costly; they also create pressure on the company to increase the size of grants to many other executives.

Finally, investors need to consider the under-reported aspect of long-term incentive plan proliferation. A company, which had been granting only stock options to its executives, begins to make grants both of stock options and restricted shares. Leaving aside the onus connected with restricted shares, that may not be all bad, provided the company cuts back on the size of its stock option grants to make room for its second long-term incentive plan. But companies rarely do cut back; they simply pile one form of long-term incentive compensation on top of another. In several studies where I have constructed a mathematical model to predict the size of stock option grants received by CEOs, I have found that knowing whether the CEO also receives a second or third form of long-term incentive compensation, and the economic value of that additional form, contributes nothing to the predictive value of the model. In other words, those second and third forms of long-term incentive compensation simply add to the costs of the CEO's pay package, as well as to the costs of the pay packages for every executive in the company who is accorded similar compensation treatment. Each added long-term incentive plan tends to increase the CEO's pay package by about 32%, while contributing to a 1.4 percentage point decline in the company's ten-year total shareholder return rate.

The fact that there is so much wrong with senior executive pay packages in the United States has been dramatically underscored by the movement to leveraged buyouts (LBOs) and leveraged recapitalizations. There, at least some companies have thrown out the rule book and have tried to take executive compensation back to a simpler past, one where earning more reward was dependent on taking on more risk.

Here's a recipe that LBO fans claim will work every time. Take your company private—or at least leverage the hell out of it. If you currently have $2 billion of equity and $1 billion of debt, go out and borrow $1.9 billion. At that point, you will have $2 billion of equity and $2.9 billion of debt. Then use the proceeds of the $1.9 billion loan to give your shareholders a one-time dividend of $1.9 billion. When you are done, you will have $0.1 billion of equity and $2.9 billion of debt. And you will be a trendy company.

You will also have just shot yourself in the gut. So, in order to stanch the copious flow of blood, you will have to cut back costs, and you will have to do it fast. You can sell assets, if that won't damage the rest of the company and if the assets can fetch a good price. You can cut out all executive bonuses—at least until the company outearns the monstrous extra costs of servicing its debt and thereby returns to profitability. And you can cut executive salaries. Hence, you can explain to one of your executives: "You are currently earning a base salary of $200,000 per year, and last year, before we leveraged the company, you received an annual bonus of $100,000. But we can no longer afford to pay you cash compensation of $300,000 per year, because we desperately need the cash to pay our interest bill. Therefore, you won't be receiving any bonus for probably the next three to five years. And your salary is going to have to be reduced to $100,000 per year."

At the conclusion of this speech, your executive—unless he is absolutely gutless, or just plain stupid—is going to grab his coat and hat and depart for some other company that has the sense not to tamper with his pay package. So you figure you're going to have to give him something to make up for the $200,000 per year decrease in his cash compensation package. You offer him a huge number of stock option shares. After all, the stock is now worth only $5 per share, and if the company can extricate itself from its self-dug hole, the stock will likely soar in value; leverage is a wonderful thing to behold—on the upside. Or, if pushed, you offer the executive some free shares; they're only worth $5 apiece, so you aren't giving away too much.

Let's review the bidding. The day before yesterday, you used to have a normal company. Executives earned hefty base salaries, they received almost guaranteed bonuses, and they flew everywhere on the company jet. What's more, the company had a fairly predictable stream of earnings, and because it wasn't leveraged all that much, its profit volatility was pretty low. Today, all bets are off. Executives have been told to expect no bonuses for the next three to five years, their salaries have been cut, and they fly in the back of an American Airlines jet because the company jets have been sold. The profit stream is now highly volatile due to that huge amount of added interest that must be paid each year, whether or not profits from operations are all that robust.

But your executives' minds are wonderfully concentrated—concentrated on survival. And when they have a free moment or two, they dream about becoming mega-multimillionaires after the company pays down it debt and its stock price soars. Because they have so little to lose, having lost it all already, and so much to gain, they shed their normally risk-averse nature and, imagining themselves to be the civilian equivalents of General "Stormin' Norman" Schwarz-kopf, sally forth in the company's tanks to assault and then vanquish their competition.

Will that recipe work every time? Possibly, it may. First, con-sider the Darwinian selection that occurs when a company leverages itself to the hilt and takes the pay actions just described. The faint of heart are doubtless motivated to leave the company and to find jobs at other companies which are willing to pay them as they were paid before. Hence, those who are left, or, to put it another way, the ones who are willing to stay, must by definition be less risk-averse than those who have departed. In turn, that means that the company will be more willing to take risks than in the past. Which is a good thing, because business-as-usual will never work in a highly leveraged or-ganization; risks must be taken if the company is to have a chance of survival, much less of eventual success.

Second, executives have the opportunity to receive future re-wards in line with the extra risks they are taking. If everything works out as planned, executives won't merely become wealthy. They will become seriously rich.

There is, of course, the possibility that unanticipated events beyond the company's control will make the recipe for success less of a sure thing. Consider the leveraged recapitalization of Carter Hawley Hale, and in the same industry, the leveraged buyout of R. H. Macy. Carter Hawley Hale, faced by a hostile takeover, spun off some of its prize divisions (Neiman, Marcus and Bergdorf Good-man) to its shareholders. Then it borrowed a huge amount of money and used the funds to pay a one-time dividend to its shareholders. That action, of course, had the effect of leveraging the company to the hilt and also reducing its stock price substantially. Nonetheless, the company's shares continued to trade publicly. Macy, for its part, also borrowed a huge amount of money. But rather than go the Carter Hawley Hale route and leave a lot of shares in the hands of the public, with each share worth only a couple of dollars, it bought all its outstanding shares and went private.

Neither Carter Hawley Hale nor Macy likely anticipated that retail sales might soften, especially at the key 1990 Christmas season.

And neither company likely anticipated the collapse of the junk market and the attendant rise in interest costs on low-grade debt. As of this writing, Carter Hawley Hale has filed for bankruptcy, and Macy is scrambling to find the funds to reduce its leverage before it suffers the same fate. Besides having Carter Hawley Hale's bankruptcy to remind it of the perils of leverage, Macy's top executives must frequently think about the sad case of Robert Campeau's takeover of Federated and Allied Department Stores. Although Federated and Allied owned such successful retailing outlets as Bloomingdale's and I. Magnin, Campeau had so leveraged the combined firm with debt that it was unable to withstand even the slightest wind of adversity.

Still, the LBO game is probably worth playing—at least for some companies, and provided that the debt load doesn't become suicidal. Executive motivation is likely to increase dramatically, as is risk-taking behavior. And company fixed costs are likely to decrease dramatically.

Nonetheless, not every company can play the LBO game. First, it does no good to add volatility on top of volatility. If the company's profit stream from basic operations is already loaded with volatility, adding even more volatility in the form of huge added interest expense may mean that any one of 500 possible future scenarios, not just five scenarios, may send the company into Chapter 11. And second, it is important not to forget that there is only a limited supply of risk takers around at any point in time. Earlier, we noted that one effect of creating an LBO environment is probably to send risk-averse executives into the arms of other companies. As company after company goes the LBO route, the dwindling supply of normally run companies begins to contain more and more risk-averse executives.

Some of those normally run companies—companies that have not undergone leveraged recapitalizations or attempted leveraged buyouts—have nonetheless thought seriously about revising their executive compensation packages so as to mimic the high-risk, high-reward packages offered elsewhere. But because there are so few risk takers around, they are in danger of sabotaging what they were seeking to accomplish. Executives, contrary to the advice of financial experts, are usually highly non-diversified. They have some equity in their house, and they have lots of company shares. And that's about it. If you cut the executive's cash flow, as happens in an LBO, what with the disappearance of bonuses and the diminution in salaries, and then if you load up the executive's portfolio with terribly high-risk stock instruments, you compound the problem of non-diversification. Of course, the executive who loves to take risks is going to be in hog heaven. But how about the executive who is just trying to keep a low profile until retirement? How will he respond? According to the psychologists, he is likely to respond by taking even less risk than before. It's sort of like moving from an ocean liner to a rowboat on the open sea. If you observe that the slightest movement produces a pronounced rocking motion in the rowboat, maybe you decide to sit as still as possible.

So the LBO concept may work beautifully for some companies, but it can't work beautifully for all companies. And it can't work beautifully even for some companies if it is bastardized from day one. Consider here the case of RJR Nabisco, perhaps the most celebrated of all the LBOs. Henry Kravis and the other senior executives who run Kohlberg Kravis Roberts (KKR), arguably the most successful investment banking firm of the 1980s, are known to be very smart. One of the things that makes them smart, apparently, is a keen knowledge of their own limitations. When they engineered the RJR Nabisco LBO, they didn't step in to run the company themselves. Rather, they hired one of the best executive recruiting firms in the United States, and that firm scoured the landscape for the best executive they could find. In due course, they came up with a name for KKR: Louis V. Gerstner, then the president of American Express and the heir apparent to James Robinson III, Amex's CEO. Perhaps the folks at KKR tried to get Gerstner to accept a traditional high-risk, low-cash pay package. But if they tried, they failed. Here is a synopsis of the king-sized pay package that Gerstner received:

- A huge base salary of $975,000 per year—no lean-and-mean thinking here;
- A guarantee that his base salary will increase at least 6% per year, no

matter what the escalation in salaries elsewhere and no matter what the performance of RJR Nabisco;
- A guaranteed bonus of at least $1.3 million in his first year of employment;
- A gift of 1.3 million restricted shares, as well as an option on a further 3.1 million shares.

The very fact that Gerstner received the pay package he did may augur poorly for the outcome of the RJR Nabisco LBO. For it sends signals to everyone in the organization that cost reduction and risk taking are perhaps not as important as Henry Kravis and Louis Gerstner say they are.

In ancient Rome, augurs spent their days examining the entrails of sacrifices to predict the future. They didn't have much luck. Examining the entrails of a company's executive compensation arrangements may prove to be a more productive undertaking. If the CEO is paid way too much, you can be reasonably sure that most of the company's senior executives are also paid too much. And that has bad implications for future costs, and hence future profits and future total shareholder returns. Fortunately, you don't have to be a compensation expert or a statistical whiz to gauge a company's executive compensation costs. Just count the number of long-term incentive plans in which a CEO participates, and you will have a pretty good notion as to whether the company's executive compensation costs are out of control.

And don't forget to look at the composition of the CEO's pay package, even if it isn't excessive. Companies that use restricted stock, for example, are implicitly sending out signals that they don't expect all that much in the way of future performance. Fortunately, you don't need a complicated antenna to pick up those signals; just look for the presence of restricted stock at top management levels and then call your broker.

Spending time analyzing the size and the composition of the pay packages of a company's CEO and its other senior executives is not going to guarantee that you will always earn a superior return on your investment. But you'll make money over time if you stick with it.

Sources

V IRTUALLY ALL of the figures used in this book were derived from two sources. The first are the proxy statements released by companies themselves. Those proxy statements yielded virtually all the information cited on executive pay levels and pay practices. The second source was Standard & Poor's Compustat, which has become the nation's premier provider of financial and stock price data. In preparing this book, I drew just about all my financial and stock price information from Compustat. As a cross-check, I compared some of Compustat's figures to the actual figures shown in company annual reports; Compustat passed with flying colors.

Other sources of information are cited in the text.

Index*

Accountants, role of in reform, 246
Accounting Principles Board, 230
  mistakes of, 231
Alcatel, and Rand Araskog, 102–103
Alternative incentives, search for, 11–12
AMR
  Crandall at, 178–182
  declining performance of, 179–180
  shareholders of, 179
Apartments, company-paid, 192–193
Apple Computer, stock swap action of, 136–137
Araskog, Rand
  base pay and bonus earnings of, 100
  compensation of, 100
  high pay for low performance of, 100–104
  incentive compensations of, 102
  income of, 29
  work of with Alcatel, 102–103
Aristotle, on equitable pay in community, 24
Arm's-length negotiations, 226–227
Atari, 52
Athletes, compensation of, 31–34

Bally Manufacturing, tax reimbursement plan of,
  157–158
Banner Investments, 91
  stock of, 92
Batman
  gross, 38
  and Jack Nicholson's salary, 37
Bear Market, of 1970s and early 1980s, 73

Bear Stearns
  Ace Greenberg at, 145–148
  going public, 139–140
  pay-for-performance philosophy of,
    146–147
  stock price of, 148
Black-Sholes option-pricing model, 114
Bludhorn, Charles, 119
Bonus plans, 56–57, 175
  front-end, 200
  of Steven Ross, 55–61
Bryan, John, Jr., 172
Bush, George, on tax fairness, 25
Buyer, informed, 224

Calloway, Wayne, 172
Canion, Joseph, 172
Canseco, Jose
  as informed seller of talent, 49
  payment of, 33, 35–37
Capital Cities/ABC, perquisites of, 203
Caplin, Mortimer, on Fairchild Corp. board,
  89
Car, private, 188
Carney, John, on CEO payment in United
  Kingdom, 210
Carter Hawley Hale, leveraged recapitalization of,
  261–262
CEO compensation
  average, 27–28
  compared with average worker, 205
  vs. entertainers and athletes, 31–32
  excessive, 23–41

*Chapter 16 not included.

and investor, 253-264
and pay of outside directors, 228-229
in U.S. vs. competitor nations, 28-29
in U.S. vs. Japanese, 30-31
workers' reaction to abuse of, 256-257
CEO disease, 23-24
CEOs
interests of vs. interests of shareholders, 14
resources of, 242-243
Chairman of board, outside director as, 245-246
Champion International
Andrew Sigler's compensation at, 96-100
rebound of performance of, 98-99
shareholder return performance of, 97-98
Charitable contribution, company paid, 193-194
Chris-Craft Industries, 80
Siegel's employment agreement with, 81-82
Chrysler
and change in tax marginal rate, 132
departure of key executive from, 129
Lee Iacocca and, 125-132
loss of profit sharing at, 129-131
restricted stock of, 128-129, 131-132
Salary Reduction Program of, 125-126
Chrysler Corporation Loan Guarantee Act, 125
Clemens, Roger, payment of, 33
Coca-Cola, Goizueta at, 150-153
Columbia Pictures, Guber and Peters at, 82-83
Comparable worth doctrine, 32-33
criticism of, 31-32
Compensation, elements for reasonable, 224-227
Compensation committees
bias of, 227-228
as culprits, 214-215
function of, 224
need for compensation consultant of, 242-243, 244
problems with, 224-226
requirement for formalistic decision making by, 244-245
Compensation consultant
decision to hire, 43
and great-performing company, 45-46
and poor-performing company, 46-47
recommendations of, 49-50
survey of competitors' pay scales, 43-44. *See also*
Compensation survey
Compensation consultants
vogue for, 217
as culprits, 214
firms employing, 219-220
reasons for hiring of, 217-219
types of, 220
Compensation consulting
growth of, 215-216
as prostitution, 12, 13
rationale of, 216
Compensation survey, 43-44
comparator group in, 29-30
comparisons in, 221-222
forms of compensation included in, 45
getting results you want from, 45-46
profitability of, 220
purpose and value of, 220-223
reporting data from to board, 45
selecting companies to include in, 44
Concorde, 190-191

Conglomerates, 119-120
and portfolio diversification, 120-121
reasons for, 120-121
Continental, Lorenzo's stock options with, 135
Corporate profits
elimination of, 88-89
potential for double taxation of, 88
Cosby, Bill, income of, 37
Country clubs, 193
Crandall, Robert
bonus plan of, 180
as CEO of AMR, 178-182
pay package of, 179-182
restricted stock grant of, 181-182
Cravath, Swaine & Moore, income of partners in, 40-41
Cruise, Tom, income of, 37, 38

Daly, Robert, at Warner Brothers, 52
Davis, Martin S.
asset sell-off by, 122
background of, 121-122
compensation of, 124-125
disclosure of, 236-238
as head of Paramount, 53-54
high performance of, 123-124
hostile bid for UAL by, 177
long-term incentives of, 124
pursuit of Time Inc. by, 122-123
safety net of, 119-125
Deferred compensation, 61-63
Denmark, marginal tax rate in, 26
Diller, Barry, move of to Twentieth Century Fox, 123
Dining rooms, private, 191-192
"Disguised dividend" issue, 88-89
Walt Disney
decline of, 163-164
Michael Eisner at, 163-167
rising stock prices of, 164-167
Drucker, Peter, on pay of CEOs, 24

Eamer, Richard
annual total compensation of, 111
compensation plans of, 111-119
forms of long-term incentive of, 115
income of, 28
long-term incentive package of, 112-117
option shares of, 114-115
restricted stocks of, 117-118
safety net of, 110-119
stock option of, 112
Egalitarianism, in Soviet Union, 25
Eisner, Michael, 45
bonus formula of, 164-166
compensation of, 164-167
income of, 29
move of to Walt Disney, 123
at Paramount, 163
pay risk assumed by, 166-167
performance of at Disney, 164-167
risk taking of, 170
stock option plan of, 171
Elevator, private, 187
Employee Retirement Income Security Act (ERISA), 195-196, 199
Entertainers, compensation of, 26, 31-34, 37-39

Index

Estate tax, proposed 100% marginal rate, 128
Executive compensation. *See also* CEO
    compensation
  and company size, 120
  elements underlying reasonable, 224
  in foreign countries, 204–213
  in France, 209
  in Germany, 207–209
  in Great Britain, 209–213
  in Japan, 205–206
  major questions of, 9–10
  need for government regulation of, 242
  problems of, 241
  rationalization for comparisons of, 221–223
  ratio of CEO to other top executives', 172–173
  reforming system of, 241–252
  upward spiraling of, 223

Fairchild Corporation
  and compensation of Jeffrey Steiner, 85–95
  family feel of, 86
  growth of sales in, 86
  Interest Reimbursement Plan of, 94–95
  1988 proxy of, 90
  1989 proxy of, 90–93
  1990 proxy statement of, 93–95
  stock price of, 86–87
Federal National Mortgage Association (Fannie
  Mae), 197–199
Financial Accounting Standards Board (FASB),
  230–235
  and stock option accounting, 234–235
Financial counseling, personal, 200
Financial risk, definition of, 174
Fireman, Paul
  employment agreement of, 160–161
  high performance of, 160–163
  income of, 29
  renegotiated employment agreement of,
    161–163
  risk taking of, 170
  stock option grant of, 162
First Boston, going public, 139
Ford, profit-sharing plan at, 129–130
France, executive compensation in, 209

Geneen, Harold, 100
General Motors, profit-sharing plan at, 129–130
Georgia-Pacific
  Marshall Hahn at, 153–157
  restricted stocks of, 155–157
  tax reimbursement plan of, 154–156
  volatility of stock prices of, 156–157
Germany
  CEO compensation in, 207–209
  long-term incentives in, 207–208
  taxation in, 208–209
Gerstner, Louis V.
  in Nabisco leveraged buyout, 263–264
  pay package received by, 264
Goizueta, Roberto, 150–151
  at Coca-Cola, 151–153
  compensation and performance of, 151–153
  tax-protective executive compensation of,
    152–153
Golden Parachute, 201–202
  for sports stars, 35

Gorbachev, Mikhail, and free market, 242
Government incentives, 248–249
Government regulation, need for, 242
Grace, J. Peter
  high pay for low performance of, 104–108
  longevity of, 104
  pay of, 28, 105–106
  Performance Unit Plan of, 106–107
  stock options of, 107–108
W.R. Grace
  performance of J. Peter Grace at, 104–108
  Performance Unit Plan of, 106–107
Grace, W.R., income of, 28
Graziano, Joseph, stock option grant of, 200
Great Britain. *See* United Kingdom
Great man theory, 159–173
Greenberg, Ace
  base salary of, 145–146
  bonus plan of, 146
  performance of at Bear Stearns, 146–148
Growth, American business bias toward, 99
Guber, Peter
  contract of with Warner Communications, 83
  pay package of with Columbia Pictures,
    82–83
Gulfstream supersonic corporate jet, 191
Gulf & Western
  asset sell-off of, 122
  in conglomerate movement, 119–120
Gutfreund, John
  compensation of, 144–145
  option swaps by, 134
  performance of at Salomon Brothers, 144–145
  reputation of, 143–144

Haas, Walter, 35
  deal with Canseco and, 35–37
  as informed buyer of talent, 49
Hahn, T. Marshall
  compensation and stock options of, 155–157
  at Georgia-Pacific, 153–157
  tax reimbursement plan of, 154–155
Hammer, Armand
  bonus compensation of, 108–109
  death of, 109
  high pay for low performance of, 105, 108–109
  longevity of, 104–105
  option swaps by, 134
  perquisites of, 195
  restricted stock grants of, 108–109
H.J. Heinz
  Anthony O'Reilly at, 167–170
  compensation committee of, 225
  shareholder returns of, 167–168
  stock split of, 169
Helicopter, corporate, 188–189
Hillhaven, spinoff of from NME, 118–119
E.F. Hutton, going public, 139

Iacocca, Lee
  and American Dream, 128
  and Chrysler Corporation Loan Guarantee Act,
    125
  compensation of during Salary Reduction
    Program, 126–127
  firing of from Ford Motor Company, 125
  restricted stock of, 131–132

safety net of, 125–132
  stock options of, 127–128
Incentive plans
  for bad times, 46–48
  search for alternative, 11–12
  side effects of, 49–50
Incentives, lack of, 35
Income control, failure of, 25
Innovators, 149
Insider trading, 121
Internal Revenue Service
  and double taxation of corporate profits by, 88
  regulation of stock options by, 248–249
  role of in reform, 246, 248
International Paper, stock option and restricted share plan of, 184
Investment bankers, income of, 39–40
Investment banking firms
  collegial pay in, 141
  flat stock prices of, 141–142
  going public for profit, 138–148
  problems with executive compensation in, 140–141
Investors
  projection of companies' earning by, 253
  selection of stock by, 253–264
Irani, Ray, 104–105
  tax reimbursement plan of, 157
ITT
  criticism of compensation committee of, 102–103
  poor earnings of, 100–101
  profit rebound of, 101–102
  Rand Araskog's performance at, 100–104
ITT Wars, The (Araskog), 104

Jackson, Michael, income of, 37
Japan
  CEO compensation in, 30–31, 205–206
  competition of, 213
  income taxes in, 206–207
  lack of long-term incentives in, 205–206
Jet, corporate, 189–190
  cost of, 190
  supersonic, 191
Johnson, F. Ross
  perquisites of, 190
  restricted stock of, 238–239
Just price doctrine, 24

Katzenberg, Jeffrey
  on money spent on movies, 38–39
  move of to Walt Disney, 123
Kaufman, Henry, prediction of lower interest rates by, 73
Kikuchi, Tarsuaki, on Japanese CEO salaries, 205
Kinney National, success of, 51
Kravis, Henry, 263
  in Nabisco leveraged buyout, 263–264

Labor, historic view of value of, 23–24
Lauver, Raymond
  on Accounting Principles Board decision, 231–232
  slogan of, 233
Lawyers, income of, 40–41

Lehn, Kenneth
  mathematical models of major league pay, 33–34
  on pay package of ballplayers, 34–35
Leveraged buyouts (LBOs)
  environment for, 262–263
  movement to, 259
  recipe for, 259–261
Life insurance, corporate-owned, 193–194
Long-term incentive plans, 175
  in Germany, 207–208
  lack of in Japan, 205–206
  to motivate performance, 75–76
  under-reporting of, 258–259
Lorenzo, Frank
  option swaps by, 134–138
  stock options of, 175, 248–249
Lorsch, Jay, on chairman of board, 245

Madonna, income of, 37
Major league ballplayers
  mathematical models for pay of, 33–34
  salaries of, 35–37
Mancuso, Frank
  departure of from Paramount, 123
  omission of from Paramount's cash compensation table, 237
Marginal tax rate, 25
  in Denmark, 26
  in United Kingdom, 26
Market forces, need to strengthen, 242
Materialism, in U.S., 26–27
Matthews, James, on CEO salary in United Kingdom, 210, 211
Maxwell, David, pension of, 197–199
Maxwell, Hamish, 172
McGovern, George, 100% estate tax proposal of, 128
Merrill Lynch
  going public, 139
  Incentive Equity Purchase Plan of, 142–143
  perquisites at, 194–195
  stock prices of, 141–142
Milken, Michael, earning of, 39
Montana, Joe, payment of, 33
Morgan, J.P., on pay for CEOs, 24
Morgan Stanley
  executive compensation in, 141
  going public, 139–140
Morita, Akio, as Sony CEO, 82
Movie stars, salaries of, 37–39
Mullane, Robert, tax reimbursement plan of, 157–158
Murphy, Thomas, perquisites of, 203

Nabisco
  leveraged buyout of, 263–264
  proxy disclosure of, 238–239
National Medical Enterprises (NME)
  restricted stock of, 117–118
  Richard Eamer's performance and compensation at, 111–119
  spinoff of Hillhaven from, 118–119
  stock prices of, 115–117
New York Stock Exchange (NYSE), loss of faith in, 73
Nicholas, Nicholas, income of, 29
Nicholson, Jack, income of, 37

Index

Nicklaus, Jack, income of, 33
Nixon, Richard, pay controls of, 24

Occidental Petroleum
  Armand Hammer's performance at, 104–105, 108–109
  tax reimbursement plan of, 157
Optimum pay ratio, 24
Option swaps, 133–137
  need to eliminate, 250
O'Reilly, Anthony
  background of, 167
  compensation plan of, 168–170
  income of, 29
  Irish heritage of, 168
  performance of at H.J. Heinz, 167–170
  risk taking of, 168–171
  stock option plan of, 170–171
O'Reilly, J.F., 45
Outside director
  as chairman of board, 245–246
  dependence of pay on CEO pay, 228–229, 245
  determination of pay of, 229–230
  pensions for, 229

Paine Webber, going public, 139
Paley, William S., 52
  perquisites of, 186–189
Palmer, Arnold, payment of, 33
Paramount Communications
  cash compensation table of, 236–237
  founding of, 119
  Martin Davis at, 119–125
  Performance Unit Plan of, 236
  proxy disclosure of, 236–238
  stock price of, 125
Pay. *See also* Compensation; Pay differentials; Pay levels; Pay package
  abuse of, central question of, 28–29
  government-imposed controls of, 24
  high for low performance, 96–109
Pay differentials
  ambivalence toward, 24–26
  in U.S. versus major competitors, 28–29
Pay-for-performance, need for, 49
Pay levels
  equity of, 9–10
  escalation of, 10–11
  in foreign countries, 204–213
  for foreign vs. U.S. CEOs, 10
  and scarcity of talent, 11
  in U.S., 204–205
Pay package
  composition of, 257–259
  size of, 253–257
Pay ratio
  optimum, 24
  tax code and, 25
Pensionable pay, redefinition of, 196–197
Pension plan
  cap on, 195–196
  for outside directors, 228–229
  redefining of pensionable pay in, 196–197
Performance
  great, 45–46
  high pay for low, 96–109

and long-term incentive plans, 75–76
  poor, 46–47
Performance shares, 258
  need for disclosure of, 247
Performance units, 247, 258
Perquisites, 25, 186–203
  cost of to shareholders, 188
  danger of, 202–203
  excessive, 194–196
  and isolation of CEO, 186–189
  need for disclosure of, 247
  new class of, 195–203
Personal financial counseling, 200
Peters, John, contract of with Warner Communications, 83
Phibro-Salomon, 139
Phillip Brothers, going public, 139
Plato, on equitable pay in community, 23–24
Portfolio diversification, 120–121
President, U.S., income of, 26–27
Price controls
  failure of, 24–25
  in Nixon administration, 24
Prodigal Son syndrome, 48
  at ITT, 103
Proxy reporting, regulation of, 237–240

Recession, 185
  of 1990s, 23
Redemption, promise of, 48
Reebok, Paul Fireman at, 160–163
Reeves, Rosser, on people as asset of company, 140
Reform, 241–252
Regulation, need for, 242
Regulators, 230–235
  failures of, 235–240
Reload option feature, 178
Restricted stocks
  economic trade-offs of, 182–183
  invention of, 149–150
  need for disclosure of, 247
  reliance on, 257–258
  risk reduction with, 178, 181–182
  of Warner Communications, 71–73
Restricted stock-stock option tandem grant, 183–185
Return on equity, incentive plan based on, 12
Revenue neutrality, 251
Rinfret, Pierre, 158
Risk
  definition of, 174
  volatility and, 174–175
Risk reduction techniques, 175–185
Risk taking, 175
Ross, Steven J.
  base salary of, 55–56
  bonus plan of, 57–61
    under Time Warner, 59–61
  Bonus Unit compensation of, 66–68
  build up of Warner Communications by, 51–53
  deferred compensation of, 61–63, 77–78
  employment agreement of with Time Warner, 83–84
  Equity Unit plan of, 73–74, 79
  formula bonus plan of, 56–57
  games played in compensation of, 76–80
  as "great man," 159–160

294

and Herbert Siegel, 79–82
income of, 28–29
  compared to sports stars, 33
long-term incentive compensations of, 68–73, 75
Long-Term Management Incentive Plan of,
  74–76, 78
performance of, 54–55
restricted stocks of, 71–73
secret weapon of in contract negotiations, 79–80
stock options of, 63–66, 78–79
success story of, 51–55

Safety nets, 110–132
Salary, bloated, 175
Salomon Brothers
  going public, 139
  John Gutfreund at, 143–145
Sandler, Herbert and Marion, on danger of
  perquisites, 203
Scandinavian Airlines Systems (SAS), swapping of
  stock of, 134–136
Schreyer, William
  compensation of, 142
  Incentive Equity Purchase Plan of, 142–143
Sculley, John, option swap of, 134, 136–137
Sears, Roebuck, Tax Benefit Right of, 200–201
Securities and Exchange Commission (SEC), 230
  authority of, 235–240
  role of in reform, 246–248
Seller, informed, 230
Shareholders, interests of vs. interest of CEOs,
  14
Shearson Lehman Hutton, perquisites of, 194
Siegel, Herbert J.
  employment agreement of with Chris-Craft,
    81–82
  and revolt against Steve Ross, 79–82
Siegel, William, bonus earning of, 82
Sigler, Andrew
  annual bonus of, 99
  high pay for low performance of, 96–100
  pay package of, 98
Signing bonus, 200
Smith, Adam, on maximizing personal gain, 41
Snyder, Richard, omission of from Paramount's
  cash compensation table, 237
Soviet Union, pay and price controls in, 25
Spiegel, Thomas, perquisites of, 194
Sports stars
  compensation of, 32–37
  pay and performance of, 34–35
Steiner, Eric, as Fairchild director, 86
Steiner, Jeffrey T.
  after-tax income of, 88–89
  background of, 85–86
  and Banner Investments stock options, 91–92
  base salary of, 89–90
  compensation of with low performance, 85–95
  control of Fairchild stocks by, 86
  employment agreement of with evergreen
    clause, 89–90
  employment of relatives of, 86
  performance of, 86–87
  and 1989 proxy, 90–92
  and 1990 proxy statement, 93–95
  performance share plan of, 90
  "special cash bonuses" of, 93

stock options of, 90, 93–94
total cash compensation of, 92–93
Stephanopoli, Vincent Regazzacci, on CEO salary
  in France, 209
Stock Depreciation Rights, 201
Stock market, as indicator of performance, 12
Stock option grants
  need for regulation of, 247–250
  number of, 257–258
Stock options, 175
  accounting for, 234–235
  need for disclosure of, 246–248
  preference for as compensation, 233–234
  rationale of, 216, 217
  reload feature of, 178
  and risk reduction, 175–185
  of Steven Ross, 63–66
  in United Kingdom, 210–211
  value of, 232
Stocks
  CEO pay and selection of, 253–264
  pricing of and CEO pay, 254–264
  volatility of, 174–175
  swapping of, 133–137
    need to eliminate, 251
Strike price
  establishing of, 249–250
  Warner Communications stock, 68–70
Supplemental Executive Retirement Plan (SERP),
  195–196
Survey ratcheting, 222

Talent
  need to keep in bad times, 47–48
  rewarding in good times, 45–46
  scarcity of, 11
Taxation, 149–158
  cash payment equal to, 152–153
  in Denmark, 26
  in France, 209
  in Germany, 208–209
  in Japan, 206–207
  need for reform of, 250
  protection from, 152–158
  in United Kingdom, 26, 211–212
Tax Benefit Right (TBR), 200–201
Tax rate, maximum, 150
Tax reimbursement plans, 152–153
  of Bally Manufacturing, 157–158
  Hahn's modification of, 154–155
Taylor, Arthur, 47
Thatcher, Margaret, 26
Thompson, J. Walter, perquisites of, 194
Time Inc., merger of with Warner
  Communications, 53–54
Time Warner
  bonus plan for Steve Ross under, 59–61
  Ross's employment agreement with, 83–84
  stock of, 54, 122–123
  stock option plan of, 63–66
Tin Parachutes, 202
Tournament Theory, 254–256
Towers Perrin, 219–220
Tully, Daniel P., perquisites of, 194–195

UAL, stock option plan of, 177–178
Unbundled Stock Unit (USU), 104

Index

United Auto Workers (UAW), negotiation of
  profit-sharing plan by, 130, 131
United Kingdom
  executive compensation in, 209–213
  high tax rates in, 26
  stock options in, 210–211
  tax structure in, 211–212
United Shareholders Association, 14
United States, high salaries in, 26–27

Vacation, company-paid, 193

Wall Street investors
  income of, 39–40
  losses by, 39–40
  volatility of environment of, 40
Warner Brothers, building up of, 51–52
Warner Communications, 51
  after-tax profits of, 56–57, 58
  board revolt against Ross in, 79–82
  bonus plan for Steven Ross, 55–61

Bonus Unit of, 66–68
contract of with Guber and Peters, 83
Equity Unit plan of, 73–74
games played in compensation of Ross by, 76–80
Long-Term Management Incentive Plan of,
  74–76
merger of with Time Inc., 53–54. *See also* Time
  Warner
record-breaking stock of, 52
restricted stock of, 71–73
strike price of stocks, 68–71
Wasserstein, Bruce
  income of, 39
  and Time Warner stocks, 54
Wasserstein Perella & Co., CEOs' income in,
  39–40
Whitney, John Hay, 53
Wolf, Stephen, 157
  stock option plan of, 177–178, 248

Zimmerman, Richard, 172